Mortgage Loan Originator

REFRESHER

3rd edition

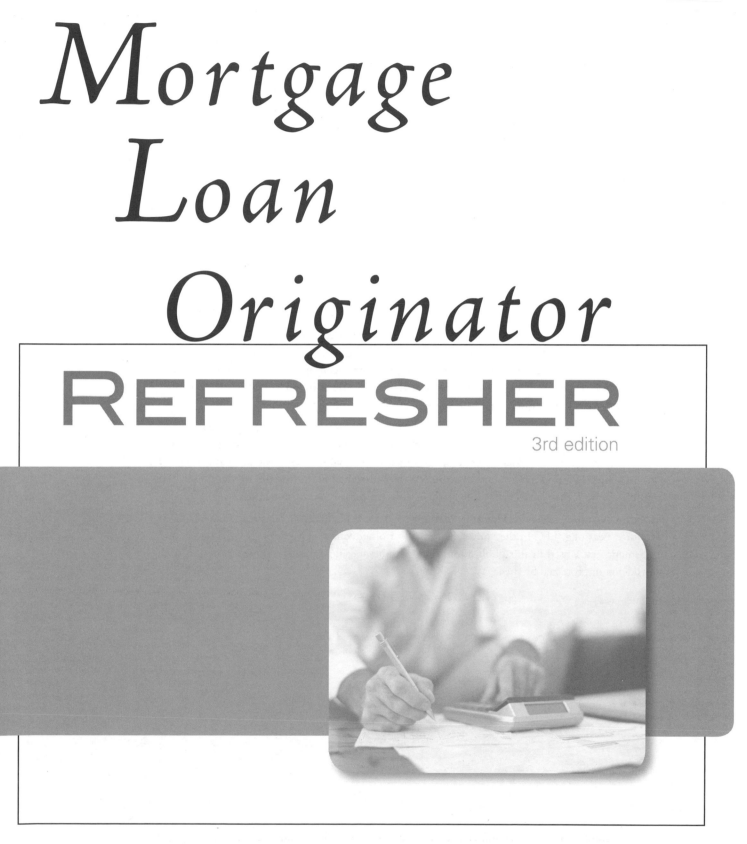

HONDROS
LEARNING™

HONDROS LEARNING™

4140 Executive Parkway

Westerville, Ohio 43081

www.hondroslearning.com

16 15 14 13   1 2 3 4

978-1-59844-217-5

For more information on, or to purchase, our products, please call 1-866-84LEARN or visit www.hondroslearning.com

Table of Contents

Preface

A mortgage loan is one of the biggest financial commitments a person will make in his or her lifetime. Because of this, mortgage professionals must be knowledgeable, ethical, and customer focused when it comes to providing home loans. To acknowledge this important responsibility, on July 30, 2008, the **Housing and Economic Recovery Act (HERA) of 2008** was signed into law by President George W. Bush, marking a significant component of mortgage reform. Title V of HERA is better known as the **Secure and Fair Enforcement for Mortgage Licensing Act of 2008 (SAFE Act)**. It establishes national minimum standards for mortgage training, including prelicensing and annual continuing education. Furthermore, under the SAFE Act, all mortgage loan originators (MLOs) must be either state-licensed or federally registered. All mortgage loan originators seeking state-licensure—or currently holding a state license—are required to pass the SAFE Mortgage Loan Originator National Test with UST, which includes both a national and uniform state content (UST) component. Title X of the Wall Street Reform and Consumer Protection Act of 2010 transfers rulemaking and enforcement authority over many consumer financial laws to the newly created **Bureau of Consumer Financial Protection**, which includes oversight of loan originator compensation.

The SAFE Act requires all states to implement a Mortgage Loan Originator (MLO) licensing process that meets certain standards through the **Nationwide Mortgage Licensing System & Registry (NMLS).** The NMLS, which was started in 2004 by the Conference of State Bank Supervisors (CSBS) and the American Association of Residential Mortgage Regulators (AARMR), is responsible for providing a centralized and standardized system for mortgage licensing that accommodates both the regulatory agencies and the mortgage industry. The NMLS online system was built and is maintained by the Financial Industry Regulatory Authority (FINRA), who operates similar systems in the securities industry.

The NMLS Resource Center contains valuable comprehensive information for all mortgage loan originators, including specific details about the steps necessary to set up an account, schedule a test appointment, and access testing and licensing requirements for your state. Use this link to access the NMLS Resource Center web site via the Internet: http://mortgage.nationwidelicensingsystem.org/Pages/Default.aspx

Using This Text

This *Mortgage Loan Originator Refresher*™ textbook is intended to serve as a refresher for all mortgage loan originators, whether experienced or new. It includes topics that map to the SAFE Mortgage Loan Originator Test - National Component with Uniform State Test Content Outline. Chapter 1 is a review of federal lending legislation, including RESPA, TILA, ECOA, and other federal laws and guidelines. Chapter 2 provides a review of nontraditional mortgage products, including mortgage programs, mortgage loan products, and terms used in the operation of the mortgage market. Chapter 3 discusses ongoing concerns with ethical behavior as well as associated acts designed to address these issues. Chapter 4 prepares the student by reviewing key terms and concepts associated with mortgage origination activities. Chapter 5 provides key terms and concepts associated with mortgage origination activities in general and covers key highlights of the SAFE Act and uniform state content topics included in the UST component of the SAFE MLO National Test with UST. The textbook also includes an appendix on financial calculations, plus chapter quizzes and a section that includes practice exams to help you gauge your knowledge in key topics areas before actually taking the SAFE Mortgage Loan Originator Test.

Course Objectives

Upon completion of this course, you will be able to:

- Define the purpose and provisions of the SAFE Act.
- Identify the disclosure requirements of RESPA and TILA.
- Describe the use of the new Good Faith Estimate and HUD-1 Settlement Statement.

- Recognize triggers for a high-cost loan and higher priced loan.
- Identify provisions of key mortgage-related federal law.
- Define nontraditional loan products.
- Compare and contrast conventional loans and nontraditional loans.
- Identify the elements in an adjustable rate mortgage.
- Describe provisions of reverse mortgages.
- Explain how a temporary buydown plan works.
- Recall TILA provisions related to advertising.
- Discuss consumer protection provisions of federal law.
- List the protected classes under federal law.
- Describe the participants in mortgage fraud schemes.
- Recognize indicators of predatory lending.
- Review the compensation rules for mortgage companies and mortgage loan originators.
- Describe and define high-level state content topics included in the UST component of the MLO exam.

Hondros Learning

Hondros Learning™ is a leading provider of classroom materials for mortgage pre-licensing and continuing education. Together with Hondros College, we have provided training and educational products for more than one million students.

Our *National Mortgage Lending CompuCram* exam prep software is the perfect companion to this book. The software is a self-paced question and answer application designed to help you study for the national mortgage lending exam. For more information about CompuCram or any of our other products, please visit www. compucram.com.

Acknowledgments

Hondros Learning™ thanks the following experts for their valuable contributions and assistance in developing this text:

Linda Heninger
Adjunct Faculty Instructor, Association of Mortgage Educators

David Hennon
Founder, Mortgage Education Training

Denise M. Leonard
Director, Massachusetts Mortgage Association

Graham Montigny
Adjunct Faculty Instructor, Hondros College

Britt Scearce
Senior Loan Advisor; Adjunct Faculty Instructor, Hondros College

Marve Stockert
Education Provider

Debbie Sousa
Director of Education and Event Planning, Massachusetts Mortgage Bankers Association

Edition of 032713

Chapter 1
Federal Lending Legislation Review

Introduction

The federal government and all state governments have enacted numerous laws that affect various aspects of the real estate industry. As a mortgage professional, not only are you obligated to know and understand the law, you have a duty to stay current with changes to the law. The following laws are reviewed here:

- Dodd-Frank Wall Street Reform and Consumer Protection Act of 2010
- Federal Reserve Loan Originator Compensation Rule
- Real Estate Settlement Procedures Act (RESPA)
- Truth in Lending Act (TILA)
- Mortgage Disclosure Improvement Act (MDIA)
- Home Ownership and Equity Protection Act (HOEPA)
- Homeowners Protection Act (HPA)
- Equal Credit Opportunity Act (ECOA)
- Home Mortgage Disclosure Act (HMDA)
- Fair Credit Reporting Act (FCRA)
- Fair and Accurate Credit Transactions Act (FACTA)
- The National Do Not Call Registry
- Mortgage Assistance Relief Service (M.A.R.S.)
- Anti-Money Laundering Act (AML)
- Consumer Financial Protection Bureau (CFPB)
- Gramm-Leach-Bliley Act (GLBA)
- Secure and Fair Enforcement for Mortgage Licensing Act (SAFE Act)

Other important federal laws will be discussed in Chapter 3, Ethics. The SAFE Act will be introduced but discussed more completely in Chapter 5, SAFE Act and UST Content Update.

Key Terms

3/7/3 Rule

Affiliated Business Arrangement (AfBA)

Annual Percentage Rate (APR)

Application

Do Not Call Registry

Good Faith Estimate (GFE)

HUD Uniform Settlement Statement (HUD-1)

Mortgage Loan Originator

Negative Amortization

Red Flag Rules

Rescind

Truth in Lending Statement (TIL)

Unique Identifier

Dodd-Frank Wall Street Reform and Consumer Protection Act of 2010

In July, 2010, the United States Congress passed the **Dodd-Frank Wall Street Reform and Consumer Protection Act** (Pub.L. 111-203, H.R. 4173). The stated purpose of this far-reaching financial legislation is

- *"To promote the financial stability of the United States by improving accountability and transparency in the financial system, to end 'too big to fail,' to protect the American taxpayer by ending bailouts, to protect consumers from abusive financial services practices, and for other purposes."*

The two titles of the Dodd-Frank Wall Street Reform and Consumer Protection Act of 2010 with the greatest impact on the mortgage industry are Title X, designated as **the Consumer Financial Protection Act**, and Title XIV, designated as the **Mortgage Reform and Anti-Predatory Lending Act**.

Title X creates the **Consumer Financial Protection Bureau** (CFPB) as an independent entity within the Federal Reserve. Effective July 2011, the rulemaking and enforcement authority over many consumer financial laws was transferred to the CFPB, including:

- Truth in Lending Act (TILA)
- Real Estate Settlement Procedures Act (RESPA)
- Homeowners Protection Act (HPA)
- Fair Credit Reporting Act (FCRA)
- Fair and Accurate Credit Transactions Act (FACTA)
- Portions of the Gramm-Leach-Bliley Act related to information privacy
- Equal Credit Opportunity Act (ECOA)
- Home Mortgage Disclosure Act (HMDA)
- Home Ownership and Equity Protection Act (HOEPA)
- Secure and Fair Enforcement for Mortgage Licensing Act (SAFE Act)

While Dodd-Frank indicates that final regulations for most of the mortgage provisions are required within 18 months of its enactment, actual implementation of all its provisions depends on the transfer of responsibility to the Consumer Financial Protection Bureau and the issuing of final rules and regulations. The expected timeline for complete implementation of Dodd-Frank may be as much as three and half years from the passage of the Act. Even so, it is possible that some provisions may never be implemented exactly as proposed in the Act. Every mortgage loan originator is responsible for staying current with the regulations as they are implemented.

Consumer Financial Protection Bureau (CFPB)

The Consumer Financial Protection Bureau (CFPB) was created to ensure that financial products and services that Americans depend on every day —including credit cards, mortgages, and loans—work better for the people who use them. The CFPB is a significant part of President Obama's historic Wall Street reforms.

Created under Title X of the Dodd-Frank Wall Street Reform and Consumer Protection Act of 2010, the CFPB is charged with overseeing the federal financial laws that specifically protect **consumers**—people who keep their money in banks and credit unions, pay for goods and services with their credit cards, and rely on loans to buy homes or pay for college, among other services.

The Bureau is tasked with making sure people understand the fine print that explains the risks involved in using these services, and ensuring the banks, credit unions, and other financial companies that provide them play by the rules.

Before the CFPB was established, seven different federal agencies were responsible for various aspects of consumer financial protection. No single agency had effective tools to set the rules or oversee the whole market, and that is part of what led to an economic crash of epic proportions.

Moving forward from July 2011 when rule making and enforcement authorities for many consumer protection laws were transferred to the CFPB, this agency will be the single, consumer-focused regulating authority, consolidating the existing authorities scattered throughout the federal government under one roof. The CFPB's oversight includes the large banks and credit unions that had historically been regulated by the federal government, as well as independent and privately owned "non-bank financial institutions" that had never been regulated before.

This means that for the first time, the federal government will be able to regulate the activities of independent payday lenders, private mortgage lenders and servicers, debt collectors, credit reporting agencies, and private student loan companies.

Source: http://www.whitehouse.gov/blog/2012/01/04/consumer-financial-protection-bureau-101-why-we-need-consumer-watchdog#What is CFPB

Qualified Mortgage (QM)

In this section, we'll discuss the Qualified Mortgage (QM) definition and rules.

◇ **Note:** Qualified Mortgage (QM) rules do **not** take effect until January 2014.

A **qualified mortgage** is a home loan that meets certain standards set forth by the federal government. Lenders that generate such loans will be presumed to have also met the **Ability-to-Repay** rule also mandated by the Dodd-Frank Act.

Qualified Mortgage (QM) rules are designed to create safer loans by prohibiting or limiting certain high-risk products and features. Lenders that make QM loans, as defined, will receive some degree of legal protection against borrower lawsuits, either in the form of a safe harbor or rebuttable presumption.

Definition of a Qualified Mortgage

The term "**qualified mortgage**" (QM) was first used within the text of the Dodd-Frank Wall Street Reform and Consumer Protection Act, which became federal law on July 21, 2010.

The Dodd-Frank Act provided a general definition (essentially an outline) of the QM loan.

The CFPB was then given the task of finalizing that definition, which they did in **January 2013.** Here are the key features of a qualified mortgage according to the update:

No Excessive Upfront Points and Fees

In this context, points and fees are *additional costs charged by the lender during mortgage application, processing, and closing.*

The QM rule puts a limit on these additional costs or charges, including those used to compensate mortgage brokers and loan originators.

- Generally speaking, the points and fees paid by the borrower **must *not* exceed 3% of the total amount borrowed**, if the loan is to be considered a qualified mortgage.

◇ **Note:** Certain exceptions have been made for **bona fide discount points** on prime loans.

No Toxic Loan Features

In this context, a **toxic loan feature** can refer to *any high-risk feature that may have contributed to the mortgage and housing collapse of 2008*. Such features are prohibited by the qualified mortgage (QM) rule.

Prohibited features include:

- **No interest-only loans.** These are mortgage products where the borrower defers the repayment of principal and pays only the interest, usually for a certain period of time.
- **No negative-amortization loans.** These are loans where the principal amount borrowed increases over time, even while monthly payments are being made. This often happens as the result of the interest-only payments mentioned above.
- **No terms beyond 30 years.** In order to meet the definition of a qualified mortgage, the loan must have a repayment term of 30 years or less.
- **No balloon loans.** In most cases, balloon loans will be prohibited by the QM rules. But some exceptions have been made. Smaller lenders in rural or underserved areas may still make such loans. Definition: A balloon mortgage is one that has a larger-than-normal payment at the end of the repayment term.

Limits on Debt-to-Income Ratios

In general, the qualified mortgage will be granted to borrowers with debt-to-income (DTI) ratios **no higher than 43%**.

As the name implies, the debt-to-income ratio compares the amount of money a person earns each month (gross monthly income) to the amount he or she spends on recurring debt obligations.

This aspect of the QM rule is intended to prevent consumers from taking on mortgage loans they cannot realistically afford.

◇ **Note:** A temporary (after January 2014) exception will be granted for loans that are eligible to be sold or insured by Freddie Mac, Fannie Mae, FHA or the VA.

More information on the Qualified Mortgage definition and rules is available by accessing the following Internet link: http://www.qualifiedmortgage.org/definition/#ixzz2MgEbICr3

The Federal Reserve Loan Originator Compensation Rule

One of the objectives of the Dodd-Frank Wall Street Reform and Consumer Protection Act of 2010 was to address perceived unfair practices by mortgage loan originators related to **compensation** paid by consumers.

The Federal Reserve Board, anticipating the Dodd-Frank amendments to the Truth in Lending Act, propagated a final rule, which became effective April 2011, as an amendment to Regulation Z, found in Part 1026, Subpart E, *Special Rules for Certain Home Mortgage Transactions*, that addresses compensation consistent with Dodd-Frank. According to the Compliance Guide prepared by the staff of the Board of Governors of the Federal Reserve System, this rule applies to transactions involving closed-end extensions of credit secured by a consumer's principal dwelling and must be followed by all persons who originate loans, including mortgage brokers and their employees, as well as mortgage loan originators employed by depository institutions and other lenders. For the purposes of this rule, loan originator is defined in Regulation Z § 1026.36 (a).

The objectives of the rule are to protect consumers from unfair, abusive, or deceptive practices that can arise from mortgage loan originator compensation agreements. Examples of abuses include:

- Any change in compensation
- Change in fees from the original good faith estimate (GFE)
- Any mortgage loan officer compensation changes because the borrower is charged additional discount fees

To clarify the objectives of the rule, note the following definitions:

- A loan originator is a person who arranges, negotiates, or otherwise obtains loans, or a producing manager, a person that has routine interaction with consumers, or a person who, for compensation or other monetary gain, arranges, negotiates, or otherwise obtains an extension of consumer credit for another person.

- A loan originator is also a table-funded creditor (loans that are funded at the closing table and *not* sold through a correspondent program or secondary market, the loans remain as creditor for disclosure purposes); also defined as a mortgage broker.

- Compensation is defined as **salary**, **commissions**, **bonuses**, **awards**, or **prizes**.

- Payments from loan proceeds are considered payments made directly by the consumer, while disclosed yield spread premium (YSP) as described under Real Estate Settlement Procedures Act (RESPA), is *not* considered a payment from the borrower.

- Transactions are described as all closed-end consumer loans secured by a one- to four-unit residential dwelling, closed end mortgages, or reverse mortgages.

It is important to know that compensation *cannot* be based differently because a loan is an FHA loan or a conventional loan, a purchase loan or a refinance, a vacation home (second home) or a primary residence, or a loan originated for delivery via wholesale vs. in-house loan.

Prohibited Practices

The following are prohibited under the rule:

- Any compensation that is based on loan terms or conditions such as interest rate, annual percentage rate (APR), loan-to-value (LTV), etc.
- Compensation received directly from consumer and from any other source on the same loan

Dual Compensation

If a mortgage loan originator receives compensation for a transaction directly from a consumer, no one else may compensate the mortgage loan originator for that transaction, either directly or indirectly (§ 1026.36 (d)(2)).

Additional Provisions

Additional provisions in the rule include the following:

- Pricing concessions for any reason are prohibited —Can't give sister a discount
- The practice of establishing "point banks" is prohibited
- An MLO cannot be penalized for GFE violations or misquotes of fees
- Net branches may *not* allow compensation based on fees or income
- Basing compensation on terms of previous transactions is prohibited

Basis for Compensation

Bonuses are allowed and are a critical part of MLO compensation. Compensation can be based on any of the following triggers:

- Overall loan volume
- Long-term loan performance
- Hourly basis
- Existing/new customer
- Flat fee
- "Pull-through" rate, i.e., quality of loan files
- Legitimate business expenses

Other terms by which compensation may be based include long-term loan performance or a different loan arrangement for each mortgage loan originator.

Steering and Safe Harbor

One of the most critical points of the Federal Reserve Loan Originator Compensation Rule is the prohibition of the practice of "steering" consumers to a lender to receive greater compensation, unless the loan is on the consumer's interest.

It would *not* be considered steering, in other words, it would be a safe harbor, if:

- The consumer is presented with loan options for each type of loan, including:
    - Lowest interest rate
    - Lowest interest rate without certain risky features
    - Lowest total for origination and discount
- The mortgage loan originator:
    - Obtains options from creditors the MLO regularly does business with.
    - Believes in good faith that the consumer qualifies for options presented.

◇ **CAUTION:** Due to the complexity of the Federal Loan Originator Compensation Rule, brokers and lenders are advised to consult with their legal counsel before entering into MLO compensation agreements to ensure that they do *not* violate the new rules.

Real Estate Settlement Procedures Act (RESPA)

The **Real Estate Settlement Procedures Act of 1974** (RESPA) (12 USC §§ 2601-2617):

- Promulgated in 1975 by the **U.S. Department of Housing and Urban Development (HUD)** as **Regulation X**.
- Implemented and enforced by the Consumer Financial Protection Bureau.
- Intended to help consumers become better shoppers for settlement services and to eliminate unnecessary increases in the costs of certain settlement services due to kickbacks and referral fees.

Covered Transactions (Regulation X 12. C.F.R § 1024.05)

Regulation X:

- Covers loans secured with a mortgage placed on **residential** properties designed for occupancy of from one to four families.
- Applies to most conventional loans and government agency loans such as FHA, VA, and USDA.
- Includes most purchase loans, assumptions, refinances, property improvement loans, and equity lines of credit.
- Amended in 1994 to extend coverage to subordinate lien loans.

Transactions *not* covered include:

- An all-cash sale
- A sale where the individual home seller takes back the mortgage
- A rental property transaction
- Temporary construction loans
- Other business purpose transaction
- Property of 25 acres or more
- Vacant or unimproved land (unless a dwelling will be constructed or moved onto the property within two years)

RESPA Provisions

Among the provisions of RESPA are sections that address compensation, title insurance, and escrow accounts.

Section 8: Kickbacks, Fee-Splitting, Unearned Fees

- Prohibits giving or accepting a fee, kickback, or **anything of value** in exchange for referrals of settlement service business involving a federally-related mortgage loan (allows for **a thing of *minimal* value** *used for promotional purposes*, such as pens, mementos, coffee cups, hats, etc.).

- Defines prohibited **thing of value** to include, *without limitation*: monies, things, discounts, salaries, commissions, fees, duplicate payments of a charge, stock, dividends, distributions of partnership profits, franchise royalties, credits representing monies that may be paid at a future date, the opportunity to participate in a money-making program, retained or increased earnings, increased equity in a parent or subsidiary entity, special bank deposits or accounts, special or unusual banking terms, services of all types at special or free rates, sales or rentals at special prices or rates, lease or rental payments based in whole or in part on the amount of business referred, trips and payment of another person's expenses, or reduction in credit against an existing obligation.

- Prohibits **fee-splitting** and receiving **unearned fees** or a percentage of any charge made or received for services *not* actually performed.

- Prohibits a **required use** of specific settlement service providers, except in cases where a lender refers a borrower to an attorney, credit reporting agency, or real estate appraiser to represent the lender's interest in the transaction.

- Does *not* prohibit the payment of fees to attorneys, title companies, or agents for **service actually performed**, the payment of a bona fide salary or compensation to a person for goods or products actually furnished or services actually performed in the making of a loan, and payments pursuant to cooperative brokerage and referral arrangements or agreements between real estate agents and brokers.

- Allows legitimate discounts on services to consumers *if a combination of settlement services is offered at a total price lower than the sum of the individual settlement services*, as long as:

  o The use of any such combination is **optional** to the purchaser, and

  o The lower price for the combination is *not* made up by higher costs elsewhere in the settlement process.

- Subjects violators to criminal and civil penalties, including:

  o Fines up to $10,000

  o Imprisonment up to one year

  o Liability up to three times the amount of the charge paid for the service (civil lawsuit)

Section 9: Title Insurance

- Prohibits a seller from requiring the home buyer to use a particular title insurance company, either directly or indirectly, as a condition of sale.

- Allows buyers to sue for an amount equal to three times all charges made for the title insurance.

Section 10: Limits on Escrow Account

- Limits the amount that a lender may require a borrower to put into an escrow account for purposes of paying taxes, hazard insurance, and other charges related to the property to **no more than 1/12 of the total** of all disbursements payable during the year, plus an amount necessary to pay for any shortage in the account.

- Allows a lender to require a cushion, *not* to exceed an amount equal to **1/6 of the total** disbursements for the year (usually two months).

- Requires the lender to perform an escrow account analysis once during the year and notify borrowers of any shortage; any excess of **$50 or more** must be returned to the borrower, as long as the borrower is *not* delinquent.

- Does *not* require lenders to impose an escrow account on borrowers; however, certain government loan programs or lenders may require escrow accounts as a condition of the loan; for example, a mortgage loan that includes mortgage insurance MUST have an escrow account. In addition, a loan that meets the definition of a "higher-priced" loan is required to have a lender-imposed escrow account for at least 12 months.

Affiliated Business Arrangements (AfBA)

While kickbacks from referrals are prohibited, Regulation X does recognize the legitimacy of affiliated business arrangements involving real estate settlement services for federally related mortgage loans (12 C.F.R.§ 1024,15. An affiliated business arrangement is a situation where a person in a position to refer settlement services—or an associate of that person—has either an affiliate relationship with or a direct or beneficial ownership interest of **more than 1%** in a provider of settlement services and who then refers business to that provider or in some way influences the selection of that provider.

Within the scope of this definition, a "person" could be an individual or a corporation, association, partnership, or trust. The term "associate" refers to someone who has one or more of the following relationships with a person in a position to refer settlement business:

- A spouse, parent, or child of that person

- A corporation or business entity that controls, is controlled by, or is under common control with such person

- An employer, officer, director, partner, franchisor, or franchisee of that person

- Anyone who has an agreement, arrangement, or understanding with that person when the purpose or substantial effect of which is to enable that person to benefit financially from the referrals

How someone with ownership interest receives compensation for settlement services is important under RESPA. Legitimate fees or wages for **services actually rendered** or hours worked are permissible. Additionally it is permissible to accept **bona fide compensation** from the ownership interest or franchise relationship between entities in an affiliate relationship, as long as it is for ordinary business purposes and is *not* a fee for the referral of settlement service business or an unearned fee. That compensation could include dividends, capital or equity distributions, business loans, advances, and capital or equity contributions.

Required Disclosures

In order to meet its objective of helping consumers understand settlement services, RESPA requires multiple disclosures related to a completed application for a federally related mortgage to be provided at various times throughout the loan process. **Application** is defined by Regulation X (12 C.F.R. § 1024.2) as the submission of a borrower's financial information in anticipation of a credit decision which includes:

- Borrower's name

- Borrower's monthly income

- Borrower's Social Security number to obtain a credit report

- Property address

- Estimate of value of the property

- Loan amount

Receipt of the above information triggers mandated disclosures. The Regulation X definition of a "business day" includes "any day on which the business entity is open to the public for carrying on substantially all of the entity's business functions" (§ 1024.2 (b)).

Within Three (3) Business Days of Completed Loan Application

- **HUD Settlement Costs Booklet**—contains consumer information regarding various real estate settlement services (required for purchase transactions only).
- **Good Faith Estimate (GFE) of Settlement Costs**—provides an estimate of each charge the buyer is likely to pay at settlement.
- **Mortgage Servicing Disclosure Statement**—discloses to the borrower whether the lender intends to service the loan or transfer servicing to another lender, and provides information about complaint resolution.

If the lender **turns down the loan** within three (3) business days, RESPA does *not* require the mortgage loan originator to provide these documents.

Before Settlement Occurs

- **Affiliated Business Arrangement (AfBA or ABA) Disclosure**—requires a settlement service provider to give an AfBA disclosure to the consumer at or prior to the time of referral to another provider with whom the referring party has an ownership or other beneficial interest; must describe the business arrangement that exists and give the borrower an estimate of the second provider's charges.
- **HUD-1 Settlement Statement**—a standard form that clearly shows all charges imposed on borrowers and sellers in connection with the settlement; allows borrower to request the HUD-1 Settlement Statement **one (1) business day before the actual settlement.**

At Settlement

- **HUD-1 Settlement Statement**—shows the actual settlement costs of the loan transaction for both the buyer and the seller.
- **Initial Escrow Statement**—itemizes the estimated taxes, insurance premiums, and other charges anticipated to be paid from the escrow account during the first 12 months of the loan, including any cushion; although usually given at settlement, the lender has 45 days from settlement to deliver.

After Settlement

- **Annual Escrow Statement**—required from loan servicers once a year; summarizes all escrow account deposits and payments during the servicer's 12-month computation year, notifies the borrower of any shortages or surpluses in the account, and advises the borrower about the course of action being taken.
- **Servicing Transfer Statement**—required if the loan servicer sells or assigns the servicing rights to a borrower's loan to another loan servicer (does *not* include transfer of ownership into the secondary market without corresponding transfer of servicing rights); generally required 15 days before the effective date of the loan transfer; must include the name and address of the new servicer, toll-free telephone numbers, and the date the new servicer will begin accepting payments; protects borrowers who make a timely payment to previous service provider within 60 days of the transfer.

Good Faith Estimate (GFE)

- The Good Faith Estimate (GFE) serves as a clear and concise form showing the dollar amount of settlement charges (§ 1024.7 of Regulation X).
- Must be provided no later than **three (3) business days** after receipt of a completed application.
- Requires the settlement charges and terms to be available for at least **ten (10) business days** after it has been issued. (Recall that the Regulation X definition of a "business day" includes any day on which the business entity is open to the public for carrying on substantially all of the entity's business functions" (§ 1024.2 (b)).
- Allows "average charge" calculations for settlement services if based on the period of time (between 30 days and six months), the type of loan, and the geographic area (*not* the size of the loan or property

value); if used, requires the same average charge to be used for all loans within a specific loan classification and requires the lender to retain all documentation use to calculate the average charge for three years after settlement.

- GFE from HUD includes:

    - Page 1: Dates, loan summary, escrow amount information, estimated settlement charges

    - Page 2: Itemized list of origination charges, credits or points for interest rate selected, and charges for other settlement services; note that the new form requires a **lump sum origination charge** that reflects the lender fee and the mortgage broker fee

    - Page 3: Tools that consumers can use to evaluate the settlement charges associated with the loan under different terms and to compare this loan and its settlement charges to other GFEs

◇ **Note:** The CFPB intends to replace this standardized form with a new integrated GFE/Truth in Lending Statement.

Settlement Services

Regulation X (12 C.F.R. § 1024.2) defines **settlement services** as any service provided in connection with a prospective or actual settlement, including, but *not* limited to, any one or more of the following:

- Origination of a federally related mortgage loan (including, but *not* limited to, the taking of loan applications, loan processing, and the underwriting and funding of such loans)
- Rendering of services by a mortgage broker (including counseling, taking of applications, obtaining verifications and appraisals, and other loan processing and origination services, and communicating with the borrower and lender)
- Provision of any services related to the origination, processing, or funding of a federally related mortgage loan
- Provision of title services, including title searches, title examinations, abstract preparation, insurability determinations, and the issuance of title commitments and title insurance policies
- Rendering of services by an attorney
- Preparation of documents, including notarization, delivery, and recordation
- Rendering of credit reports and appraisals
- Rendering of inspections, including inspections required by applicable law or any inspections required by the sales contract or mortgage documents prior to transfer of title
- Conducting of settlement by a settlement agent and any related services
- Provision of services involving mortgage insurance
- Provision of services involving hazard, flood, or other casualty insurance or homeowner's warranties
- Provision of services involving mortgage life, disability, or similar insurance designed to pay a mortgage loan upon disability or death of a borrower, but only if such insurance is required by the lender as a condition of the loan
- Provision of services involving real property taxes or any other assessments or charges on the real property
- Rendering of services by a real estate agent or real estate broker
- Provision of any other services for which a settlement service provider requires a borrower or seller to pay

Tolerances

Charges that may *not* exceed the GFE amount include:

- Origination charges, which may be for any service involved in the creation of a mortgage loan, including but *not* limited to the taking of the loan application, loan processing, and the underwriting and funding of loan, and the processing and administrative services required to perform these functions.

- Credit or charge for interest rate chosen/adjusted origination charge while interest rate is locked.
- Transfer taxes.

Charges that cannot exceed **10%** of GFE include:

- Lender-required settlement services, where the lender selects.
- Lender-required services, title services and required title insurance, and owner's title insurance, when borrower uses provider identified by loan originator.
- Government recording charges.

Amounts disclosed and charged for all other settlement services may change at settlement.

Binding

The terms in a GFE are binding, unless a new GFE is provided. An updated GFE is required within **three (3) business days** of learning of changed circumstances. The reason for the change must be documented and retained for at least three years.

Among the reasons for changing GFE are:

- Changed circumstances that increase settlement costs to exceed tolerances.
- Changed circumstances affecting eligibility for the specific loan terms identified in the GFE.
- Borrower-requested changes affecting charges/terms.
- Changes to the charge or credit for the interest rate chosen, the adjusted origination charges, per diem interest, and loan terms related to the interest rate if the interest rate has ***not*** **been locked** by the borrower or if a locked interest rate has **expired.**

Changed Circumstances

Regulation X (12 C.F.R. § 1024.7 (f)(i)) defines "changed circumstances" as:

- Acts of God, war, disaster, or other emergency.
- Information particular to the borrower or transaction that was relied on in providing the GFE—such as credit quality of the borrower, the amount of the loan, value of the property, or other information that was used in providing the GFE—that changes or is found to be inaccurate after the GFE has been provided.
- New information particular to the borrower or transaction that was *not* relied on in providing the GFE.
- Other circumstances that are particular to the borrower or transaction—such as boundary disputes, the need for flood insurance, or environmental problems.

Changed circumstances do *not* include:

- The borrower's name, the borrower's monthly income, the property address, an estimate of the value of the property, the mortgage loan amount sought, and any information contained in any credit report obtained by the loan originator prior to providing the GFE, unless the information changes or is found to be inaccurate after the GFE has been provided
- Market price fluctuations by themselves

Other Provisions

The original **GFE expires in ten (10) business days** (or longer as specified by mortgage loan originator) if borrower does *not* intend to continue with an application.

If charges at settlement exceed the charges listed on the GFE by more than the permitted tolerances within the ten (10) business-day period, the MLO must cure the discrepancy by reimbursing to the borrower the amount of the excess either:

- At settlement.
- Within thirty (30) calendar days after settlement.

HUD-1 Settlement Statement

The **HUD-1** Settlement Statement used for RESPA compliance under Regulation X (12 C.F.R. § 1024.8) is completed by the person conducting the closing (settlement agent) and must clearly itemize all charges imposed upon the borrower and the seller by the mortgage loan originator, including all sales commissions. It shows:

- Buyers how much money they will have to bring to settlement.

- Sellers how much money they will walk away with (or sometimes, have to bring to settlement).

The **HUD-1** Settlement Statement is used for transactions with a borrower and seller. The **HUD-1A** may be substituted for transactions with a borrower and *no seller*—for example, refinancings and subordinate lien loans. No settlement statement is required for open-end home equity plans subject to the Truth in Lending Act and Regulation Z. However, the HUD-1 form may be used for loans *not* subject to RESPA without subjecting the transaction to the provisions of RESPA.

◇ **Note:** The CFPB intends to replace this standardized form with a new integrated GFE/Truth in Lending Statement.

HUD-1 Page 1

Page 1 contains identification such as the borrower's name and address, the address or other location information on the property, the lender's identifying loan number, the settlement date, and the name and address of the lender. This page also provides a notice related to charges paid outside of closing (P.O.C.).

Section J, Summary of Borrower's Transaction. Indicates the details of the borrower's transaction, including the gross amount due from the borrower, adjustments for items paid by the seller in advance, amounts paid by or on behalf of the borrower, adjustments for items unpaid by the seller, and the cash at settlement paid by—or in some cases, to—the borrower.

Section K, Summary of Seller's Transaction. Indicates the details of the seller's transaction, including the gross amount due to the seller, adjustments for items paid by the seller in advance, reductions in amount due to the seller, adjustments for items unpaid by the seller, and the cash at settlement paid to—or in some cases, by—the seller.

HUD-1 Page 2

Itemizes settlement charges paid by the borrower and the seller, including:

- Items paid in connection with the loan
- Items required by the lender to be paid in advance
- Reserves deposited with the lender
- Title charges
- Government recording and transfer charges
- Any additional settlement charges

HUD-1 Page 3

The last page of the HUD-1 offers a comparison of the exact amounts from the Good Faith Estimate (GFE) and the actual settlement charges indicated on the HUD–1 or HUD-1A Settlement Statement, including:

- Charges that cannot increase
- Charges that cannot increase more than 10%
- Charges that can change
- Loan terms

Truth in Lending Act (TILA)

The Truth in Lending Act is administered by the Consumer Financial Protection Bureau (CFPB). The specific provisions of the Act, which is contained in Title I of the Consumer Credit Protection Act, as amended (15 U.S.C. 1601 et seq.), are implemented by Regulation Z (12 C.F.R. 1026). TILA has been amended numerous times, most recently with the Housing and Economic Recovery Act of 2008, the Mortgage Disclosure Improvement Act (MDIA), which went into effect in 2009, and the Dodd-Frank Wall Street Reform and Consumer Protection Act of 2010.

Purpose of TILA

TILA's intended purpose is to:

- Promote the informed use of consumer credit.
- Provide a standard way to inform consumers of the true cost of borrowing money by requiring the disclosure of the **annual percentage rate (APR)**.
- Assure meaningful disclosure of credit terms to allow consumer to compare more readily the various options available and avoid the uninformed use of credit.

Overview of TILA

TILA:

- Does *not* set limits on interest rates or other finance charges imposed by lenders, but regulates the disclosure of these items.
- Establishes a three (3) business-day right of rescission in certain transactions.
- Applies to all real estate loans made to consumers (*not* companies) primarily for personal, family, or household purposes (*not* for business or commercial purposes) if loan is:
  - Subject to a finance charge, or
  - Payable by written agreement in **more than four installments**.

Disclosures

Disclosures are required by TILA in two general areas:

- **When creditors offer credit but before the transaction is consummated.** Disclosures must be made clearly, conspicuously, in writing, and in a form the consumer may keep and read prior to the loan closing.
- **When credit terms are advertised to potential customers.** Requires advertisers of consumer credit to clearly and conspicuously provide certain information if they use specific triggering terms in their credit ads.

The following are the specific disclosures required by the Truth in Lending Act that must be given **no later than three (3) business days** after the creditor receives the consumer's completed application:

- **Truth in Lending Disclosure Statement** (TIL) and a guide on how to read the TIL.

Most creditors give the applicant the TIL disclosure statement when applying for the real estate loan. If any of the estimated figures change over the course of the transaction, **new disclosures must be made at least three (3) business days before loan consummation, which could trigger an additional waiting period.** A creditor must retain evidence of compliance with these disclosure requirements for at least **two (2) years** after the disclosures were required to be made.

Regulation Z (12 C.F.R. § 1026.19) prohibits mortgage loan originators and servicers from charging a fee for the preparation of the Truth in Lending Statement (TIL) or other disclosures required by the Truth in Lending Act or the disclosures and statements required by RESPA, such as the GFE, HUD-1 Settlement Statement, or annual escrow account statements. Furthermore, the only fee that may be collected prior to these mandated disclosures is a fee for **a credit report**. Other loan origination fees may be collected after these disclosures are hand-delivered to the borrower or three (3) business days after they are mailed.

Other Required Disclosures

Other required disclosures, when applicable, include:

- **Consumer Handbook on Adjustable Rate Mortgages** (CHARM booklet), **ARM Disclosure**, and ARM loan program details for ARM loans
- **Balloon Disclosure**
- **Prepayment Disclosure**
- **Notice of Right to Rescind**
- **When Your Home is on the Line** Booklet for home equity loans and lines of credit

Truth in Lending Disclosure Statement (TIL)

The Truth in Lending Disclosure Statement:

- Is required for mortgage loans subject to RESPA secured by consumer's dwelling (other than HELOCs).
- Must be given (along with other required disclosures) at application or placed in the mail no later than **three (3) business days** after the creditor receives the consumer's written application.
- Must be delivered no later than 7th business day before consummation of the transaction.

> **Note:** This means that in order to comply with the Mortgage Disclosure Improvement Act, the earliest a loan may close is the seventh business day after initial disclosures are delivered or placed in the mail (12 C.F.R. § 1026.19 (a) (2)(i)).

Fees

The only fee that may be collected prior to these mandated disclosures is a fee for a credit report, assuming the fee is bona fide and reasonable in amount. Other loan origination fees may be collected after these disclosures are hand-delivered to the borrower or three (3) business days after they are mailed (12 C.F.R. § 1026.19 (a) (1) (ii) (iii).

> **Note:** Mortgage loan originators and servicers are prohibited from charging a fee for the preparation of the Truth in Lending Statement (TIL) or other disclosures required by the Truth in Lending Act or the Real Estate Settlement Procedures Act (12 C.F.R. § 1024.12).

Data in the "Federal Box"

The TIL must include the following items:

- Finance charge expressed as an **annual percentage rate** (the APR is labeled with a phrase such as "The cost of your credit as a yearly rate")
- Total **finance charges** (amount of money paid toward interest over the life of the loan plus the upfront fees, e.g., origination fee, loan fee, commitment fee, assumption fee, prepaid interest, prepaid PMI, prepaid credit life insurance, etc.)
- **Amount financed**—the total amount of credit the lender extends to the borrower, reflecting the subtraction of any prepaid finance charges the borrower paid and the addition of other amounts financed
- **Total of payments** paid at the end of the loan term
- **Mandatory statement**—"You are *not* required to complete this agreement merely because you have received these disclosures or signed a loan application."

Other Required Data for Closed-End Transactions

According to Regulation Z § 1026.18, the following must be disclosed on closed-end transactions:

- Name of the lender/creditor
- Notice of a right to receive an itemization of the amount financed, including the principal amount, all finance charges detailed, and any discounts, points, fees, mortgage insurance premiums, etc., that are financed
- Number, amount, and timing of payments scheduled to repay the obligation
- New payment, late payment, and prepayment provisions
- Description and identification of the security (there will be a phrase such as "There is a security interest in the property purchased")
- Whether the loan may be assumed by a subsequent buyer
- Notice that consumers may *not* be able to refinance to a lower rate in the future (previously required only for adjustable rate loans)
- Payment summary table indicating initial interest rate and corresponding monthly payment

In addition, for adjustable or step-rate mortgages, the payment summary table must include the maximum interest rate and payment that can occur during the first five years and a "worst case" example showing the maximum rate and payment possible over the life of the loan, for example:

	Introductory Rate and Monthly Payment (first period)	Maximum During First Five Years (date)	Maximum Ever as early as (date)
Interest Rate	_____ %	_____ %	_____ %
Principal + Interest Payment	$ _____	$ _____	$ _____
Est. Taxes + Insurance (Escrow) [Includes Private Mortgage Insurance]	$ _____	$ _____	$ _____
Total Est. Monthly Payment	$ _____	$ _____	$ _____

Annual Percentage Rate (APR)

The **annual percentage rate** (APR) tells a borrower the total cost of financing a loan in percentage terms, as a relationship of the total finance charges to the total amount financed. APR includes *not* just the interest rate on the note, but the total cost of the loan, including all other finance charges spread out over the life of the loan. For example, a mortgage loan with a 6% interest rate may have an APR of 6.5%, representing the total cost of the loan, including all finance charges spread over the life of the loan.

Whenever a mortgage loan originator quotes an interest rate to a consumer—whether orally or in writing, including advertisements, websites, etc.—the Truth in Lending Act requires that APR must also be disclosed, even when a consumer just calls for an interest rate quote. Note that even when different interest rates may apply during the loan term, the loan only has one annual percentage rate.

Finance Charges

It can be a challenge to explain closing costs and fees to consumers, especially to define those fees that are considered finance charges for the purposes of calculating the APR. Regulation Z (12 C.F.R. § 1026) defines the **finance charge** (§ 1026.4) as the *cost of consumer credit as a dollar amount*. It includes any charge payable directly or indirectly by the consumer and imposed directly or indirectly by the creditor as an incident to or a condition of the extension of credit. It does *not* include any charge of a type payable in a comparable cash transaction.

The finance charge includes fees and amounts charged by someone other than the creditor, (unless otherwise excluded) if the creditor:

- Requires the use of a third party as a condition of or an incident to the extension of credit, even if the consumer can choose the third party; or
- Retains a portion of the third-party charge, to the extent of the portion retained.

Fees charged by a third party that conducts the loan closing (such as a settlement agent, attorney, or escrow or title company) are finance charges only if the creditor:

- Requires the particular services for which the consumer is charged;
- Requires the imposition of the charge; or
- Retains a portion of the third-party charge, to the extent of the portion retained.

Fees charged by a mortgage broker (including fees paid by the consumer directly to the broker or to the creditor for delivery to the broker) are finance charges even if the creditor does *not* require the consumer to use a mortgage broker and even if the creditor does *not* retain any portion of the charge.

Examples of Finance Charges

According to Regulation Z § 1026.4 (b), the following are examples of finance charges (*not* an all-inclusive list):

- Interest, time price differential, and any amount payable under an add-on or discount system of additional charges
- Service, transaction, activity, and carrying charges, including any charge imposed on a checking or other transaction account to the extent that the charge exceeds the charge for a similar account without a credit feature
- Points, loan fees, assumption fees, finder's fees, and similar charges (note that a finder's fee is *not* the same as a referral fee or a kickback as defined by RESPA; a finder's fee given to a properly licensed individual, such as mortgage broker, for bona fide services rendered, such as finding a lender, is acceptable)
- Appraisal review, investigation, and credit report investigation fees (may be exempt from inclusion in APR if bona-fide third party fees)
- Premiums or other charges for:
  - Any guarantee or insurance protecting the creditor against the consumer's default or other credit loss
  - Credit life, accident, health, or loss-of-income insurance, written in connection with a credit transaction
  - Insurance against loss of or damage to property, or against liability arising out of the ownership or use of property, written in connection with a credit transaction
- Charges imposed on a creditor by another person for purchasing or accepting a consumer's obligation, if the consumer is required to pay the charges in cash, as an addition to the obligation, or as a deduction from the proceeds of the obligation
- Discounts for the purpose of inducing payment by a means other than the use of credit
- Debt cancellation fee, including charges or premiums paid for debt cancellation coverage written in connection with a credit transaction, whether or *not* the debt cancellation coverage is insurance under applicable law

Charges Excluded from the Finance Charge

According to Regulation Z § 1026.4 (c) (d) (e), the following are excluded from being part of the finance charge (*not* an all-inclusive list):

- Application fees charged to all applicants for credit, whether or *not* credit is actually extended
- Charges for actual unanticipated late payment, for exceeding a credit limit or for delinquency, default, or a similar occurrence

- Charges imposed by a financial institution for paying items that overdraw an account, unless the payment of such items and the imposition of the charge were previously agreed upon in writing
- Fees charged for participation in a credit plan, whether assessed on an annual or other periodic basis
- Seller's points
- Interest forfeited as a result of an interest reduction required by law on a time deposit used as security for an extension of credit
- These fees in a transaction secured by real property or in a residential mortgage transaction, if bona fide and a reasonable amount:
  - Fees for title examination, abstract of title, title insurance, property survey, and similar purposes
  - Fees for preparing loan-related documents, such as deeds, mortgages, and reconveyance or settlement documents
  - Notary and credit report fees
  - Property appraisal fees or fees for inspections to assess the value or condition of the property if the service is performed prior to closing, including fees related to pest infestation or flood hazard determinations
  - Amounts required to be paid into escrow or trustee accounts if the amounts would *not* otherwise be included in the finance charge
- Discounts offered to induce payment for a purchase by cash, check, or other means
- Premiums for voluntary credit life, accident, health, loss-of-income insurance, or debt cancellation coverage if the following conditions are met:
  - The insurance coverage or debt cancellation agreement or coverage is *not* required by the creditor, and this fact is disclosed in writing
  - The fee or premium for the initial term of insurance coverage or debt cancellation coverage is disclosed, as well as the term of insurance or coverage when less than the term of the transaction
  - Any consumer in the transaction signs or initials an affirmative written request for the insurance or debt cancellation coverage after receiving the specified disclosures
- Premiums for insurance against loss of or damage to property, or against liability arising out of the ownership or use of property when the following conditions are met:
  - The insurance coverage may be obtained from a person of the consumer's choice, and this fact is disclosed
  - When the coverage is obtained from or through the creditor, the premium for the initial term of insurance coverage is disclosed, as well as the term of the insurance if less than the term of the transaction
- If itemized and disclosed, the following security interest charges may be excluded:
  - Taxes and fees prescribed by law that actually are or will be paid to public officials for determining the existence of or for perfecting, releasing, or satisfying a security interest
  - The premium for insurance in lieu of perfecting a security interest to the extent that the premium does *not* exceed fees described above that otherwise would be payable
  - Taxes on security instruments or on documents evidencing indebtedness if the payment of such taxes is a requirement for recording the instrument

APR Accuracy and Redisclosure

According to the Regulation Z (§ 1026.22), the annual percentage rate (APR) is generally considered accurate if it does *not* vary above or below the APR initially disclosed by more than:

- 1/8% (.125) for a regular transaction.
- 1/4% (.25) for an irregular transaction.

TILA defines an "irregular" transaction as one that includes one or more of the following features:

- Multiple advances
- Irregular payment periods
- Irregular payment amounts (other than an irregular first period or irregular first and final payment)

If a change renders the APR inaccurate prior to loan consummation, the Mortgage Disclosure Improvement Act requires that the borrower be given corrected disclosure of all terms. The consumer must receive the corrected disclosures no later three (3) business days prior to loan consummation. If the corrected disclosures are mailed or delivered by some method other than in person, the consumer is considered to have received them three (3) business days after they were mailed (12 C.F.R. § 1026.19 (a) (2)(ii)).

The loan generally cannot be consummated until both waiting periods have expired. However, a borrower may be able to **waive** the waiting periods and expedite the closing if there's a **bona fide personal financial emergency**, such as to avoid foreclosure. This requires a dated written statement from the borrower with the details of the emergency (12 C.F.R § 1026.19 (a)(3)).

3/7/3 Rule

You can remember the disclosure requirements of TILA as the 3/7/3 Rule:

- Initial disclosure must be given (or placed in the mail) within **three (3) business days** of receipt of a completed application.

- The earliest a loan may be consummated is on the **seventh (7th) business day** after disclosures are delivered/mailed.

- Any corrected disclosures must be received by the consumer at least **three (3) business days** before the loan is consummated.

The loan cannot be consummated until both waiting periods have expired.

Also, remember that consumers are *not* required to continue with the loan during these waiting periods simply because the creditor provided these disclosures.

When considering these waiting periods, Regulation Z 12 C.F.R. § 1026 defines a **business day** to be all calendar days **except** Sundays and the legal public holidays specified in 5 U.S.C. 6103(a), such as New Year's Day, the birthday of Martin Luther King, Jr., Washington's Birthday, Memorial Day, Independence Day, Labor Day, Columbus Day, Veterans Day, Thanksgiving Day, and Christmas Day (12 C.F.R. § 1026.2 (a)(6)).

Right of Rescission

Under Regulation Z (§§ 1026.15 and 1026.23) consumers may have the right to rescind, or withdraw, from certain credit transactions involving the establishment of a security interest (usually a mortgage) of their existing **principal residence**, such as:

- Home equity loans.
- Home improvement loans.
- Refinances.

This right of rescission does *not* apply to the following:

- Purchase loans
- Construction loans
- Commercial loans
- Loans on vacation or second homes

- A refinancing or consolidation by the same creditor of an extension of credit already secured by the consumer's principal dwelling unless the new amount financed exceeds the unpaid principal balance, any earned unpaid finance charge on the existing debt, and amounts attributed solely to the costs of the refinancing or consolidation

- A transaction in which a state agency is a creditor

Note that for the purposes of rescission, the term **consumer** is expanded to include any "natural person in whose principal dwelling a security interest is or will be retained or acquired, if that person's ownership interest in the dwelling is or will be subject to the security interest" (12 C.F.R. § 1026.2 (a) (11)).

Provisions

- Consumers may exercise the right to rescind the credit transaction until midnight of the third business day following loan consummation, delivery of the required rescission notice, or delivery of all material disclosures, whichever occurs last. For example:

Wednesday	Thursday	Friday	Saturday	Sunday	Monday
Loan Consummation SIGNING	Day 1	Day 2	Day 3	--	$$ Disbursed

- Creditors must **inform consumers** of their right to rescind by providing **two copies** of a **Notice of Right to Rescind** document to each consumer entitled to rescind that is separate from the sale or credit document at loan consummation.

- The notice must identify the transaction or occurrence and conspicuously disclose the following:

  o The retention or acquisition of a security interest in the consumer's principal dwelling

  o The consumer's right to rescind

  o How to exercise the right of rescission, with a form to use that designates the address of the creditor's place of business

  o The effects of rescission

  o The date on which the rescission period ends

- When more than one consumer has the right to rescind, the exercise of the right by one consumer is effective for all consumers.

- If the borrower does choose to exercise his right to rescind, the mortgage is void and the creditor must return any money it collected related to the loan **within 20 calendar days**. The borrower has no liability for the loan, including finance charges.

Extended Right of Rescission

Borrowers may have the right to an extended rescission period of up to **three years** under these circumstances:

- The creditor fails to properly notify consumers of the right to rescind.

- The creditor does *not* provide all parties on title with the required material disclosures (or the required corrected redisclosures). "Material" refers to annual percentage rate, finance charge, amount financed, total payments, or payment schedule within the acceptable tolerances.

For the purposes of extended rescission, the acceptable **tolerances** for accuracy include:

1/2 of 1 percent tolerance. The finance charge and other disclosures affected by the finance charge (such as the amount financed and the annual percentage rate) shall be considered accurate if the disclosed finance charge:

- Is understated by no more than **0.5%** of the face amount of the note or **$100**, whichever is greater, or

- Is greater than the amount required to be disclosed.

1 percent tolerance. In a refinancing of a residential mortgage transaction with a new creditor, if there is no new advance and no consolidation of existing loans, the finance charge and other disclosures affected by the finance charge (such as the amount financed and the annual percentage rate) is considered accurate if the disclosed finance charge:

- Is understated by no more than 1 percent of the face amount of the note or $100, whichever is greater, or
- Is greater than the amount required to be disclosed.

The extended right to rescind expires three years after the occurrence giving rise to the right of rescission, upon transfer of all of the consumer's interest in the property, or upon sale of the property, whichever occurs first.

Additional Rescission Considerations for Foreclosures

After the initiation of foreclosure on the consumer's principal dwelling that secures the credit obligation, the consumer shall have the right to rescind the transaction if:

- A mortgage broker fee that should have been included in the finance charge was *not* included.
- The creditor did *not* provide the properly completed Notice of Rescission.

Tolerance for disclosures. After the initiation of foreclosure on the consumer's principal dwelling that secures the credit obligation, the finance charge and other disclosures affected by the finance charge (such as the amount financed and the annual percentage rate) shall be considered accurate if the disclosed finance charge is:

- Understated by no more than $35; or
- Greater than the amount required to be disclosed.

Higher Priced Loans

"Higher priced loans," defined by 2009 amendments to Regulation Z (12 C.F.R. § 1026.35), include closed-end home purchase loans where the APR exceeds the average prime offer rate by at least:

- 1.5 percentage points for first lien loans, or
- 3.5 percentage points for junior lien loans.

These are known as Section 35 loans and can be found in section 35 of Regulation Z of the Truth in Lending Act.

The APR is measured against the applicable average prime offer rate, which is an annual percentage rate derived from average interest rates, points, and other loan pricing terms that are currently offered to consumers by a representative sample of lenders for mortgage transactions that have low-risk pricing characteristics. The average prime offer rate for both fixed and adjustable rate loans is published in a table and updated at least weekly.

This does *not* apply to loans used to finance:

- The initial construction of a dwelling.
- A temporary or "bridge" loan with a term of 12 months or less, such as a loan to purchase a new dwelling where the consumer plans to sell a current dwelling within 12 months.
- A reverse-mortgage transaction.
- A home equity line of credit.

Restrictions

TILA imposes the following restrictions on loans that meet the definition of a higher-priced mortgage loan:

- **Repayment Ability.** Lenders are obligated to verify the repayment ability of the borrower.
- **Prepayment Penalties.** These are generally prohibited unless it is limited to the first two years of the loan. A prepayment penalty is prohibited if the amount of the periodic payment of principal, interest, or

both, can change at any time during the first four years of the loan. It is also prohibited if the source of the prepayment funds is a refinance by the lender or its affiliate.

- **Escrow Accounts.** An escrow account must be established for property taxes and premiums for mortgage-related insurance required by the lender when the loan is a first lien that secures the borrower's principal dwelling. Escrow accounts are *not* required for loans secured by shares in a cooperative. Insurance premiums are *not* required to be included in the escrow account on loans for condominium units if the homeowners' association is required to maintain a master policy insuring all units.

Escrow Requirements on Jumbo Loans

In response to the Dodd-Frank Wall Street Reform and Consumer Protection Act of 2010 (Pub.L. 111-203, H.R. 4173), a final rule was adopted related to escrow requirements on higher-priced first lien loans that exceed Freddie Mac's conforming loan limit (jumbo loans). The rule relates to a 2008 rule implementing the Home Ownership and Equity Protection Act (HOEPA) which prohibits a creditor from extending such a higher-priced mortgage loan unless an escrow account is established for payment of required property taxes and premiums for mortgage-related insurance.

This rule, which became effective April 1, 2011, revised § Sec. 1026.35(b)(3) of Regulation Z, as proposed, to provide a higher APR threshold for determining whether jumbo mortgage loans secured by a first lien on a consumer's principal dwelling are higher-priced mortgage loans for which an escrow account must be established.

As revised, the threshold for coverage of the escrow requirement for jumbo loans is 2.5 percentage points (rather than 1.5 percentage points) in excess of the average prime offer rate for a comparable transaction, as of the date the transaction's rate is set. Raising the APR threshold applicable to jumbo loans eliminates the mandatory escrow requirement for loans with an APR above the existing threshold but below the new threshold. Creditors may, at their option, elect to continue to use the 1.5 percentage point threshold for these loans.

Other TILA Provisions Related to Servicing

Regulation Z implementing the Truth in Lending Act was amended, effective in 2009 (12 C.F.R. § 1026.36), to specifically address perceived abuses in the mortgage industry. The following prohibitions apply to any **closed-end** mortgage loan that is subject to TILA and that is secured by **the consumer's principal dwelling**, regardless of pricing or loan purpose.

Servicing may be defined as receiving any scheduled periodic payments from a borrower according to the terms of any mortgage loan—including amounts for escrow accounts—and making the payments to the owner of the loan or other third parties of principal and interest and such other payments. The following servicing practices would be a violation of the Truth in Lending Act:

- Failing to credit a payment as of the date of receipt (unless the delay results in no adverse consequences to the borrower) when the payment complies with the terms of the legal contract between the lender and the borrower. However, if a servicer accepts a payment that does *not* conform to the requirements, the servicer may credit the payment as of five days after receipt (which may result in a late fee being assessed).

- Imposing any late fee or delinquency charge in connection with a payment, when the only delinquency is attributable to late fees or delinquency charges assessed on an earlier payment, and the payment is otherwise a full payment for the applicable period and is paid on its due date or within any applicable grace period. This prohibited practice may be referred to as "pyramiding" late fees.

- Failing to provide, within a reasonable period of time, statements showing the payoff amounts as of a specified date in time.

Mortgage Disclosure Improvement Act (MDIA)

The Mortgage Disclosure Improvement Act (12 C.F.R. § 1026.16):

- Amends Regulation Z, the Truth in Lending Act (TILA).

- Is intended to ensure accuracy of the disclosures used by a consumer to make a decision and to ensure that the required disclosures are delivered in a timely fashion.

- Gives consumers the right to cancel at any point and not proceed with the transaction if they so choose.

- Specifies that prior to delivery of the mandated disclosures, the only fee that may be charged to a borrower is for a **credit report.**

- Requires added language to the initial and final TIL: *"You are not required to complete this agreement merely because you have received these disclosures or signed a loan application."*

- Requires a **seven business day waiting period** once the initial disclosure is provided before closing a home loan to give the consumer client time to review the loan terms offered to them.

Redisclosure

If the final annual percentage rate APR is off by more than .125% from the initial GFE disclosure, the lender must redisclose and wait another three business days after the consumer receives the revised disclosures before closing on the transaction.

Higher Priced Loans

MDIA defines **higher-priced mortgage loans** as *closed-end mortgage loans secured by the borrower's principal dwelling where the APR—as measured against the applicable average prime offer rate—exceeds the applicable average prime offer rate by at least 1.5% for first lien loans or 3.5% for junior lien loans.*

◇ **Note:** The definition of higher priced loans does not apply to the initial construction of a dwelling, a temporary or "bridge" loan with a term of 12 months or less, a reverse mortgage transaction, or a home equity line of credit.

Restrictions

MDIA imposes the following restrictions on loans that meet the definition of a higher-priced mortgage loan:

- Lenders are obligated to verify the repayment ability of the borrower

- Prepayment penalties are generally prohibited unless limited to the first two years of the loan

- An escrow account must be established for property taxes and premiums for mortgage-related insurance required by the lender when the loan is a first lien that secures the borrower's principal dwelling

Home Ownership and Equity Protection Act (HOEPA)

The **Home Ownership and Equity Protection Act** (HOEPA), **Section 32** of Regulation Z, is a 2002 amendment to the Truth in Lending Act.

HOEPA:

- Establishes disclosure requirements and prohibits deceptive and unfair (predatory) practices in lending by defining restrictions on high cost loans.

- Contains requirements for certain loans with high interest rates and/or fees.

- Is enforced by the **Consumer Financial Protection Bureau** (CFPB) as of July 2011.

- Mandates additional disclosure of terms and consumer protection at least three business days prior to close for high cost loans that meet one of two defined triggers for high interest and/or fees.

- Allows consumers to sue lenders who violate HOEPA for recovery of statutory and actual damages, court costs, and attorney's fees.

- May enable a consumer to rescind the loan for up to **three (3) years** if the lender is in violation of HOEPA.

High Cost Loan Triggers

HOEPA provisions must be complied with once the triggers for a "high cost loan" have been met. A high cost loan, according to HOEPA, is based on the **annual percentage rate (APR)** or the total amount of finance charges (percent or total dollar amount).

Trigger #1: APR Trigger

HOEPA is triggered when the APR exceeds more than 8% on first lien loans or 10% on second lien loans (6.5% on first lien of $50,000 or more and 8.5% on smaller and second lien loans after provisions of Dodd-Frank are implemented via regulation) of the rates in Treasury securities of comparable maturity—based on the 15yh of the month before the month in which the application was received.

Trigger #2: Total Finance Charge Trigger

If the total points and fees paid by the consumer exceed **the larger of $611** for 2012 (adjusted annually) or 8% of the loan amount (5% on loans of at least $20,000 after the provisions of Dodd-Frank are implemented via regulation).

Fulfilling the Mandates of the Dodd-Frank Act

Title XIV of the Dodd-Frank Wall Street Reform and Consumer Protection Act of 2010, designated as the Mortgage Reform and Anti-Predatory Lending Act (§ 1431), amends the Truth in Lending Act (TILA) so that, when implemented via regulation, the triggers that define a high cost loan are lowered to:

- Trigger #1: APR exceeding average prime offer rate by **6.5%** on first lien loans for $50,000 or more or 8.5% on smaller and second lien loans.

- Trigger #2: Total points and fees exceeding **5%** on mortgage loan of at least $20,000 or 8% or a certain dollar amount on loans below $20,000.

- Prepayment penalty applicable for more than three years after closing or that exceed 2% of the prepayment.

The Act also expands the definition of points and fee used for calculating the HOPEA loan trigger and requires the borrower to present certification from an approved loan counselor.

Prohibited Practices

A loan transaction subject to the Home Ownership and Equity Protection Act (HOEPA) may *not* include the following terms (12 C.F.R. § 1026.32 (d)):

- **Balloon payments:** *Where the regular payments do not fully pay off the principal balance and a lump sum payment of more than twice the amount of the regular payments is required* —on HOEPA loans having terms of less than five (5) years. HOEPA-covered loans must also have regular payments to pay down the principal or at least pay interest. **Note:** There is an exception for bridge loans of less than one year used by consumers to buy or build a home: In that situation, balloon payments are *not* prohibited.

- **Negative amortization:** *Where smaller monthly payments that do not fully pay off the loan and that cause an increase in the borrower's total principal debt.* Any interest rate changes and payment schedule caps must be coordinated to avoid this situation.

- **Default interest rates:** *Where there are higher than pre-default rates.* Also, rebates of interest upon default calculated by any method less favorable than the actuarial method.

- A **repayment schedule**: *That consolidates more than two periodic payments that are to be paid in advance from the proceeds of the loan*. The borrower should get the maximum use of the funds and have a legitimate opportunity to use the loan proceeds.

- **Prepayment penalties: Generally prohibited** *unless* limited to the first five (5) years of the loan. A prepayment penalty is also prohibited if the consumer's total monthly debts including the HOEPA loan exceed 50% of the consumer's gross monthly income verified by the creditor.

- **Due on demand clauses** (*including any provision that would enable the creditor to call the loan before maturity*): *Strictly prohibited*. Only certain behavior of the consumer would permit the lender to call the loan, such as fraud, material misrepresentation, default, or damage to the security property.

Additional Prohibitions

Additionally, according to Regulation Z 12 C.F.R. § 1026.34, creditors granting loans meeting HOEPA criteria may *not*:

- Grant loans solely based on the collateral value of the borrower's property without regard to the borrower's **ability to repay** the loan (using the largest payment of principal and interest scheduled in the first seven years following consummation).

- Disburse proceeds from home improvement loans to anyone other than the borrower, jointly to the borrower and the home improvement contractor, or, in some instances, to the escrow agent.

- Refinance a HOEPA loan into another HOEPA loan within the first 12 months of origination, unless the new loan is in the borrower's best interest. The prohibition also applies to assignees holding or servicing the loan.

- Wrongfully document a closed-end, high cost loan as an open-end loan. For example, a high cost mortgage may *not* be structured as a home equity line of credit if there is no reasonable expectation that repeat transactions will occur.

Required Disclosures

Creditors granting loans meeting HOEPA criteria must disclose certain facts about the loan in a written notice as part of the loan package in addition to the normal Regulation Z disclosures. The HOEPA notice, sometimes called **Section 32 Disclosures**, is intended to protect consumers from pressure tactics that imply the consumer is already locked into the agreement, or that canceling will be prohibitively complex or expensive. The notice, which must be in a conspicuous font size, is required to include the exact language as mandated by HOEPA:

Disclosure Form

You are not required to complete this agreement merely because you have received these disclosures or signed a loan application.

If you obtain this loan, the lender will have a mortgage on your home.

You could lose your home, and any money you have put into it, if you do not meet your obligations under the loan.

You are borrowing $ _____ . [Optional credit insurance ☐ is ☐ is not included in this amount.]

The annual percentage rate on your loan will be _____ %.

Your regular _____ frequency _____ payment will be $_____ .

[At the end of the loan, you will still owe us $ balloon amount _____ .]

[Your interest rate may rise. Increases in the interest rate could raise your payment. The highest amount your payment could increase is to $ _____ .]

Homeowners Protection Act (HPA)

The federal **Homeowners Protection Act** of 1998, or HPA, (Pub. L. No. 105-216, 112 Stat. 897) requires lenders or servicers to provide certain disclosures and notifications concerning **private mortgage insurance** (PMI) on residential mortgage transactions. Most provisions of the Act do *not* apply to home loans made before July 29, 1999.

- Lenders / servicers must provide notify borrower of rights related to private mortgage insurance (PMI), including:
    - Initial written disclosure
    - Annual reminders
- Covers lenders that grant residential mortgages, defined as a mortgage, loan, or other evidence of a security interest created with respect to a single-family dwelling that is the primary residence of the borrower.
- Does *not* apply to VA loans, FHA loans, or loans with no PMI.
- Borrower may request cancellation of mortgage insurance when mortgage loan is paid down to 80% LTV of original purchase price of appraised value of the home at the time the loan was obtained whichever is less, provided the borrower has not been 30 days late within a year of the request or 60 days late within two years. Note: New Rules for FHA loans effective April 2013 require that PMI be paid for a minimum of 11 years.
- Mortgage insurance is automatically canceled (terminated) when LTV is 78% of original value if the borrower is current on the loan. Note: New Rules for FHA loans effective April 2013 require that PMI be paid for a minimum of 11 years.
- Lenders may require evidence that the value of the property has not declined below its original value and that the property does not have a second mortgage, such as a home equity loan.
- Borrower may accelerate cancellation date with additional payments.

Equal Credit Opportunity Act (ECOA) — REG B

The **Equal Credit Opportunity Act** (15 U.S.C. § 1691 et seq.) is a federal law that *ensures that all consumers are given an equal chance to obtain credit.* ECOA. Let's review some key points:

- Applies to any creditor who regularly extends credit, including banks, small loan and finance companies, retail and department stores, credit card companies, credit unions, and real estate brokers who arrange financing.
- Implemented as **Regulation B** and enforced by the **Consumer Financial Protection Bureau (CFPB)**, with each financial institution falling under the authority of its respective regulatory agency.
- Was originally passed in 1974 to prohibit lending discrimination on the basis of sex or marital status.
- Requires creditors to disclose to consumers what their rights are under ECOA, including a notice to the applicant of their right to receive a copy of any appraisal report on the property that was used in the credit decision-making process.
- Requires credit bureaus to maintain separate credit files on married spouses, if requested.
- Allows credit applicants to file discrimination complaints or bring a civil lawsuit for alleged discrimination.
- Requires creditors to maintain records of application and related information for **25 months** (12 months for business credit) after notifying applicant of action taken.

Protections

ECOA prohibits discrimination in granting credit to **individuals** and **businesses** based on:

- Sex
- Age (provided the applicant has the capacity to contract)
- Marital status
- Race

- Color
- Religion
- National origin
- Receipt of public assistance
- Exercised rights under the Consumer Credit Protection Act

[handwritten: IF SUED ANOTHER LENDER PREVIOUSLY]

Generally, ECOA prohibits a creditor from inquiring about a consumer's marital status or intentions related to having or raising children.

ECOA also prohibits creditors from making any oral or written statement, in advertising or otherwise, to applicants or prospective applicants that would discourage them from making or pursuing an application on a prohibited basis, such as membership in a protected class.

Marital Status

To comply with ECOA, a mortgage loan originator should *not* ask about **marital status** or a spouse *unless:*

- It is a joint application,
- The applicant is relying on their spouse's income or alimony or child support from a former spouse to qualify,
- It is in a community property state, and the loan is secured by property, as with a mortgage.

When permitted to ask about marital status, use only these terms:

- Married
- Unmarried (single, divorced, or widowed)
- Separated

> ◇ **Note:** In states that recognize **dower or curtesy rights** of spouses, it is acceptable to ask about marital status even if only one person is applying for the loan. In such states, the non-borrowing spouse must consent, since the non-borrowing spouse has an interest in the security instrument.

Income Evaluation

When evaluating a borrower's gross income, a creditor may *not* discount or refuse to consider:

- Public assistance income.
- Income because of sex or marital status.
- Income from verifiable and consistent part-time employment, overtime, pension, annuity, or retirement benefits programs.
- Regular alimony, child support, or separate maintenance payments **if the applicant chooses to disclose it.** (Nor can a creditor discriminate against applicants who exercise their good faith rights of nondisclosure of those sources of income.)

Required Disclosures

Creditors must disclose customer's rights under ECOA.

Creditors must notify applicants of lending decision within **thirty (30) days** of filing a completed application as follows:

- Approved—**Commitment Letter**
- Incomplete—**Notice of Incomplete Application**
- Denied or offered less favorable terms or if there was a change of terms of an existing credit agreement— **Statement of Adverse Action**, in writing

Statement of Adverse Action must include specific reasons for the decision or inform the applicant of the right to request specific reasons for the decision within **60 days** of a credit decision.

Borrowers have a right to request a copy of the **appraisal report** used in the decision process **within 90 days** of a credit decision.

Home Mortgage Disclosure Act (HMDA) — *REF C*

The Home Mortgage Disclosure Act (12 U.S.C. § 2801-2810) was enacted to discover discriminatory practices, including **redlining**, by analyzing whether an institution turns down a disproportionate percentage of applications by race, gender, or ethnicity or by certain neighborhoods.

HMDA:

- Was enacted by Congress in 1975 and enforced by the **Consumer Financial Protection Bureau (CFPB)** as **Regulation C.**

- Applies to certain financial institutions, including banks, savings associations, credit unions, and other mortgage lending institutions including, but *not* limited to, mortgage lenders, mortgage bankers, and mortgage brokers, if they do a sufficient amount of business to be subject to Regulation C reporting requirements.

- Does *not* prohibit any specific activity of lenders nor does it establish a quota system of mortgage loans to be made in any metropolitan statistical area (MSA) or other geographic area as defined by the Office of Management and Budget.

- Requires a lending institution to post a general notice about the availability of HMDA data in the lobby of its home office and of each branch office located in a metropolitan area. Such data must be maintained and made available, upon request, for **three years**.

- Information gathered in part from Section X (Information for Government Monitoring Purposes) of the Uniform Residential Loan Application.

- Provides loan data that can be used by the public to assist in:

    - Determining whether financial institutions are serving the housing needs of their communities.

    - Aiding public officials in targeting public-sector investments so as to attract private investment to areas where it is needed.

    - Identifying possible discriminatory lending patterns through the collection and disclosure of data about applicant and borrower characteristics.

◇ **Note:** HMDA was one factor that led to the passage of the Community Reinvestment Act (CRA) in 1977, which was enacted to reduce discriminatory credit practices against low-income neighborhoods and to encourage financial institutions to help met the credit needs of the communities in which they operate.

Covered Properties

HMDA applies to applications for **one- to four-family residential** loans, including:

- Home purchase
- Home improvement
- Refinancing
- Subordinate financing

◇ **Note:** It does *not* apply to loans on vacant land, new construction, or on loans that are sold as part of a pool for servicing.

Data Reporting

Regulation C requires financial institutions to submit a report—called a **Loan/Application Register** or **LAR**—to their supervisory agencies on a loan-by-loan and application-by-application basis every March. A LAR includes the following data:

- Loan originations
- Applications
- Loan purchases
- Requests under a pre-approval program, if the pre-approval request is denied or results in the origination of a home purchase loan

The application, lending, and denial data that lending institutions subject to HMDA are required to report for all borrowers includes:

- Loan type, amount, and purpose
- Interest rate and rate spread, the difference between the annual percentage rate (APR) and the applicable Treasury yield if the spread is equal to or greater than three (3) percentage points for first-liens and five (5) percentage points for subordinate loans
- Property type and occupancy
- Ethnicity, race, and sex of applicant and co-applicants
- Applicant gross income
- Loan decision, including denial reason(s)
- Population and the percentage of which is minority (census tract)
- Whether or *not* the loan is subject to the Home Ownership and Equity Protection Act (HOEPA) controls related to predatory lending
- The type of purchaser for mortgage loans that they sell

◇ **Note:** Mortgage loan originators must ask the applicant for the information needed for the Loan/Application Register (LAR) whether the application is taken in person, by mail, telephone, or on the Internet—but cannot require the applicant to provide it. If the applicant declines to answer these questions or fails to provide the information on an application taken by mail or telephone or on the Internet, the data need *not* be provided. If the applicant chooses *not* to provide the information for an application taken in person, however, this fact must be noted on form, as well as the applicant's ethnicity, race, and sex on the basis of visual observation and surname, to the extent possible.

Additional Data

Title X of the Dodd-Frank Wall Street Reform and Consumer Protection Act of 2010, which is designated the Consumer Financial Protection Act, includes provisions that, when implemented via regulation, will also require MLOs to collect the following data about mortgage loan applicants in order to comply with HMDA, including:

- Age
- Credit score
- Total points and fees
- Loan term and pricing
- Prepayment penalty information
- Loan-to-value (LTV)
- Period of any introductory interest rate or interest only
- Negative amortization information
- Channel of origination

Role of the FFIEC

Supervisory agencies, through the **Federal Financial Institutions Examination Council** (FFIEC):

- Compile this information in the form of individual disclosure statements for each institution, and in the form of aggregate reports for all covered institutions within each MSA.
- Produces other aggregate reports that show lending patterns by median age of homes and by the central city or non-central city location of the property.

The analysis of HMDA data is a critical component to determine if there is compliance with ECOA as well as fair lending laws.

Fair Credit Reporting Act (FCRA) — REG V

Regulation V (12 C.F.R. 1022) implements the **Fair Credit Reporting Act** (15 U.S.C. § 1681), a federal law dealing with the granting of credit, access to credit information, the rights of debtors, and the responsibilities of creditors.

FCRA:

- Gives consumers access to the same information about themselves that lenders use when making credit decisions.

The Consumer Financial Protection Bureau (CFPB) publishes guides for consumers that explain all of their rights under FCRA, including

- the ability to seek damages for violations of their rights
- additional rights for identity theft victims and active duty military personnel

Consumer Rights: Copy of Consumer Credit File

Consumers are entitled to a free copy of their **credit report** under these circumstances:

- Information in a credit report resulted in **adverse action.** Adverse action requires the creditor to provide the consumer with the name, address, and phone number of the agency that provided the information. The requirements under FCRA differ somewhat from those under the ECOA, although both laws can be satisfied with a single Adverse Action Notice (sometimes called a Statement of Credit Denial).
- The consumer was a victim of **identify theft** and a fraud alert was inserted in credit file.
- The credit file contains inaccurate information as a result of fraud.
- The consumer is on **public assistance** or is **unemployed.**

Other Consumer Rights — CREDIT SCORE != credit report

- **Request a Credit Score.** Although it is *not* free, consumers have the right to ask for a **credit score** from any consumer reporting agencies that create or distribute scores used in residential real property loans. Title X of the Dodd-Frank Wall Street Reform and Consumer Protection Act of 2010, § 1100F, amends the Fair Credit Reporting Act to require a creditor to provide a consumer with a written or electronic disclosure of the numeric credit score used in taking any adverse action, including a risk-based pricing notice.
- **Dispute Incomplete or Inaccurate Information.** Consumers have the right to dispute any incomplete or inaccurate information that they find in their credit report. The consumer reporting agency must correct or delete inaccurate, incomplete, or unverifiable information.
- **Limit Prescreened Offers.** Consumers may choose to limit "prescreened" offers of credit and insurance based on information in their credit report. Unsolicited prescreened offers for credit and insurance must include a toll-free phone number to call to be removed from the lists on which these offers are based.

Consumer Reporting Agency Obligations

Under the Fair Credit Reporting Act, consumer reporting agencies:

- May *not* **report outdated negative** information. In most cases, a consumer reporting agency will *not* report negative credit information that is more than **seven (7) years old** or bankruptcies that are more than **ten (10) years old**. Credit reporting agencies generally remove Chapter 13 bankruptcies after seven (7) years, however, and Chapter 7 bankruptcies after ten (10) years.

> **Note:** The timing begins from discharge or dismissal date, *not* the date the case was filed.

- There is no time limit on the reporting of criminal convictions.
- Must **limit access** to a credit file. A consumer reporting agency may provide information to people with a valid need—usually to consider an application with a creditor, insurer, employer, landlord, or other business. The FCRA specifies those with a valid need for access.
- May *not* give out consumer credit information to an employer, or a potential employer, without written consent given to the employer by the consumer.

Fair and Accurate Credit Transaction Act (FACTA)

The **Fair and Accurate Credit Transaction Act** of 2003 (Pub.L. 108-159):

- Amended the federal Fair Credit Reporting Act.
- Referred to as either the FACT Act or, more commonly, FACTA.
- Is intended primarily to help consumers fight the growing crime of **identity theft** and to dispute inaccurate credit information.
- Contains seven major titles: Identity Theft Prevention and Credit History Restoration, Improvements in Use of and Consumer Access to Credit Information, Enhancing the Accuracy of Consumer Report Information, Limiting the Use and Sharing of Medical Information in the Financial System, Financial Literacy and Education Improvement, Protecting Employee Misconduct Investigations, and Relation to State Laws.
- Applies to federal and state-chartered banks and credit unions, non-bank lenders, mortgage brokers, any person that regularly participates in a credit decision, including setting the terms of credit, and any person who requests a consumer report.

Provisions

FACTA includes provisions related to:

- Accuracy.
- Privacy.
- Limits on information sharing.
- New consumer rights to disclosure.

Access to Credit Reports (Section 211)

- Requires that consumers applying for credit receive the **Home Loan Applicant Credit Score Information Disclosure** notice, which explains their rights
- Allows consumers to obtain a free copy of their credit report **once every twelve (12) months** from each of the three credit bureaus—Equifax, Experian, and TransUnion—by contacting a centralized website, (maintained in cooperation with the Federal Trade Commission): www.annualcreditreport.com
- Allows consumers to request that the first five digits of their Social Security number (or similar identification number) are *not* included in the credit report file they receive

Fraud Alerts and Freezes (Section 112)

- Allows consumers who believe they have been a victim of identity theft to contact the Credit Bureau and place a **fraud alert**
- Requires creditors running a credit report with a fraud alert to contact the person whose name is on the account at a number he provided to the credit bureau or take other reasonable steps to ensure that the person applying for a mortgage loan is *not* really an identity thief
- Allows consumers to place a **credit freeze** in order to prevent the information from showing on a credit report. The consumer may then "thaw" the credit report when they apply for a loan
- Allows members of the military who are deploying overseas to place a credit freeze, thereby making fraudulent applications for credit more difficult

Truncation of Credit and Debit Card Numbers (Section 113)

FACTA also prohibits businesses from printing more than five digits of any customer's card number or card expiration date on any receipt provided to the cardholder at the point of sale or transaction. Note: The provision excludes receipts that are handwritten or imprinted, if that is the only method of recording the credit card number.

Security and Disposal (Section 216)

Requires businesses to take measures to responsibly **secure and dispose** of sensitive personal information that is found in a consumer's credit report. Reasonable methods for security and disposal include:

- Burning or shredding papers that contain consumer report information so that information cannot be reconstructed
- Destroying or erasing electronic files or media so that information cannot be recovered or reconstructed
- Placing all pending loan documents in locked desks, cabinets, or storage rooms at the end of the work day

Red Flags Rules (Section 114)

Section 114 of FACTA, known as the **Red Flags Rules**, applies to federal and state-chartered banks and credit unions, non-bank lenders, mortgage brokers, any person that regularly participates in a credit decision— including setting the terms of credit, and any person who requests a consumer report.

Red Flags Rules require:

- Financial institutions and creditors to implement a written identity theft prevention program that is appropriate to the size and operation of their particular business.
- Card issuers to assess the validity of change of address requests.
- Users of consumer reports to reasonably verify the identity of the subject of a consumer report in the event of a notice of address discrepancy.

Types of Red Flags

Red flags generally fall into these categories:

- Alerts, notifications, or warnings from a consumer reporting agency
- Suspicious documents
- Suspicious personally identifying information, such as a suspicious address
- Unusual use of—or suspicious activity relating to—a covered account
- Notices from customers, victims of identity theft, law enforcement authorities, or other businesses about possible identity theft in connection with covered accounts

The National Do Not Call Registry

- A provision of the federal Telemarketing Sales Rule (16 C.F.R. Part 310), the National Do Not Call Registry, is managed by the **Federal Trade Commission** (FTC), the nation's consumer protection agency and enforced by the FTC, the Federal Communications Commission (FCC), and state law enforcement officials.

- Applies to any plan, program, or campaign to sell goods or services through interstate phone calls. This includes telemarketers who solicit consumers, often on behalf of third party sellers. It also includes sellers who provide, offer to provide, or arrange to provide goods or services to consumers in exchange for payment. The National Do Not Call Registry does *not* limit calls by political organizations, charities, or telephone surveyors.

- Requires companies to maintain national and internal lists of customers and prospects and keep them updated regularly (national list every three months; internal every 30 days).

- Prohibits calls to consumers no later than 31 days after consumer asks to be included on the registry.

- Allows consumers who receive a telemarketing call despite being on the registry to file a complaint with the FTC. Violators could be fined up to **$16,000 per incident.**

Established Business Relationship

A telemarketer or seller may call a consumer with whom it has an **established business relationship** (EBR) for up to **eighteen (18) months** after the consumer's last purchase, delivery, or payment, even if the consumer's number is on the National Do Not Call Registry. In addition, a company may call a consumer for up to **three (3) months** after the consumer makes an inquiry or submits an application to the company. Obtaining the name, phone number, and **signature** from a consumer provides written consent that does *not* expire until rescinded.

One warning: If a consumer has asked to be put on the company's internal Do Not Call list, the company may *not* call, even if there is an EBR. The prohibition on calling applies only to sales or business solicitation. One may call regarding an existing business relationship for collection purposes or other similar actions.

Mortgage Assistance Relief Services (M.A.R.S.)

Homeowners are protected by a Federal Trade Commission (FTC) rule that bans providers of mortgage foreclosure rescue and loan modification services from collecting fees until homeowners have a written offer from their lender or servicer that they decide is acceptable.

"At a time when many Americans are struggling to pay their mortgages, peddlers of so-called mortgage relief services have taken hundreds of millions of dollars from hundreds of thousands of homeowners without ever delivering results," FTC Chairman Jon Leibowitz said. "By banning providers of these services from collecting fees until the customer is satisfied with the results, this rule will protect consumers from being victimized by these scams."

The intent of the Mortgage Assistance Relief Services (MARS) Rule is to protect distressed homeowners from mortgage relief scams such as the ones that sprung up during the mortgage crisis.

These fraudulent mortgage relief schemes involved bogus operations falsely claiming that, for a fee, they would negotiate with the consumer's mortgage lender or servicer to obtain a loan modification, a short sale, or other relief from foreclosure. Many of these operations pretended to be affiliated with the government and government housing assistance programs.

The FTC has brought more than 30 cases against operations like these, and state and federal law enforcement partners have brought hundreds more. The MARS Rule was established to combat this predatory practice

Key Provisions

The following are among the key provisions of the final MARS rule (12 C.F.R. § 1015):

- A ban on those who provide mortgage foreclosure rescue and loan modification services from collecting fees until homeowners have a written offer from their lender or servicer that they decide is acceptable.

- A requirement that mortgage relief companies disclose key information to consumers to protect them from being misled and to help them make better informed purchasing decisions, for example, the company's fee, the fact that the company is not associated with the government, and that the consumer has the right to discontinue doing business with the company at any time.

- A prohibition against making any false or misleading claims about their services, for example, any guarantees or the amount of money the consumer will save.

- A prohibition barring mortgage relief companies from advising consumers to discontinue communication with their lenders.

◇ **Note:** For additional information about the MARS Rule, use this link to access the FTC's web page: http://www.ftc.gov/opa/2010/11/mars.shtm

Advance Fee Ban

The most significant consumer protection under the FTC's MARS rule is the **advance fee ban**. Under this provision, mortgage relief companies may *not* collect any fees until they have provided consumers with a written offer from their lender or servicer that the consumer decides is acceptable, and a written document from the lender or servicer describing the key changes to the mortgage that would result if the consumer accepts the offer. The companies also must remind consumers of their right to reject the offer without any charge.

This ruling *not* only applies to loan modifications, but also to short sales. Fines of $11,000 per occurrence and $11,000 per day may be incurred for violations, so it is important that you understand the new regulations and are compliant.

For more information, refer to the FTC's update: *FTC Issues Final Rule to Protect Struggling Homeowners from Mortgage Relief Scams on the following web page:* http://www.ftc.gov/opa/2010/11/mars.shtm

Bank Secrecy Act (BSA)/Anti-Money Laundering Act

The Currency and Foreign Transactions Reporting Act of 1970 is commonly referred to as the "Bank Secrecy Act" or "BSA"). The BSA requires financial institutions in the United States to assist U.S. government agencies to detect and prevent money laundering. The BSA was originally passed by the Congress of the United States in 1970, and amended several times since then, including provisions in Title III of the USA PATRIOT Act. (See 31 USC 5311-5330 and 31 CFR Chapter X.) The BSA is often referred to as the Anti-Money Laundering Law ("AML"), or sometimes as "BSA/AML."

Specifically, the Act requires financial institutions to:

- Keep records of cash purchases of negotiable instruments.
- File reports of cash transactions exceeding $10,000 (daily aggregate amount).
- Report suspicious activity that might signify money laundering, tax evasion, or other criminal activities.

Gramm-Leach-Bliley Act (GLBA)

Various laws have been passed that address the disclosure and protection of private information, including the Fair Credit Reporting Act (FCRA) and the Fair and Accurate Credit Transactions Act (FACT Act).

The Gramm-Leach-Bliley Act (GLB) (15 U.S.C. § 6801), also known as The **Financial Services Modernization Act of 1999,** was another piece of legislation that was enacted to provide additional consumer protection with regard to financial transactions. This Act includes provisions in **Title V** to protect and regulate the disclosure of consumers' personal financial information.

There are three principal parts to the Title V privacy requirements:

- Financial Privacy Rule.
- Safeguards Rule.
- Pretexting Provisions.

Financial Privacy Rule

The Financial Privacy Rule (15 U.S.C. § 6801–6809) governs the collection and disclosure of customers' personal financial information—known as **nonpublic personal information.** This rule restricts when and under what circumstances such information may be disclosed to affiliates and to nonaffiliated third parties.

Nonpublic Personal Information

Nonpublic personal information is defined as: Any personally-identifiable financial information that a financial institution collects about an individual in connection with providing a financial product or service, such as:

- Information on an application.
- Data from a credit reporting agency.
- Transactions between individuals and companies such as an account balance, payment history, or debit/credit card purchase information.
- Whether or not an individual is a consumer or customer of a particular financial institution.

Prohibited Practices

The Financial Privacy Rule:

- Prohibits financial institutions from disclosing—other than to a consumer reporting agency—access codes or account numbers to any nonaffiliated third party for use in telemarketing, direct mail marketing, or other marketing through electronic mail.
- Requires a **Consumer Privacy Policy** notice that explains the lender's information collection and information sharing practices be provided to **consumers before** the company discloses personal information. Note: **Customers** must receive this notice **annually** for the duration of the financial relationship.
- Allows consumers to **opt out** of having their private information shared.

Safeguards Rule

The Safeguards Rule (15 U.S.C. § 6801–6809) requires all financial institutions and institutions that receive consumer's financial information to design, implement, and maintain safeguards to protect customer information while it is in the custody and control of the institution and its agents.

A written Safeguards Policy must include provisions that:

- Ensure the security and confidentiality of customer records.
- Protect against any anticipated threats or hazards to the security of such records.
- Protect against the unauthorized access or use of such records or information in ways that could result in substantial harm or inconvenience to customers.

Pretexting Provisions

Pretexting provisions:

- Protect consumers from individuals and companies that obtain their personal financial information under false, fictitious, or fraudulent pretenses (15 U.S.C. § 6821–6827).

The SAFE Mortgage Licensing Act

The **Housing and Economic Recovery Act of 2008 (HERA)** is a major housing law designed to assist with the recovery and the revitalization of America's residential housing market (Pub.L. 110-289). HERA has multiple purposes: The modernization of the Federal Housing Administration, foreclosure prevention, and the enhancement of consumer protections.

Title V, the **Secure and Fair Enforcement for Mortgage Licensing Act** or **SAFE Act:**

- Requires all states to implement a SAFE-compliant Mortgage Loan Originator (MLO) licensing process that meets certain minimum standards through the **Nationwide Mortgage Licensing System & Registry (NMLS).**

- **Provisions of the SAFE Act are implemented as Regulation G (12 C.F.R. 1007) for federal licensing and as Regulation H (12 C.F.R. 1008) for state licensing.**

- Requires that all mortgage loan originators (MLOs) must be either state-licensed or federally registered.

- Is designed to enhance consumer protection and reduce fraud by requiring national minimum standards for mortgage training, including prelicensing education and annual continuing education.

- Requires all mortgage loan originators seeking state licensure, or currently holding a state license, to pass the SAFE Mortgage Loan Originator Test, which includes a national test component and, effective as of April 2013, a uniform state component (UST).

Fulfilling the Mandates of the SAFE Act

With the enactment of the SAFE Act, the Conference of State Bank Supervisors (CSBS) and the American Association of Residential Mortgage Regulators (AARMR) worked with the Department of Housing and Urban Development (HUD) to fulfill the mandates of the Act, including the requirements that states establish minimum standards for the licensing or registration of all mortgage loan originators. To that end, CSBS and AARMR developed a model state law that met the minimum standards in the SAFE Act, including definitions, education and testing requirements, and financial responsibility and criminal background standards for mortgage loan originators. HUD reviewed the model legislation and determined that it did indeed meet the requirements of the SAFE Act. Therefore, any state legislation that follows the model will also have met the applicable minimum requirements of the SAFE Act.

Uniform State Test (UST)

On April 1, 2013, the NMLS will launch the Uniform State test or UST. The UST will become Section V of the National Mortgage Loan Originator Test, adding 25 questions on high level state-related content. This brings the length of the national MLO test to 125 questions, of which, 115 will be scored and 10 will be unscored. After the launch of the UST, all applicants must take and pass the UST section of the national exam regardless of which state they are seeking licensure in. In addition, a short version of the UST, called the Standalone UST, will be introduced and it will include 25 questions, all of which will be scored. Twenty-four states have elected to adopt the UST as their state test component by June 2013; selected other states or territories may require an additional state-specific test component.

The new UST material will test applicants on their knowledge of high level state-related content that is based on the SAFE Act and the CSBS/AARMR Model State Law (MSL) which many states used to implement the SAFE Act. More information about the new SAFE MLO National Test with UST, and the Standalone UST, including the content outline and references for study can be found in Chapter 5.

◇   **Note:** The April 2013 launch of the UST is the first major change to SAFE mortgage loan originator test requirements since July 2009. In Chapter 5, we include complete review of the objectives and requirements of the SAFE Act, as we discuss the recent implementation of the UST (Section V) component of the SAFE Mortgage Loan Originator Test.

Federal Mortgage-Related Law Summary

Requiring Financial Disclosures		
Federal Law	**Highlights**	**Disclosures/Notices**
Truth in Lending Act (Regulation Z, TILA) 1968; amended by Mortgage Disclosure Improvement Act (MDIA) 2009 Enforced by Consumer Financial Protection Bureau	• Promotes the informed use of credit by disclosing costs in a uniform manner • Applies to loans with more than four installments • Provides right of rescission for three business days after loan consummation on refinance of owner-occupied property • Completed application requires use of TIL Statement (credit terms, including APR and total finance charges, payment amounts, and due dates) • Imposes a prescribed tolerance between TIL APR and final APR • 3/7/3 Rule – initial disclosure within 3 business days; earliest close 7th business day after initial disclosure; 3 business-day waiting period before consummation if redisclosure required	Within 3 Business Days of Completed Application: • TIL disclosure statement / guide to TIL Statement • When Home is on the Line (home equity loans) • CHARM booklet (ARM loans) At Settlement (for loans on primary residence): • Notice of right to rescind (2 copies) General • Disclosure of APR in advertising with certain triggering terms
Real Estate Settlement Procedures Act (Regulation X, RESPA) 1974 Enforced by Consumer Financial Protection Bureau	• Helps consumers compare settlement services and eliminate unnecessary increases in the costs of certain settlement services • Covers loans secured with a mortgage placed on a one- to four-family residential property • Prohibits kickbacks, fee-splitting, and unearned fees • Sets limits on escrow accounts • Prohibits sellers from requiring home buyers to use a particular title insurance company • Requires Good Faith Estimate (GFE) showing amount of settlement charges the borrower is likely to pay; includes tools for consumers to compare • Requires use of HUD-1 or HUD-1A Settlement Statement to clearly show all charges imposed on borrowers and sellers in connection with the settlement (except for open-end home equity)	Within 3 Business Days of Completed Application: • Good Faith Estimate • Mortgage Servicing Disclosure • HUD Booklet on Settlement Costs Before Settlement: • Affiliated Business Arrangement Disclosure • HUD-1 Settlement Statement (within 1 business day of settlement if requested) At Settlement: • HUD-1 Settlement Statement • Initial Escrow Statement After Settlement: • Annual Escrow Statement • Servicing Transfer Statement
Homeowners Protection Act (HPA) 1998 Enforced by Consumer Financial Protection Bureau	• Applies to single-family residential dwellings	• Initial disclosure of HPA provisions with annual reminders

FLASH CARDS

Privacy and Consumer Identification

Federal Law	Highlights	Disclosures/Notices
Fair Credit Reporting Act (Regulation V, FCRA) 1968 Enforced by Consumer Financial Protection Bureau	• Gives consumers access to the same information about themselves that lenders use when making credit decisions • Entitles consumers to free credit report upon adverse action or identity theft • Allows consumers to dispute credit report • Provides additional rights for identity theft victims and active duty military personnel	• One-time written notice of derogatory information, separate from Truth in Lending disclosures
Fair and Accurate Credit Transaction Act of 2003 (FACT Act) Enforced by Consumer Financial Protection Bureau	• Amends the Fair Credit Reporting Act to help consumers fight identity theft • Mandates limits on information sharing • Entitles consumers to annual free credit report • Allows consumers to place fraud alerts and credit freezes • Requires businesses to truncate credit/debit card numbers on receipts • Mandates businesses to secure and properly dispose of sensitive personal information in a consumer's credit report • Red Flag Rules require financial institutions and creditors to implement a written identity theft prevention program	When Applying for Credit: • Home Loan Applicant Credit Score Information Disclosure
Gramm-Leach-Bliley Act or Financial Services Modernization Act of 1999 (The Privacy Act) Privacy of Consumer Financial Information (Reg P) provisions enforced by Consumer Financial Protection Bureau	Financial Privacy Rule: • Restricts when and under what circumstances personal financial information may be disclosed to non-affiliated third parties • Allows consumers to opt out of allowing information to be shared Safeguards Rule: • Requires all financial institutions to design, implement, and maintain safeguards to protect customer information while it is in the custody and control of the institution and its agents and in the transfer of such information Pretexting Provisions: • Protects consumers from those who obtain personal information under false, fictitious, or fraudulent pretenses	Before Disclosing Information to Non-Affiliated Third Parties: • Consumer Privacy Policy (and annually to customers as long as the relationship continues)
National Do Not Call Registry Enforced by Federal Trade Commission	• Allows consumers to put phone numbers on a national Do Not Call list • Applies to any plan, program, or campaign to sell goods or services through interstate phone calls • Requires companies to maintain national and internal lists of customers and prospects and keep them updated regularly • Allows business to call a consumer with whom it has an established business relationship (EBR) for up to 18 months after the consumer's last purchase, delivery, or payment; or up to 90 days after an inquiry • Imposes fines of up to $16,000 per violation	None
U.S. Patriot Act (Uniting and Strengthening America by Providing Appropriate Tools Required to Intercept and Obstruct Terrorism Act) 2001	• Requires lenders and banks to create and maintain customer identification programs (CIPs) to verify identity of customers entering into a "formal relationship" • Mortgage brokers must also perform the lender's CIP	Patriot Act Information Disclosure

Prohibiting Discrimination		
Federal Law	**Highlights**	**Disclosures/Notices**
Civil Rights Act 1866	• Prohibits all racial discrimination, private or public, in the sale and rental of property • Allows someone claiming unlawful discrimination to sue only in federal district court	None
Fair Housing Act 1968	• Prohibits any discrimination in the sale, lease, or loan terms for residential property based on race, color, religion, sex, national origin, disability, or familial status • Allows someone claiming discrimination to file a written complaint to the nearest HUD office within one year of the alleged violation	• Fair/Equal Housing/Lending posters and logos • Post availability of information in lobby (depository institutions)
Equal Credit Opportunity Act (Regulation B, ECOA) 1974 Enforced by Consumer Financial Protection Bureau	• Prohibits discrimination in granting credit to people based on sex, age (if at least 18), marital status, race, color, religion, national origin, receipt of public assistance, or exercised rights under the Consumer Credit Protection Act • Requires credit bureaus to keep separate files on married spouses, if requested • Prohibits creditors from refusing to consider or discounting income from alimony, child support, maintenance if borrower chooses to disclose it • Allows borrowers to request copy of appraisal report used in credit decision within 90 days	• ECOA statement of rights, including right to receive a copy of appraisal report • Notification of credit decision within 30 days of application (statement of adverse action if declined, incomplete, or change of terms offered)
Home Mortgage Disclosure Act (Federal Reserve Board's Regulation C, HMDA) 1975 Enforced by B Consumer Financial Protection Bureau	• Determines if financial institutions are serving the housing needs of their communities • Applies to financial institutions and non-depository institutions with assets in excess of $10 million or who originate more than 100 loans/year • Identifies possible discriminatory lending patterns through the collection and disclosure of data about applicant and borrower characteristics	Loan/Application Register (LAR): Report to supervisory agencies on a loan-by-loan and application-by-application basis every March
Community Reinvestment Act (CRA) 1977	• Encourage financial institutions to help meet the credit needs of the communities in which they operate. • Requires periodic examinations by federal agencies responsible for supervising depository institutions	None

Against Predatory Lending		
Federal Law	**Highlights**	**Disclosures/Notices**
Home Ownership and Equity Protection Act (HOEPA) 1994 Enforced by Consumer Financial Protection Bureau	• Amends Regulation Z (Section 32) to prohibit deceptive and unfair practices in lending • Establishes additional disclosure requirements for high cost loans • Defines high cost loan as: The APR exceeds the rates on Treasury securities of comparable maturity by more than eight percentage points for a first mortgage or more than ten percentage points for a second mortgage; or the total points and fees exceed 8% of the loan amount, or total dollar amount exceeds $611 for 2012 • Uses some different criteria to define total finance charges, e.g., counts optional credit insurance premiums • Prohibits balloon payments (on loans of less than 5 years), negative amortization, demand clauses • Limits prepayment penalties • Allows three business-day right of rescission for HOEPA loans	Section 32 disclosures include: • Notice that consumer is not required to complete the transaction • Warning that the lender will have a mortgage on the home and the borrower could lose it and equity if in default • The annual percentage rate (APR) • The regular payment amount (including any balloon payment where the law permits balloon payments) • The loan amount • Credit insurance premiums, if applicable • For variable rate loans, the amount of the maximum monthly payment and the fact that the rate and monthly payment may increase
Higher-Priced Loans – Regulation Z § 1026.35 as amended by Housing and Economic Recovery Act of 2008 Enforced by Consumer Financial Protection Bureau	• Closed-end mortgage loan secured by borrower's principal dwelling where APR exceeds applicable average prime offer rate by at least 1.5% for first lien loans or 3.5% for junior lien loans • Creditors obligated to verify repayment ability • Prepayment penalties generally prohibited • Escrow account must be established for property taxes and mortgage-related insurance premiums required by creditor	None
MLO Compensation Rule –Regulation Z § 1026.36 Enforced by Consumer Financial Protection Bureau	• Amends Regulation Z (12 C.F.R. § 1026.36) • Prohibits compensation based on loan interest rates or other terms/conditions other than loan amount • Prohibits dual compensation (borrower paid and lender paid) to MLOs • Prohibits steering consumers to specific lenders to gain greater compensation unless loan is in borrower's interest • Sets safe harbor rules for presenting loan options to consumers	Present loan options from significant number of creditors

MLO Licensing		
Federal Law	**Highlights**	**Disclosures/Notices**
The Secure and Fair Enforcement for Mortgage Licensing Act of 2008 (SAFE Act, Title V of Housing and Economic Recovery Act); Regulation G (federal) and Regulation H (state) Enforced by Consumer Financial Protection Bureau	• Establishes minimum standards for the licensing of state-licensed mortgage loan originators and registered mortgage loan originators • Provides for the establishment and maintenance of a Nationwide Mortgage Licensing System and Registry for the residential mortgage industry • Requires 20 hours of prelicensing education for state-licensed MLO applicants • Requires background checks for applicants • Requires passage of National MLO Exam with UST, which after April 2013, includes a new Section V comprised of 25 additional questions on uniform high-level state content. Note: Selected states may require an additional state or territory-specific test component • Requires at least 8 hours of annual continuing education for state-licensed MLOs • Requires contractor loan processors and underwriters to have MLO license	• Display of license • Use of NMLS unique ID on applications and other documents

Key Term Review

3/7/3 Rule A provision of the Truth in Lending Act related to required disclosures and waiting periods. Initial disclosure to be delivered within three business days of receipt of an application; earliest to close a loan is the seventh business day after disclosures are provided; a three business-day waiting period imposed after borrower receives redisclosures before a loan can close (only if redisclosures required).

Affiliated Business Arrangement A situation where a person in a position to refer settlement services—or an associate of that person—has either an affiliate relationship with or a direct or beneficial ownership interest of more than **1%** in a provider of settlement services and who then refers business to that provider or in some way influences the selection of that provider.

Annual Percentage Rate (APR) Total cost of financing a loan in percentage terms, as a relationship of the total finance charges to the total amount financed.

Application The submission of a borrower's financial information in anticipation of a credit decision relating to a federally related mortgage loan which includes the borrower's name, monthly income, social security number to obtain a credit report, the property address and estimate of value, the loan amount, and any other information deemed necessary by the loan originator. This triggers mandated disclosures.

Do Not Call Registry National registry managed by the Federal Trade Commission that limits commercial telemarketers from phoning consumers who place their phone numbers on a list.

Good Faith Estimate (GFE) An estimate by the mortgage loan originator of the closing costs that the borrower must pay for a real estate loan. The MLO must give this to the borrower within three business days of a completed application. Often referred to as **Good Faith Statement**.

HUD Uniform Settlement Statement (HUD-1) Required under RESPA; details a complete disclosure of all costs associated with a closing, showing what was paid, to whom, and for what.

Mortgage Loan Originator As defined by the SAFE Act, an individual who either takes a residential mortgage loan application or offers or negotiates terms of a residential mortgage loan for compensation or gain.

Negative Amortization When a loan balance grows because of deferred interest.

Red Flag Rules Section 114 of the Fair and Accurate Credit Transaction Act requiring financial institutions to implement identity theft prevention programs.

Regulation Z Federal guidelines under Truth-in-Lending Act requiring full disclosure of all credit terms for consumer loans.

Rescind To take back or withdraw an offer or contract. (For up to 3 business days, consumers may have right to rescind credit transactions when the security interest—usually a mortgage—is in their principal residence, except for the initial purchase or construction of a home.)

Truth in Lending Statement (TIL) Disclosure of the true costs associated with a residential loan, including the annual percentage rate that is required to be given to prospective borrowers within three business days of a completed application.

Unique Identifier A number or other identifier assigned by protocols established by the Nationwide Mortgage Licensing System and Registry that permanently identifies a mortgage loan originator.

Chapter 1 Quiz

1. **How long prior to closing does RESPA require that the HUD-1 Settlement Statement be provided to the borrower, if requested?**

   A. 6 hours
   B. 12 hours
   C. 1 business day
   D. 2 business days

2. **Under ECOA, which of the following may NOT be considered adversely when underwriting the loan?**

   A. borrower's employment history
   B. borrower's history of making payments on past obligations
   C. borrower's receipt of public assistance
   D. economic health of the borrower's field of employment

3. **According to the Truth in Lending Act, a borrower on a refinance transaction to whom the APR has NOT been disclosed has the right to rescind the loan for**

   A. three business days.
   B. thirty days.
   C. one year.
   D. three years.

4. **The Privacy Rule of the Gramm-Leach Bliley Act requires financial institutions to provide the borrower with a Consumer Privacy policy?**

   A. before disclosing information to non-affiliated third parties
   B. each time the servicing is transferred
   C. one business day prior to closing
   D. three business days prior to closing

5. **What law defines a high cost loan, also known as a Section 32 loan?**

   A. Home Mortgage Disclosure Act
   B. Home Ownership and Equity Protection Act
   C. Homeowners Protection Act
   D. Mortgage Reform and Anti-Predatory Lending Act

6. **While it is unlawful to consider race when underwriting a loan, what federal legislation requires that this information be included on the loan application?**

   A. Equal Credit Opportunity Act
   B. Fair Credit Reporting Act
   C. Home Mortgage Disclosure Act
   D. Truth in Lending Act

7. **What is the more common name of Title V of the Housing and Economic Recovery Act of 2008?**

   A. FACTA
   B. Gramm-Leach-Bliley Act
   C. Red Flag Rules
   D. SAFE Act

8. **Which federal law requires financial institutions to file reports of cash transactions exceeding a daily aggregate amount of $10,000?**

   A. BSA/AML
   B. RESPA
   C. SAFE
   D. TILA

9. **ABC Mortgage Company has been accused of inappropriately calling two consumers on the National Do No Call Registry. What is the total maximum fine ABC could incur for this?**

   A. $11,000
   B. $16,000
   C. $32,000
   D. $34,000

10. **Which rule requires all financial institutions to design, implement, and maintain safeguards to protect customer information while it is in the custody and control of the institution and its agents?**

    A. Financial Privacy Rule
    B. MARS Rule
    C. Red Flags Rule
    D. Safeguards Rule

11. **Which federal act created the Consumer Financial Protection Bureau?**

    A. Bank Secrecy Act/Anti-Money Laundering Act
    B. Dodd-Frank Act
    C. Fair Credit Reporting Act
    D. Gramm-Leach-Bliley Act

12. **The rule that bans providers of mortgage foreclosure rescue and loan modification services from collecting fees until homeowners have a written offer from their lender or servicer that they decide is acceptable is the**

    A. 3/7/3 Rule.
    B. Loan Originator Compensation Rule.
    C. MARS Rule.
    D. Safeguards Rule.

13. **What loan type is NOT included in the Home Mortgage Disclosure Act?**

    A. owner-occupied refinances
    B. purchase of existing housing
    C. second mortgages
    D. vacant land loans

14. **A borrower is refinancing her house, which gives the right to rescind the loan for**

    A. three business days excluding Saturday, Sunday, and federal holidays.
    B. three business days including Saturday, and excluding Sunday and federal holidays.
    C. three business days including Saturday and Sunday, excluding federal holidays.
    D. five business days including Saturday, and excluding Sunday and federal holidays.

15. **A lender has how many days to notify the borrower of an underwriting decision?**

    A. 3
    B. 10
    C. 30
    D. 60

16. **RESPA applies to all**

    A. business loans with collateral.
    B. commercial real estate loans.
    C. real estate credit transactions for one- to four-family dwellings.
    D. real estate purchase transactions.

17. **A loan's APR must be disclosed to the consumer on the**

    A. GFE.
    B. initial escrow statement.
    C. Loan/Application Register (LAR).
    D. TIL Statement.

18. **According to the FCRA, how many days does a credit information provider usually have to respond to the consumer after receiving a notice of a dispute?**

    A. 30
    B. 60
    C. 90
    D. 120

19. **To comply with the FACTA, a mortgage loan originator should**

    A. consider all legal forms of income when evaluating a loan application.
    B. note the race of all loan applicants on the LAR.
    C. place all loan applications and documentation in a secure place when not working on them.
    D. send loan applicants an adverse action notice within 30 days.

20. **As a result of the Mortgage Disclosure Improvement Act, how soon can a residential loan close?**

    A. the next business day
    B. after three business days for a refinance or home equity loan
    C. within three business days of applying
    D. on the seventh business day after delivery of required disclosures

21. **Of these settlement charges, which is allowed to show a 10% tolerance between the GFE and the actual charge at closing?**

    A. charge for the interest rate chosen when locked
    B. government recording charges
    C. origination fee
    D. transfer taxes

22. **The estimate for most settlement charges shown on a GFE must be available for at least _____ business days.**

    A. 3
    B. 7
    C. 10
    D. 14

23. **Which fee can be imposed prior to delivery of a Truth in Lending Statement and a Good Faith Estimate?**

    A. appraisal fee
    B. credit report fee
    C. origination fee
    D. No fees can be imposed prior to delivery of these disclosures.

24. **A mortgage broker rents office space from a title company at a discount in exchange for referring customers for settlement services. Which federal law does this arrangement violate?**

    A. RESPA
    B. SAFE Act
    C. TILA
    D. It does not violate any federal law.

25. *The APR on an initial TIL for a 30-year fixed rate loan is 5.99%, and the APR on the final TIL is 6.25%. After redisclosure, how long must the borrower wait to close the loan?*

   A. 1 business day
   B. three business days after redisclosure
   C. seven business days after redisclosure
   D. There is no waiting required since the difference is within the acceptable tolerance.

26. *According to MDIA, a "higher-priced loan" is one that has*

   A. an APR that exceeds the applicable average prime offer rate by at least 1.5% on first liens.
   B. an APR that exceeds the rates on Treasury securities of comparable maturity by more than 8%.
   C. total points and fees greater than 8% of the loan amount.
   D. total points and fees greater than 10% of the loan amount for junior liens.

27. *The Dodd-Frank Act definition of a qualified mortgage includes all of these features EXCEPT*

   A. interest-only loan offerings.
   B. limits on debt-to-income ratios.
   C. no excessive upfront points and fees.
   D. no terms beyond 30 years.

28. *To comply with the Bank Secrecy/Anti-Money Laundering Act, financial institutions must keep records of any*

   A. affiliate relationship with or a direct or beneficial ownership interest of more than 1% in a provider of settlement services.
   B. cash purchases of negotiable instruments.
   C. established business relationship (EBR) for up to eighteen (18) months even if the consumer's number is on the National Do Not Call Registry.
   D. ethnicity, race, and sex of loan applicant and co-applicants.

29. *Which of these circumstances would NOT be an acceptable reason to provide a revised GFE to a borrower?*

   A. The borrower lost the income from a part-time job and so was no longer eligible for the specific loan terms identified in the GFE.
   B. The borrower requested to change the loan term from 15 to 30 years.
   C. The loan originator regretted overlooking certain liabilities in order to qualify the borrower for a better interest rate.
   D. The title company discovered a junior lien on the property that was not considered when preparing the GFE.

30. *Which of the following is an acceptable condition on which to base a mortgage loan originator's compensation?*

   A. a fixed percentage of the loan amount
   B. a percentage of all fees collected on the loan
   C. a premium based on the interest rate selected
   D. a premium for lower LTV loans

Chapter 2
Nontraditional Mortgage Products Overview

Introduction

Mortgage professionals need to be familiar with vast amounts of information on varied topics, from finances to contracts, property law to lending law. Familiarity with specific terminology and concepts is critical to a lending professional's long-term success. While this chapter does include definitions of many types of nontraditional mortgage products, it focuses more specifically on two: Adjustable rate mortgages and reverse mortgages. We'll also look at temporary buydown plans.

Key Terms

Mortgage Products

Lenders offer multiple mortgage loan programs in order to meet the varied needs of borrowers. Loan programs are generally broadly classified as either conventional or government agency-sponsored, conforming or nonconforming. There are many variations within each of these broad categories to review. The focus of this chapter, however, will be on **nontraditional mortgage products**, which are defined by the **Secure and Fair Enforcement for Mortgage Licensing Act** (12 C.F.R. § 1008.23) as **anything other than a 30-year fixed rate mortgage loan**.

Conventional Loans

Conventional financing refers to real estate that is paid for or financed with a **conventional loan**, one that is usually made by a bank or institutional lender, and that is not insured or guaranteed by a government entity or agency, such as FHA, VA or USDA. Most conventional loans are purchased by government-sponsored enterprises (GSEs) in the secondary market, such as Freddie Mac and Fannie Mae, however. Traditionally speaking, conventional loans are:

Long Term. Long-term real estate loans generally have total payments generally spread out over **30 years** but may extend out as far as 40 years.

Fully Amortizing. Total payments over the life of a loan pay off the entire balance of principal and interest due at the end of the term. This is also known as **self-liquidating**. The payments stay constant for the entire loan term, although the amounts applied to principal and interest are adjusted each month. At the beginning of the loan term, most of the monthly payment goes toward interest. As the loan liquidates, the amount applied to interest drops in relation to the amount applied to principal.

Fixed Rate. Interest rates remain constant for the duration of the loan.

Borrowers can significantly reduce the interest paid with a **15-year fixed rate** mortgage. Also, lenders typically offer a better interest rate since the shorter term also means less risk from the lender. The disadvantage for the buyer is that payments are higher.

Conforming loans meet Fannie Mae/Freddie Mac standards, and therefore can be sold on the secondary market. Jumbo loans also may be sold in the secondary market, but that is considered private secondary markets. Most lenders prefer conforming loans because they can **liquidate** (sell for cash) their real estate loans on the secondary market.

Nonconforming

Nonconforming loans do **not** meet the standards necessary to be sold to Fannie Mae or Freddie Mac. There are other secondary markets where nonconforming loans can be sold, however, and lenders that have the option of keeping loans in their own portfolio (mostly banks and S & Ls) can, within the limits of the law, deviate from the standards set by secondary markets. There are two main reasons why a loan would be classified as nonconforming:

Size of the Loan. So-called **jumbo loans** exceed the maximum loan amount established by Fannie Mae and Freddie Mac for conforming mortgage loans. Currently for 2013, the general maximum loan limit is $417,000 on a single-family home, while higher limits apply in localities such as Hawaii, Alaska, Guam, the U.S. Virgin Islands, and some other specific areas in states where home prices are generally higher.

Credit Quality of Buyer. You may see a borrower who does not meet the minimum standards established by Fannie Mae or Freddie Mac classified as a **B or C borrower**. This might be someone who has had a credit problem in the past, such as a bankruptcy within the past seven to ten years or uncollected medical bills, or someone whose credit scores are low because they own lots of investment property or have been self-employed for too short a period of time. Lenders, such as neighborhood banks, may still offer loans to these borrowers, but the loans cannot be sold to Fannie Mae or Freddie Mac.

Subprime Loans

Subprime loans have more risks than are allowed in the conforming loan market. Subprime loans—also called **B-C loans** or B-C credit—fill a need for those with less than perfect credit who want to own a home or refinance for debt consolidation purposes. Subprime loans may also be made to borrowers who cannot or choose not to provide as much documentation. Some lenders and investors are willing to make these riskier loans because they can get higher interest rates and fees than they can with other real estate loans. With subprime lending, criteria for who gets approved—and at what interest rate—vary greatly. Sometimes, larger down payments or secondary financing are required by lenders who want to be sure the collateral can cover the first mortgage loan amount.

Secondary Financing

One way a buyer can get a conventional loan without a 20% down payment is through **secondary financing**, where a buyer borrows money from another source (other than the primary lender) to pay part of the purchase price or closing costs.

- Often the **seller** carries the extra financing.

- Lender could offer **conventional 80-20 loans** (essentially a 100% loan, as the same lender does both the 80% loan and 20% loan), which can be sold to Fannie Mae and Freddie Mac on the secondary market if the loans meet all standards and criteria.

- Could be a simple second mortgage or additional **junior liens**, such as with a down payment assistance program or even a third or fourth mortgage.

- The **combined loan-to-value** (CLTV) is the percentage of the property value borrowed through a combination of more than one loan, such as a first mortgage and a second mortgage home equity loan.

- While today's mortgage climate continues to be uncertain, traditionally for secondary financing, the secondary lender might require:

  - 5% down payment,

  - No prepayment penalty,

  - Regularly scheduled payments, and

  - No negative amortization.

Mortgage Repayment

Mortgages may be classified based on how the borrower repays the principal and interest portions of the loan.

Fixed Rate Mortgages

Fixed rate loans have an interest rate that remains constant for the duration of the loan. This is both good and bad for the borrower and the lender. The biggest advantage is that a borrower doesn't need to worry about rates going up, and if rates go down enough, the borrower can refinance. From the lender's perspective, there is a guaranteed rate of return but the rate is locked-in for the loan period even if interest rates should go up during the loan term.

A fixed-rate mortgage keeps the debt service, the monthly principal and interest payment, the same over the life of the loan. It is a fully amortizing loan, meaning the last payment of principal and interest satisfies or pays off the mortgage note. A 30 year, Fixed-rate conventional mortgage (meeting Fannie Mae or Freddie Mac guidelines) is the only form of a Traditional Mortgage. With each and every subsequent monthly payment, more of the debt service is applied to the principal and less is applied to the interest.

Adjustable Rate Mortgages (ARMs)

ARMs have an interest rate that may periodically adjust to reflect fluctuations in the cost of money. ARMs pass the risk of fluctuating interest rates on to borrowers—if rates climb, payments go up; if they decline, payments go down. Lenders usually follow secondary market guidelines so they can sell ARMs just as they do fixed rate loans, although the guidelines for ARMs are generally stricter.

Hybrid Mortgages/Interest Only

Mortgages that are a combination of fixed, adjustable, and/or interest only; for example, a 5/25 Interest Only/Fixed, where the borrower pays only interest for the first five years of the loan term, then a fixed rate for 25 years until the loan is paid off.

Graduated Payment Mortgages (GPM)

This is a specialized payment structure that allows the borrower to make smaller payments in the early years of the mortgage, with payments increasing yearly until they are sufficient to fully amortize the loan. The lower payments in the early years of a mortgage structured in the note as a GPM are not sufficient to cover the interest due on the loan, and so the unpaid interest is added to the loan balance, resulting in a scheduled period **negative amortization**. At a predetermined point in the loan term, the payments escalate on a scheduled basis until they eventually reach the point in which they are sufficient to fully amortize the loan over the remainder of its term.

Growth Equity Mortgage (GEM)

This is a fixed rate mortgage set up like a 30-year conventional loan, but payments increase regularly, like an ARM. GEMs can help a borrower pay off a mortgage faster and save interest since the fixed interest rate allows 100% of the annual payment increases to reduce the principal balance. There are many variations that work similarly, e.g., building equity mortgages (BEMs), rapidly amortizing mortgages (RAMs).

Intragency Guidelines

The federal financial regulatory agencies occasionally issue guidelines, recommendations, and policy statements for their member institutions. One example is the 2006 Guidance on Nontraditional Mortgage Product Risks, which was jointly published by the following agencies:

- The Office of the Comptroller of the Currency (OCC)
- The Board of Governors of the Federal Reserve System (Board)
- The Federal Deposit Insurance Corporation (FDIC)
- The Office of Thrift Supervision (OTS)
- The National Credit Union Administration (NCUA)

The final version of this statement reflects the comments and input from financial institutions, trade associations, consumer and community organizations, state and financial regulatory organizations, and other members of the public.

Guidance on Nontraditional Mortgage Product Risks

The Guidance applies to **nontraditional mortgage products** (NMPs), which they define *as mortgage products that allow borrowers to defer principal and, sometimes, interest.* The agencies are primarily concerned about payment shock, competitive pressures, and ceding underwriting standards to third-party originations. This includes products with an interest only (I/O) feature and products with the potential for negative amortization (including those with flexible payment options). While the NMP Guidance may not explicitly pertain to subprime mortgage lending, it does outline prudent underwriting and consumer protection principles that institutions also should consider.

Qualification Standards

An institution's qualifying standards should recognize the potential impact of payment shock and should recognize that nontraditional mortgage loans often are not appropriate for borrowers with high loan-to-value (LTV), high debt income ratios, and low credit scores. The analysis of borrowers' repayment capacity should include an evaluation of their ability to repay the debt by final maturity at the fully indexed rate and should avoid "over-reliance" on credit scores.

The NMP Guidance includes several guiding principles:

- **Collateral-Dependent Loans.** Acknowledging that loans to borrowers who do not show capacity to repay the loan from sources other than the collateral are unsafe and unsound, institutions should avoid loan terms that rely on property sale or refinancing once amortization begins.

- **Risk Layering.** Risk layering features—such as low- or no-document loans or simultaneous seconds—should be compensated with risk mitigating features, such as high credit scores, lower LTV, lower debt-to-income ratios, credit enhancements, and mortgage insurance.

- **Reduced Documentation.** Should be governed by clear guidelines and accepted only if there are other risk mitigating factors, such as lower LTV.

- **Simultaneous Second Lien Loans.** Loans with minimal owner equity should generally not have a payment structure that allows for delayed or negative amortization.

- **Introductory Interest Rates.** In setting introductory interest rates, institutions should consider ways to minimize the probability of disruptive early re-castings or extraordinary payment shock.

Underwriting Standards

The NMP Guidance indicates that mortgage loan underwriting standards should address the effect of a substantial payment increase on the borrower's capacity to repay a nontraditional mortgage loan when amortization begins. For example:

Interest Only. For mortgage loans with an interest only (I/O) feature, an analysis of a borrower's repayment capacity should include an evaluation of the borrower's ability to repay the debt by final maturity at the fully indexed rate (if adjustable rate), or note rate (if fixed rate), assuming a fully amortizing repayment schedule based on the term of the mortgage. The fully indexed rate generally equals the index value prevailing at the time of underwriting plus the applicable margin that will apply after the expiration of any introductory interest rate period.

Negative Amortization. For mortgage loans with a negative amortization feature, the repayment analysis should be based upon the initial loan amount plus any balance increase that may accrue from the negative amortization provision. The balance that may accrue from the negative amortization provision may be calculated by taking the lesser of the negative amortization cap per the mortgage note (the highest percent the loan amount can increase through negative amortization), or the maximum negative amortization percentage that the loan may accrue based on the spread between the introductory or "teaser" rate and the accrual rate before the end of the initial payment option period.

Adjustable Rate Mortgages (ARMs)

The interest rate on an adjustable rate mortgage (ARM) is adjusted periodically to reflect fluctuations in the cost of money. The interest rate on an ARM is determined by the current value of the selected **index** (a statistical report that is generally a reliable indicator of the approximate cost of money) plus the agreed to **margin** indicated in the note. Margins remain constant throughout the term of the loan.

ARM Elements

An ARM is made of these elements:

- **Index.** Once the initial interest rate for the loan is set, the rate of the loan is tied to a widely recognized and published **index**, a statistical report that is generally a reliable indicator of the approximate cost of money. The loan interest rate will rise and fall with the rates reported by that index. Among the most common indexes used are: Average One-Year Treasury Constant Maturity Index (TCM), Cost of Funds Index (COFI), and London Interbank Offering Rate (LIBOR), and 10-year Treasury Bill.

- **Margin.** The difference between the index value and the interest rate charged on an ARM, sometimes called the **spread**. The lender adds a margin to the index to ensure sufficient income for administrative expenses and profit. The selected margin generally remains fixed for the duration of the loan, and is not impacted by the movement of interest rates or other factors in the financial markets.

◇ **Note:** The margin is expressed as Basis Points. 1 basis point is 1/100th of a %. Therefore, 50 bps would be .50 %' 100 bps would be 1%; and 150 bps would be 1.5%.

- **Rate Adjustment Period.** The length of time between interest rate changes with ARMs. This interval can range from a few months up to seven years. The most common rate adjustment periods are every six months or one year.
- **Mortgage Payment Adjustment Period.** The length of time between mortgage payment changes with ARMs. Here the borrower's actual principal and interest payments are recast, usually for loans with negative amortization. Like the rate adjustment period, this payment adjustment interval can range from a period of months up to seven years.
- **Interest Rate Caps.** Used with ARMs to limit the number of percentage points an interest rate can be increased or decreased during the term of each adjustment period, helping to eliminate large and frequent mortgage payment increases.
- **Mortgage Payment Caps.** Used with ARMs to protect a borrower from large payment increases. This is another way lenders limit the magnitude of payment changes that occur with interest rate adjustments and limit negative amortization.
- **Negative Amortization Cap.** When a loan balance grows from deferred interest, because payments do not cover the interest on the loan. Negative amortization caps do not stop a loan from accruing interest, but require the loan payments to be adjusted or recast when the cap is reached so that larger payments again retire a portion of the principal.

Example

Index Rate + Margin = Fully Indexed ARM Interest Rate

Initial Index Value:	5.75%
Margin:	+ 2.25%
Fully Indexed Rate:	8.00%

Initial ARM rates are usually discounted:

Initial Index Value:	5.75%
Margin:	+ 2.25%
Discount Rate:	- 1.25%
Initial Interest Rate:	6.75%

If the index rate does **not** change at the first adjustment period:

Initial Index Value:	5.75%
Margin:	+ 2.25%
Fully Indexed Rate:	8.00%

If the index rate increases to 6.25% at the first adjustment period:

Current Index Value:	6.25%
Margin:	+ 2.25%
Current Index Rate:	8.50%

ARM Provisions

ARM Caps. Caps on interest rates and mortgage payments keep ARMs from growing out of control. If the ARM has a 2/6 cap, there is a maximum 2% increase at any adjustment with a lifetime cap of 6% above the initial rate.

Example

Initial Rate:	6.75%
Lifetime Cap:	+ 6.00%
Max. Interest Rate:	12.75%

Periodic Re-Amortization. Like mandatory re-amortization lenders impose when loan balances reach the negative amortization cap, ARMs provide for regularly scheduled, periodic re-amortization of the loan, generally at every interest rate adjustment unless there are payment caps but no interest caps. This can be instead of, or in addition to, any negative amortization caps, payment caps, or rate caps.

Convertible ARMs. A **conversion option** in an ARM gives the borrower the right to convert from an adjustable rate loan to a fixed rate loan. ARMs with a conversion option normally include a higher interest rate (often the initial rate and converted rate are higher), limited time to convert (e.g., between the first and fifth year), and a conversion fee (typically several hundred dollars).

Disclosures

The Truth in Lending Act requires these disclosures for ARMs:

- Consumer Handbook on Adjustable Rate Mortgages (**CHARM**), prepared by the Federal Reserve and the Federal Home Loan Bank Board; must be provided when the loan application is made or before payment of any non-refundable fee, whichever occurs first.

- Reg Z requires that the APR in the federal box on the Truth in Lending Statement (TIL) be based on the lender's margin and the **composite annual percentage rate**, which is based on the initial payment rate and the fully indexed rate that would exist for the remaining years on the loan term.

- Advance notice of any change in payment or interest rate must be given at least 25 days, but not more than 120, before a new payment level takes effect, as well as an example, based on a $10,000 loan, showing how the payments and loan balance will be affected by changes in the index used.

ARM Programs

Payment Option ARM. An adjustable rate mortgage that allows borrowers to choose among several payment options each month, such as traditional payment of principal and interest, an interest-only payment, or a minimum (or limited) payment that may be less than the amount of interest due that month and may not reduce the amount owed, adding unpaid interest to the loan balance. Such ARMs are rare—if not non-existent—in today's marketplace.

Hybrid Mortgage. A combination of fixed and adjustable rates, meaning that the loan has a fixed rate for a specified number of years, and then the interest rate adjusts for the remainder of the loan term; for example, a 3/27 ARM is a mortgage that has a fixed rate for the first three years, and then adjusts for the next 27 years.

Buydown Plans

Discount points are additional funds paid to a lender at the beginning of a loan to lower the interest rate and monthly payments. A **point** is simply **one percent of the loan amount**. The effect of discount points, also called a **buydown**, could make it easier for a borrower to qualify for the loan. A buydown can be paid for either by the borrower or by the seller, which may sometimes be a builder/developer. Typically, a borrower would pay for a buydown by simply increasing the cash down payment. There are two main advantages to a buydown plan:

- The borrower's monthly payment is lower than normal.
- The lender may evaluate the borrower for loan qualification on the basis of the reduced payment after the buydown.

A buydown shows as a charge to the borrower on the GFE.

CASE IN POINT

Let's see how this helps the borrower afford the home. Suppose that a borrower financing $180,000 was quoted an interest rate of 6.5% for a 30-year conventional loan. The payments on that loan would be $1,137.72 per month. At 6.25% for the same $180,000 30-year loan, the payments would be only $1,108.29. So by paying discount points up front to buy down the interest rate 1/4%, the buyer pays $29.43 per month less.

However, when you consider that a discount point is typically quoted as 1 point per 1/8 rate reduction, the borrower would have likely paid an additional $3,600 at closing to get this interest rate (2 points at $1,800 per point). That means the borrower must stay in the mortgage for at least 123 months ($3,600 / $29.43 = 122.3) to realize the advantages of the buydown. If the borrower refinances or sells the house in the first 10 years of that loan, therefore, he will not recapture what he paid for the upfront discount points. Qualifying at the lower payment rate will be contingent upon a lender and its underwriting standards.

Seller Paid Buydowns

Another option is for the seller to pay discount points to buy down the interest rate for the buyer. While this means less money in the seller's pocket, it may be necessary to make the deal. The lender determines what the buydown amount is and subtracts that amount from the loan proceeds paid to the seller for the property. The buyer, however, still signs a note for the full amount. The seller just agrees to receive less.

CASE IN POINT

The sale price of a home is $120,000. The buyer is making a $20,000 down payment but would like to have the interest rate 1/2% lower to reduce the monthly payment. While qualifying at the lower payment rate will be contingent upon a lender and its underwriting standards, the seller agrees to pay for a permanent 1/2% buydown of the loan. For the sake of this scenario, let's say that the lender determines that 1/2% is equal to 6 points, so:

$100,000 (loan amount) x 0.06 (points) = $6,000

Thus, the lender deducts $6,000 from the amount actually advanced to the borrower, so only the balance of $94,000 is delivered to the borrower to finance the home. The borrower still signs a promissory note and mortgage agreeing to repay the entire $100,000 at the agreed upon (1/2% lower) interest rate. The borrower then transfers the loan proceeds ($94,000) to the seller without making up the difference. In effect, the seller paid the lender $6,000 to raise the lender's return so the lender would make the loan with a lower interest rate.

Permanent Buydown

Buydowns can be paid to reduce the borrower's payments early in the loan (temporary buydown) or throughout the life of the loan (permanent buydown). Regardless, if permanent or temporary, the cost of the buydown is considered prepaid interest. Again, note that qualifying at the lower payment rate will be contingent upon a lender and its underwriting standards.

A **permanent buydown** is when points are paid to a lender to reduce the interest rate and loan payments *for the entire life of the loan.* When a buyer's interest rate is reduced for the life of the loan, the lender will write that interest rate into the promissory note. Thus, the nominal rate (or coupon rate) stated in the note will be the actual reduced interest rate.

Temporary Buydown

One way to think of a **temporary buydown** is that a borrower or a third party is *prepaying some of the interest on the loan.* This strategy allows points to be paid to a lender to reduce the interest rate and loan payments *early in a loan, with the interest rate or payments rising at a predetermined point later in the loan term.* When interest rates are high, temporary buydowns are a popular means of reducing a borrower's payments in the early months or years of a loan. When qualifying a borrower who is using a temporary buydown, underwriters will generally consider the payments using the **note rate**, *not* the starting rate. The note rate stated in the promissory note is the interest rate that is used to amortize the mortgage loan. Since a loan with a temporary buydown has different interest rates, it would be considered a nontraditional loan. Temporary buydown plans can take two forms:

- Level payment.
- Graduated payment.

Level Payment

A **level payment buydown** is a plan with the *interest rate reduction remaining constant throughout the buydown period.* This constant interest rate keeps the payments the same (level) during the buydown period, as the name implies. For example, the lender makes a 30-year loan for $165,000 at 9% interest rate. The seller agrees to buy down the buyer's interest rate to 7% for three years.

	Note Interest Rate	Buydown %	Effective Interest Rate	Monthly Payment at 9%	Actual Monthly Payment	Monthly Subsidy	Annual Subsidy
Year							
1	9%	2%	7%	$1,328	$1,098	$230	$2,760
2	9%	2%	7%	$1,328	$1,098	$230	$2,760
3	9%	2%	7%	$1,328	$1,098	$230	$2,760
4	9%	-0-	9%	$1,328	$1,328	-0-	-0-

LEVEL PAYMENT EXAMPLE

TOTAL BUYDOWN: $8,280

FIGURE 2.1: *Level Payment Example.*

Graduated Payment

A **graduated payment buydown** is a plan for which payment subsidies in the early years keep payments low, but payments increase each year as indicated in the note until they're sufficient to fully amortize the loan. Usually there's a definite structure to the loan such that the subsidy may last for only two or three years. The two most common types of graduated payment buydown plans are often referred to as 2-1 buydowns and 3-2-1 buydowns.

2-1 buydown is a graduated payment buydown with the payments subsidized for only two years—for example, 2% below the interest rate in the first year and 1.5% the second year.

3-2-1 buydown is a graduated payment buydown with the payments subsidized for three years—for example, 2.5% below the interest rate the first year, 2% the second year, and 1.5% the third year.

The subsidies for graduated payment buydowns may be a buyer's upfront escrow deposit of extra cash that earns interest, or the subsidy may be from a seller or builder trying to help the buyer with lower payments early in the loan. No matter who pays for the buydown (buyer, seller, builder, etc.), if the subsidy buys down the interest rate more than 2%, lenders will usually only let the borrower qualify at up to 2% below the current market interest rates. For example, the lender makes a 30-year loan for $170,000 at 8.75% interest rate. The builder agrees to do a 3-2-1 buydown of the buyer's interest rate.

GRADUATED PAYMENT EXAMPLE

Year	Note Interest Rate	Buydown %	Effective Interest Rate	Monthly Payment at 9%	Actual Monthly Payment	Monthly Subsidy	Annual Subsidy
1	8.75%	3%	5.75%	$1,337	$ 992	$345	$4,140
2	8.75%	2%	6.75%	$1,337	$1,103	$234	$2,808
3	8.75%	1%	7.75%	$1,337	$1,218	$119	$1,428
4	8.75%	-0-	8.75%	$1,337	$1,337	-0-	-0-

TOTAL BUYDOWN: $8,376

FIGURE 2.2: Graduated Payment Example.

Reverse Mortgages

Another type of nontraditional mortgage is the "reverse" mortgage. The purpose of a reverse mortgage is to provide a vehicle for a borrower who has substantial equity in a property to convert that accumulated equity—at a cost—to cash and additional debt without selling the property and without making payments to the lender. Seniors, those adults age 62 or older, can use the equity in their home for any use, including but not limited to health care, home repairs and upkeep, and/or to maintain a lifestyle that is otherwise unaffordable. Note that a borrower is still responsible for paying real estate taxes and homeowners insurance. A "reverse mortgage" may also be called a reverse equity mortgage or a reverse annuity mortgage.

Contrast with a Traditional Mortgage

To contrast, with a traditional, fully amortizing "forward" mortgage for a purchase, a homebuyer makes a down payment and borrows the rest of the money needed to purchase the home. They then pay off the loan every month over the course of many years. During the life of the loan, the debt decreases, and the home equity increases. Once the final mortgage payment is made, the homeowner owes nothing and, in theory, the home equity equals the value of the home. You can think of this as a "falling debt, rising equity" scenario.

On the other hand, with a typical reverse mortgage, the balance of the loan rises as the borrower receives money from the lender and incurs interest to the outstanding loan balance. Since the borrower is not making any payments, by the time a reverse mortgage becomes due, for whatever reason, the borrower may owe a lot of money and have a small amount of equity. It is even possible, depending on the length of the loan and other factors, that there is no equity left when the loan becomes due.

For most reverse mortgages, the amount owed grows and the equity shrinks, which creates a "rising debt, falling equity" scenario.

Eligibility Requirements

Reverse mortgages have some very specific requirements, and some less stringent requirements.

Income

Another key way in which a reverse mortgage differs from a traditional mortgage relates to income requirements. With a traditional mortgage, the income of the borrower is critical in determining the terms of the loan, the amount that can be borrowed, etc. A reverse mortgage, on the other hand, has no income requirements to qualify. If the interested borrower meets the other criteria, their income, or lack of income, is not relevant. This is because the borrower does not make monthly payments with a reverse mortgage.

Age

In order to qualify for a reverse mortgage, **all persons with an ownership interest in the property**—for example, a husband and wife—must meet the age requirement of **62**. If one of the owners is under the age of 62, the younger owner(s) would have to relinquish all ownership interest in the property in order for the other person to qualify for a reverse mortgage.

Home

Although the specific type of reverse mortgage may impose different standards, in general, single family, one-unit dwellings are considered eligible properties for a reverse mortgage. Depending on the program, condominiums, planned unit developments (PUDs), and manufactured homes may be acceptable. Mobile home and cooperative apartments are *not* generally eligible, although HUD may approve some types of mobile homes.

Note that, as with a traditional mortgage, the lender will require that the borrower maintain a **homeowners insurance** policy that is sufficient to cover the replacement value of the collateral property. This protects the lender's interest in the event of damage that causes a loss of value, such as a fire, tornado, etc. The lender may also require a separate flood insurance policy. Since borrowers obtaining a reverse mortgage may have had the same insurance policy in place for years, they are urged to review their policies to ensure the insurance in place provides adequate coverage.

Ownership

To be eligible for a reverse mortgage, the home must be considered the principal residence, and any debt on the home should *ideally* be paid off. This does not automatically prevent someone from getting a reverse mortgage if there is debt on the home, however. Generally, homeowners may be able to get a lump sum advance from the reverse mortgage to pay off any remaining debt on the home or subordinate the original debt to the new reverse mortgage, if acceptable to both the reverse mortgage lender and the existing debt holder that would be subordinating.

Meeting with a Counselor

Most reverse mortgage programs impose an additional condition on prospective borrowers by requiring them to participate in a consumer counseling session given by an approved counselor. The counselor will be able to explain the costs of the loan and the financial implications as well as provide guidance and advice in selecting a program and/or a lender.

This unbiased, independent counselor can help guide the borrower through what can be a confusing process and a lot of difficult decisions. And at the end of the session, the counselor must provide any required certification of counseling. A counselor may even point the homeowner to other programs or assistance that might be a better solution than a reverse mortgage. An application for FHA insurance for a reverse mortgage may not be submitted without proof of counseling.

Amount Available with a Reverse Mortgage

Many factors determine how much money a homeowner can receive with a reverse mortgage. For example, a required appraisal will determine the value of the home. The more the home is worth, the more cash that can borrowed with the reverse mortgage.

Other factors that could impact the amount of money available include the amount of equity that has been built up, the location of the home, the payment options, the interest rates, the program costs and/or loan financing fees. And of course, the specific program selected has much to do with determining the impact of these factors.

Age of the Homeowner

Another important factor that figures into the determination of the amount of money available is the **age** of the homeowner. Typically, an older homeowner would have a *higher dollar amount* available to them with a reverse mortgage than a younger homeowner since an older person has a shorter life expectancy and, therefore, the loan would be for a shorter term.

Note that when the reverse mortgage is in more than one name, it is the age of the *youngest* that factors into the amount of money available.

For example, Margaret (age 65), Thomas (age 75), and Laura (age 85) own their homes, each of which is valued at $100,000. All three have qualified for a reverse mortgage loan at an interest rate of 9%. All other things being equal, Margaret might be able to borrow only 58% of her home's value; Thomas might be able to borrow up to 70% of his home's value; while Laura might be able to borrow as much as 80% of her home's value.

Payment Options

The homeowner who takes out a reverse mortgage generally gets to decide how to receive the money. The payment options include:

- **Fixed monthly payments** for either a predetermined period or for as long as the homeowner remains in the home
- A **lump sum** payment up front
- A **line of credit** that allows the homeowner to have access to funds on an "as-needed" basis

A homeowner may also choose to receive some **combination** of these options. However, you should note that the payment option that a homeowner chooses could affect the amount of cash they may be eligible to receive from the loan.

Spending Options

Typically, the homeowner who takes out a reverse mortgage also gets to determine how to **spend** the money. It may be that the majority of those who get reverse mortgages do so primarily to supplement a fixed retirement income, cover the costs of healthcare, or make much-needed improvements to their home. But the funds from a reverse mortgage can be used for virtually anything. A homeowner may choose to make that lifelong vacation dream a reality. Another could choose to start a small business, pay off credit card debt, or contribute to a grandchild's college tuition.

Tax Implications

For the most part, the funds paid out with a reverse mortgage are *not* considered income by the IRS, and so they are not taxed. And unlike a typical house mortgage, the interest that the lender charges on the reverse mortgage can be deducted only at the *conclusion* of the loan at the point when the loan principal and the interest are repaid.

Although the funds paid out from a reverse mortgage are generally tax-free, homeowners should get advice from a qualified reverse mortgage counselor to determine whether or not the income received could in any way affect their eligibility for any needs-based public assistance benefits such as Medicaid or Supplemental Social Security.

◇ **Important:** Do not offer tax advice unless properly trained or licensed to do so.

Repayment

Assuming the borrower upholds the terms of the contract, a typical reverse mortgage becomes due when the last surviving borrower:

- Dies,
- Sells the home, or
- Ceases to live in the home for 12 consecutive months.

At that point, the homeowner or the homeowner's heirs must repay the total loan amount, which includes the money that was paid out as well as any interest, insurance, closing costs, or other fees as stipulated in the terms of the loan.

Of course, it is often the case that the proceeds from the sale of the home are used to repay the reverse mortgage. Any remaining equity belongs to the estate (in event of death) or the homeowner (if they sold and moved).

Non-Recourse Loans

A reverse mortgage is considered a "non-recourse" loan, and so a lender cannot force a borrower out of his or her home during the life of the loan. Nor can the lender simply sell the home when a reverse mortgage comes due as they are NOT the homeowners. Usually the lender will allow up to 12 months for payment in the event of death. If the home is not sold or is not deeded back to the lender, a formal foreclosure process will be started in the county where the home is located.

Even in the rare instance that the amount of money distributed over the life of the reverse mortgage exceeds the value of the home, the borrower or the borrower's heirs cannot owe more than fair market sale price of the home, minus reasonable sales expenses. The lender has no claims on any other assets that may be held by the borrower or the borrower's heirs.

Accelerating Repayment

As with any mortgage situation, however, there are some circumstances that might cause the lender to require immediate repayment. A few situations that could accelerate the repayment might be:

- The homeowner fails to make necessary repairs to the property.
- The property is condemned.
- The homeowner does not pay the mandatory property taxes.
- The homeowner ceases to pay the appropriate homeowners insurance premiums.
- A government entity claims eminent domain over the property.
- The borrower ceases to live in the property or it is discovered the property is no longer the borrower's principal residence.

Truth in Lending Requirements

The Truth in Lending Act (§ 1026.33) requires creditors to provide additional disclosure (a model is found in Appendix K to Part 226) for reverse mortgage transactions that include:

- **Notice.** A statement that the consumer is not obligated to complete the reverse mortgage transaction merely because the consumer has received the disclosures required by this section or has signed an application for a reverse mortgage loan.

- **Total annual loan cost rates.** A good-faith projection of the total cost of the credit and expressed as a table of "total annual loan cost rates," using that term.
- **Itemization of pertinent information.** An itemization of loan terms, charges, the age of the youngest borrower, and the appraised property value.
- **Explanation of table.** An explanation of the table of total annual loan cost rates.

TILA further indicates that the projected total cost of credit must reflect the following factors, as applicable:

- **Costs to consumer.** All costs and charges to the consumer, including the costs of any annuity the consumer purchases as part of the reverse mortgage transaction.
- **Payments to consumer.** All advances to and for the benefit of the consumer, including annuity payments that the consumer will receive from an annuity that the consumer purchases as part of the reverse mortgage transaction.
- **Additional creditor compensation.** Any shared appreciation or equity in the dwelling that the creditor is entitled by contract to receive.
- **Limitations on consumer liability.** Any limitation on the consumer's liability (such as nonrecourse limits and equity conservation agreements).
- **Assumed annual appreciation rates.** Each of the following assumed annual appreciation rates for the dwelling: 0 percent, 4 percent, 8 percent.
- **Assumed loan period.** Each of the following assumed loan periods: Two years, the actuarial life expectancy of the consumer to become obligated on the reverse mortgage transaction as of that consumer's most recent birthday (in the case of multiple consumers, the period shall be the actuarial life expectancy of the youngest consumer (as of that consumer's most recent birthday), and that actuarial life expectancy multiplied by a factor of 1.4 and rounded to the nearest full year; OR, at the creditor's option, the actuarial life expectancy multiplied by a factor of .5 and rounded to the nearest full year.

Timing of Disclosures

The creditor shall furnish the required disclosures **at least three (3) business days** prior to:

- Consummation of a closed-end credit transaction; or
- The first transaction under an open-end credit plan.

Home Equity Conversion Mortgages (HECMs)

One of the most popular reverse mortgage programs is the Home Equity Conversion Mortgage (HECM) from the U.S. Department of Housing and Urban Development (HUD). HUD first introduced the HECM in November 1989. HECM reverse mortgages are offered through the Federal Housing Administration (FHA) and are funded by a lending institution such as a mortgage lender, bank, credit union, or savings and loan institution. This reverse mortgage is a **federally insured private loan**, making it safe for both the senior borrower and the lender.

Basic Features

- Borrowers must be age 62 years or older.
- They must own the property and occupy the property as their primary residence.
- They generally must have only a small mortgage balance or no mortgage at all.
- They must participate in a consumer information session given by an approved HECM counselor.
- There are no income or credit qualifications required.
- No repayment is required as long as the property is the primary residence.
- Closing costs can be financed in the mortgage.

HECM Eligible Properties

The eligible properties for an HECM reverse mortgage include:

- Single family homes
- to 4-unit homes in which one unit is occupied by the borrower
- Condominiums or planned unit developments (PUDs) that are HUD-FHA approved
- Mobile homes that meet HUD guidelines (generally, they must be on a permanent foundation)

Mortgage Amount

As with any reverse mortgage, the HECM mortgage amount is based on the age of the youngest borrower and the current interest rate. In addition, FHA defines the maximum claim amount on an HECM reverse mortgage as the **lesser** of the:

- Appraised value of the property.
- Sales price of the property, or
- National maximum loan limit established under Section 305(a)(2) of the Federal Home Loan Mortgage Corporation Act for a one-family residence.

HECM Payment Options

The participants in the HECM program can select from a variety of different payment plans to borrow against the equity in their homes:

- **Tenure** provides equal monthly payments as long as at least one borrower lives and continues to occupy the home as a primary residence.
- **Term** provides equal monthly payments for a fixed number of months.
- **Line of credit** allows the borrower to request a loan advance at any up to the approved credit line. A unique feature of the HECM program is the cash growth opportunities of the line of credit. As the credit line grows over time, the amount of cash available increases by the same total rate being charged on the loan balance until the borrower withdraws it all.

The HECM program is extremely flexible, so in addition, borrowers can choose a modified option that is a hybrid of two other options:

- **Modified tenure** is a combination of the line of credit with monthly payments for as long as the borrower lives in the home.
- **Modified term** is a combination of the line of credit with monthly payments for a fixed period of months selected by the borrower.

The HECM program allows homeowners to restructure their payment options for a nominal fee if their circumstances change.

Loan Origination Fees

A borrower pays an origination fee to compensate the lender for making an HECM loan. The fee is based on the appraised value of the home. If the home's appraised value is:

- Less than $125,000, the HECM origination fee is capped at $2,500.
- More than $125,000, lenders can charge 2% of the first $200,000 of the home's value plus 1% of the amount over $200,000, up to a cap of $6,000.

Mortgage Insurance Premiums

HECM borrowers must also pay a nonrefundable **upfront** mortgage insurance premium (MIP):

- **2% of the lesser** of the home's value or the FHA HECM mortgage limit for the area for HECM Standard.
- **.01% of the lesser** of the home's value or the FHA HECM mortgage limit for the area for HECM Saver.

The annual premium is equal to **1.25% of the outstanding mortgage balance** and is collected monthly.

Other Types of Mortgage Products

Although mortgages are primarily security devices used to collateralize real estate loans, the word mortgage is often prefaced with adjectives that describe the particular function the mortgage is serving, or the nature of the circumstances surrounding its use.

Some mortgage loans can be more than one type of mortgage loan at the same time, plus some share many different mortgage features. For example, you can have a conventional mortgage loan that is a first mortgage (and thus a senior mortgage), and this same mortgage can also be an adjustable rate mortgage that is a construction mortgage. Of course, some of the mortgage types and features are mutually exclusive, for example, a construction mortgage can't also be a reverse equity mortgage.

Balloon

- Also known as a partially amortized loan.
- Has periodic payments that do **not** fully amortize the loan by the end of the loan term.
- The final payment is larger than the others and is known as a **balloon payment**.
- Sometimes set up to contain a **straight term** mortgage, which means the borrower is making payments to interest only; the last payment is the interest for the last period plus the entire principal amount (an interest only or I/O loan).

Bi-Weekly Mortgage

- Technically, just a payment plan with a fixed rate mortgage set up like a standard 30-year conventional loan but payments are made every two weeks instead of every month.
- The 26 annual payments equal one extra monthly payment each year.
- Can help a borrower reach a goal of paying off a mortgage earlier and saving interest.

Blanket Mortgage

- Covers more than one parcel of land or lot, and is usually used to finance subdivision developments.
- Usually have a **partial release clause**, allowing the borrower to pay a certain amount to release some of the lots with the mortgage continuing to cover the remaining lots.

Bridge Mortgage

- Occurs between the termination of one mortgage and the beginning of the next.
- When the next mortgage is taken out, the bridge mortgage is repaid.
- Designed to be temporary, and are used most commonly for construction financing; a less common use for a bridge mortgage is for someone buying a new home before selling the old one.

Cash-Out Mortgage

- Allows borrower to get cash for the equity that has built up in a property, as when a property owner takes out a home equity loan for a specific purpose or refinances and receives cash at the closing.
- Allows owners to tap into the equity built up in the property over the years, but still retain ownership.
- Could be either a first or second (junior) mortgage.

Construction Mortgage

- Also called an interim loan, this is a temporary loan used to finance the construction of improvements and buildings on land.
- Generally, an appraiser will value the property for a construction loan by evaluating the building plans and specifications, completing a "subject to" appraisal.

- When construction is complete, the appraiser verifies that specifications have been met and the original opinion of value is valid; then the loan is replaced by permanent financing, called a **take out loan**.
- Usually requires extended rate locks.
- A **fixed disbursement plan** pays a percentage of funds at a set time; a series of predetermined disbursements, called **obligatory advances,** are paid out at various stages of construction.
- A **permanent construction loan** is a special type of construction loan where there is only one loan and one closing, with no take out loan; there is a fixed disbursement schedule for loan funds, and the loan automatically converts to a permanent first mortgage when construction is finished.

Easy Qualifier Loans

- May be referred to as stated-income, no-ratio, low-doc, no-doc, NINA (no income/no asset verification), or easy qualifier mortgages.
- Intended for borrowers who have less than perfect credit but have a larger down payment or borrowers whose credit is good but have difficulty proving the stability of their income because they are self-employed.
- Lenders typically modify their qualifying standards or loan criteria based on the customer's needs, such as relaxing documentation requirements.
- Generally has higher interest rates and fees.
- Availability of such loans depends on current market conditions; very rare, if not completely unavailable, today.

Equity Participation Mortgage

- Permits the lender to share part of the earnings, income, or profits from a real estate project.
- Usually in addition to collecting principal and interest payments on the loan; for example, the lender may receive 5% of gross rents.
- Done mostly for commercial real estate projects.
- Also known as a participation plan.

Home Equity Loan/Home Equity Line of Credit

- A loan usually secured by a mortgage on one's principal residence.
- Home equity loan is usually a one-time loan for a specific amount of money (and often for a specific purpose).
- Home equity line of credit (HELOC) is money that is available to the homeowner to be borrowed as needs arise; an open-end loan.
- Both vehicles take advantage of the equity that a homeowner has in the property by attaching a junior mortgage (unless the property is free and clear) to the property.
- May be a senior or junior lien.

Interest Only (I/O) Loans

- One with scheduled payments that pay only accrued interest, and not any portion of principal.
- Reduces monthly payments significantly.
- When making interest-only payments, the loan amount **never** decreases.
- No amortization is used; payment is determined by multiplying the interest rate by principal then dividing by 12 (months).
- Since no principal is paid during the loan term, the balloon payment is the original amount borrowed.
- Availability of such loans depends on current market conditions; very rare, if not completely unavailable, today.

Open-End Mortgage

- Allows the borrower to request additional funds from the lender, up to a certain pre-defined limit, even reborrowing part of the debt that's been repaid (at the lender's discretion) without having to renegotiate the loan.
- Popular with builders and farmers, who have recurring needs for money.
- The lender rarely gives consent to a person borrowing more funds without reassessing the borrower's situation and renegotiating the loan.
- Frequently requires a borrower to get a home equity line of credit, because the interest rate is adjustable.

Package Mortgage

- A mortgage that includes personal property, like appliances, in the property sale and all are financed together in one contract.
- The personal property also serves as collateral for the loan.
- A common use for this type of mortgage is to buy a furnished condominium, where the loan and mortgage documents may also recite appliances and/or furniture as part of the transaction.

Purchase Money Mortgage

- Usually used to describe a mortgage given by a buyer to a lender or a seller to secure part or all of the money that's borrowed to purchase property.
- A seller may take part of the purchase price as a mortgage to help the sale; if given to a seller, a purchase money mortgage can be called a **soft money mortgage**, because the borrower receives credit instead of actual cash.
- Can be a first mortgage or a junior mortgage, depending on its lien priority.
- Also known as a seller-held mortgage.

Reduction Option Mortgage

- A fixed rate loan that gives a borrower a limited opportunity to reduce the interest rate without paying refinancing costs.
- The Freddie Mac-approved program is a 30-year, fixed rate loan with an option to reduce the interest rate once between the 13th and 59th month of the loan:
  - Market interest rates must decline at least 2% before the borrower can reduce the rate.
  - The fee for this is about $100, plus 1/4% of the original loan amount.
  - Other costs, like appraisals and credit checks, are also avoided.

Refinance Mortgage

- Borrower pays off existing mortgage and replaces it with a new loan.
- Allows borrower to get better loan terms, for example, to lower the interest rate, change an adjustable rate to a fixed rate, change a 30-year loan to a 15-year loan, combine multiple mortgages into one, or remove private mortgage insurance.
- Could involve no cash-out or could be a cash-out mortgage.
- Is *not* the same thing as a loan modification, which is a change to the terms of an existing mortgage.
- Mortgage loan originator should be able to show a net tangible benefit to the borrower.

Variable Balance Mortgage (VBM)

- A loan with an adjustable interest rate, but with payments that never change; instead, as the rate increases or decreases, the balance due on the mortgage changes.
- Mortgage may last for a longer or shorter period of time than what is stated in the note.
- Generally for people who want the advantage of a variable interest rate, but are worried about payment increases.

Wraparound Mortgage

- When an existing loan on a property is retained, while the lender gives the buyer another, larger loan.
- The total debt (new second loan plus existing loan) is treated as a single obligation by the buyer, with one payment made on the entire debt.
- Often done by a seller when there's an existing loan with a lower interest rate that makes the property more attractive to the buyer.
- Requires an assumable first mortgage, with bank approval for the wraparound loan, to be proper and legal.

KEY TERM REVIEW

2-1 Buydown A graduated payment buydown that provides for subsidized payments in the first two years of the loan.

3-2-1 Buydown A graduated payment buydown that provides for subsidized payments in the first three years of the loan.

Amortization The decrease of a loan balance due to periodic installments paid on the principal and interest. Compare to Negative Amortization.

Buydown Additional funds in the form of points paid to a lender at the beginning of a loan to lower the interest rate and monthly payments.

Buydown, Permanent The payment of points by a borrower to a lender to reduce the interest rate and loan payments for the entire life of the loan.

Buydown, Temporary The payment of points by a borrower to a lender to reduce the interest rate and payments early in a loan, with interest rate and payments rising later.

Conforming Loan Loans that meet Fannie Mae/Freddie Mac standards and which can be sold on the secondary market.

Conventional Loan Loans not insured by a government entity.

Equity The difference between market value of a property and the sum of the mortgages and liens against it.

Fixed Rate Loan Loans with a constant interest rate remaining for the duration of the loan.

Fully Amortizing Loans Loans for which the total payments over the life of the loan pay off the entire balance of principal and interest due at the end of the loan term.

Home Equity Line of Credit (HELOC) Available money that can be borrowed by a homeowner, secured by a second mortgage on the principal residence. Home equity lines of credit can be accessed at any time up to a predetermined borrowing limit and are often used for non-housing expenditures. Compare to Home Equity Loan.

Index A statistical report that is generally a reliable indicator of the approximate change in the cost of money, and is often used to adjust the interest rate in ARMs.

Interest 1. A right or share in something, such as a piece of real estate. 2. A charge a borrower pays to a lender for the use of the lender's money. Compare to Principal.

Interest Rate The rate which is charged or paid for the use of money, generally expressed as a percentage of the principal.

Jumbo Loans Loans that exceed the maximum loan amount that Fannie Mae/Freddie Mac will buy, making them nonconforming.

Margin The difference between the index value and the interest rate charged to the borrower with an ARM loan.

Negative Amortization A situation that occurs when the minimum required periodic payment for principal and interest does not cover the accrued interest due for that period, resulting in the unpaid interest being added to the principal balance.

Nonconforming Loans Loans that do not meet Fannie Mae/Freddie Mac standards, and thus cannot be sold to them but can be sold to other secondary markets.

Nontraditional Loans Anything other than 30-year fixed rate loans.

Partially Amortizing Loans Loans for which payments are applied to principal and interest, but the payments do not retire the debt when the agreed upon loan term expires, thus requiring a balloon payment at the end of the loan term.

Points One percent of the loan amount. Points are charged for any reason, but are often used for buydowns (where they may also be called discount points).

Principal With regard to a loan, the amount originally borrowed, or the current balance.

Reverse Mortgage A loan used by qualified homeowners age 62 or older to convert equity in the home into a lump sum, a monthly cash stream, and/or a line of credit; generally repaid when the last surviving borrower dies, sells the home, or ceases to live in the home for 12 consecutive months.

Secondary Financing The borrowing of money from another source in addition to the primary lender to pay for part of the purchase price or closing costs.

Self-liquidating Description of a fully amortizing loan for which the total payments over the life of the loan pay off the entire balance by the end of the loan's term.

Subprime Loans Loans that have more risks than allowed in the conforming market. Also called B-C Loans or B-C Credit.

Teaser Rates A low initial rate on an ARM. The rate usually returns to normal at the first adjustment date.

CHAPTER 2 QUIZ

1. *Each of these are characteristics that could make a loan nontraditional EXCEPT*

   A. 15-year term.
   B. adjustable rate.
   C. fixed rate.
   D. temporary buydown.

2. *In which federal law would you find the definition of a nontraditional loan?*

   A. Homeowners Equity Protection Act
   B. Real Estate Settlement Procedures Act
   C. Secure and Fair Enforcement for Mortgage Licensing Act
   D. Truth in Lending Act

3. *A "jumbo" loan is also known as a(n)*

   A. conforming loan.
   B. FHA loan.
   C. nonconforming loan.
   D. subprime loan.

4. *The type of mortgage that covers more than one parcel or lot and is often used for financing subdivision developments is called a*

   A. blanket mortgage.
   B. equity participation mortgage.
   C. open-end mortgage.
   D. package mortgage.

5. *Initial interest rates that are much lower than the normal interest rate, with the rate usually returning to the normal interest rate at the first adjustment, is known as a*

   A. par rate.
   B. premium rate.
   C. teaser rate.
   D. yield spread premium.

6. *6. Which would be considered a toxic feature under the qualifying mortgage rule definition?*

   A. adjustable rate
   B. defeasance clause
   C. interest only payments
   D. short term

7. *A mortgage loan, typically a second mortgage, that has a predetermined maximum loan amount, has an adjustable rate, can be borrowed against and paid off as needed, and has an interest only minimum monthly payment, is known as a(n)*

   A. HELOC.
   B. installment second mortgage.
   C. reverse mortgage.
   D. revolving mortgage.

8. *If a borrower exercises his right to change from an adjustable rate mortgage to a fixed rate mortgage one time during the loan term, provided certain conditions are met, he has what type of mortgage?*

   A. convertible ARM
   B. fixed ARM
   C. hybrid ARM
   D. option ARM

9. *A conforming loan*

   A. exceeds the maximum loan amount established by Fannie Mae/Freddie Mac.
   B. follows the secondary market criteria set by Fannie Mae/Freddie Mac.
   C. is for more than $417,000 on a single family home and also called a jumbo loan.
   D. is offered to borrowers who do not meet qualifications for Fannie Mae/Freddie Mac.

10. *According to the Interagency Guidance on Nontraditional Mortgage Product Risks, nontraditional mortgage loans may be LEAST risky for borrowers with*

    A. high debt income ratios.
    B. high loan-to-value.
    C. low credit scores.
    D. low debt income ratios.

11. *Borrower Stan is considering a simultaneous second loan. Each of these are risk mitigating factors that might help him get this loan EXCEPT*

    A. high housing expense ratio.
    B. high credit score.
    C. low LTV.
    D. low debt to income ratio.

12. *The difference between the index and the interest rate charged to the borrower with an ARM is known as the*

   A. cap.
   B. discount.
   C. margin.
   D. note rate.

13. *The type of mortgage that provides the borrower with a monthly check instead of the borrower paying a monthly payment is known as a*

   A. conforming loan.
   B. graduated payment mortgage.
   C. nonconforming loan.
   D. reverse mortgage.

14. *A loan in which total payments over the life of the loan pay off the entire balance of principal and interest due at the end of the term is called*

   A. amortized.
   B. fixed rate.
   C. fully amortizing.
   D. long term.

15. *Which element of an ARM is a statistical report that is a generally reliable indicator of the approximate change in the cost of money and may be used to adjust interest rates?*

   A. discount
   B. index
   C. margin
   D. prime rate

16. *During the life of a typical reverse mortgage, which of the following factors is decreased?*

   A. debt
   B. equity
   C. interest
   D. monthly payments

17. *Which statement about reverse mortgages is FALSE??*

   A. A borrower's credit card debt and other debt are not considered.
   B. A homeowner must own her home free and clear in order to qualify.
   C. The home should be considered the primary residence.
   D. Title to the home must be held by the borrower.

18. *A reverse mortgage must be repaid if the home is unoccupied by the borrower for how long?*

   A. 3 consecutive months
   B. 6 consecutive months
   C. 12 consecutive months
   D. 18 consecutive months

19. *Which property would NOT be eligible for an HECM loan?*

   A. condominium
   B. cooperative
   C. duplex
   D. manufactured home on a permanent foundation

20. *Which factor is NOT taken into consideration when determining the mortgage amount for an HECM?*

   A. age of the youngest borrower
   B. credit history of the borrower
   C. current interest rate
   D. lesser of the appraised value or the FHA insurance limit

Chapter 3
Ethics: Ongoing Concerns

Introduction

Ethics and fair lending are two very important issues. To avoid potential liability, mortgage professionals need to know what conduct violates anti-discrimination laws. They must also know what constitutes fraud to prevent engaging in any illegal mortgage activity. And, it's important to be able to recognize practices that are considered predatory lending so that they may be avoided. This module includes a quick review of two federal laws covered in Chapter 1—as well as some additional federal laws—as it addresses these associated topics:

- Advertising
- Consumer protection
- Discrimination
- Appraisal
- Fraud
- Predatory lending

Blockbusting

Ethics

Flipping

Flipping, Illegal

Fraud

Fraud, Actual

Fraud, Constructive

HOEPA Loan

Junk Fees

Kickbacks

Negligence

Predatory Lending

Redlining

Steering

Straw Buyer

Suspicious Activity Reports (SARs)

Key Terms

Codes of Ethics

Ethics in the mortgage industry may seem like a complex issue, but it really boils down to a few simple points:

- Treat everyone equally.
- Be honest.
- Give full disclosure.
- Don't take advantage of people.
- Keep good documentation.

If you do these things, follow the law, and adhere to a code of ethics put forth by your state or local mortgage board and other industry groups, then you shouldn't have any problems. For example, the **Association of Mortgage Brokers or NAMP** (which was known previously as NAMB or the National Association of Mortgage Brokers) has promulgated a **Code of Ethics**:

- **Honesty and Integrity**. Mortgage professionals should conduct business in a manner reflecting honesty, honor, and integrity. Not only must you act with integrity, but you should insist that those with whom you do business act with integrity as well.
- **Professional Conduct.** Reasonable care and skill must always be used when acting on behalf of a customer. Never take on tasks beyond your ability or claim expertise where you have no special training or skills. And never pressure any provider of services, goods, or facilities to circumvent industry professional standards.
- **Honesty in Advertising.** Mortgage professionals should strive to be truthful in all advertisements and other solicitations for business that they make.
- **Confidentiality.** Personal and financial information given by the customer or gained from other sources can be used only for the business purpose for which it was intended and must be kept confidential and protected.
- **Compliance with the Law.** Not only are you obligated to know and understand the law, you have a duty to stay current with changes to the law.
- **Disclosure of Financial Interests.** Avoid all situations that might lead to a real or apparent conflict between your self-interest and your duty as a mortgage professional. Any equity or financial interest in a property being offered as collateral to secure a loan must be disclosed.

Truth in Lending Act

In an earlier chapter, we looked that provisions and disclosure requirements of **Regulation Z** (the Truth in Lending Act) as found in the Code of Federal Regulations (C.F.R.), Title 12 Banks and Banking, Part 1026. While adhering to this important law is certainly part of your ethical duty, in this chapter, we'll focus just on the advertising provisions relating to real estate finance and mortgage loans as required by TILA.

Prior to the passage of the Truth in Lending Act, an advertiser might have disclosed only the most attractive credit terms, distorting the true cost of financing. For example, the ad could have included the low monthly payments (e.g., $275 a month) without indicating the large down payment necessary to qualify for that payment level. Advertisers did not have to disclose the APR or whether the transaction was a credit sale or lease. TILA requires the advertiser to tell the whole story, and tell it **clearly** and **conspicuously**. Also, **if** an advertisement for credit states specific credit terms, it must state only those terms that are **actually are available** or **will be arranged or offered** by the creditor.

Triggering Terms

If an advertisement is for credit secured by a dwelling, the advertisement may not state any other rate, except that a simple annual rate that is applied to an unpaid balance may be stated in conjunction with, but not more conspicuously than, the annual percentage rate. If an advertisement contains any one of the triggering terms about the loan as specified in the Truth in Lending Act, that advertisement must also include the required disclosures. Examples of triggering terms in advertisements include:

- The amount of the down payment (e.g., "20% down")
- The amount of any payment (e.g., "Pay only $700 per month")
- The number of payments (e.g., "Only 360 monthly payments")
- The period of repayment (e.g., "30-year financing available")
- The amount of any finance charge (e.g., "1% finance charge")

Required Advertising Disclosures

If any triggering terms are used in an ad, *all* of these disclosures must be made:

- Amount or percentage of down payment.
- Terms of repayment, e.g., payment schedule, including any balloon payments.
- Annual percentage rate, using that term spelled out in full or APR.
- If the rate may increase (e.g., for ARMs), that fact must also be disclosed.

Required disclosures must be made clearly and conspicuously.

If an ad discloses only the APR, the additional disclosures are *not* required.

Terms That Do NOT Trigger Disclosure

Examples of terms that do *not* trigger required disclosures include:

- "No down payment"
- "5% Annual Percentage Rate loan available here"
- "Easy monthly payments"
- "FHA financing available." or "100% VA financing available"
- "Terms to fit your budget"

Triggering Terms (require disclosure)	Non-Triggering Terms (do not require disclosure)
"20% down"	"No down payment"
"Pay only $700 per month"	"We'll work with you"
"Only 360 monthly payments"	"Easy monthly payments"
"30-year financing available"	"FHA financing available"
"1% finance charge"	"100% VA financing available"

Advertising Closed-End Credit

A **closed-end** credit transaction is one in which the balance is expected to be repaid—along with any interest and finance changes—by a specified future date. Most real estate loans are closed-end. Additional advertising provisions in the Truth in Lending Act (12 C.F.R. § 1026.24) related to these loans include:

Rate. If an advertisement states a simple annual rate of interest and more than one rate will apply over the term of the loan, the advertisement must also disclose—with equal prominence and in close proximity to the advertised rate—this information:

- Each simple annual rate of interest that will apply; if a variable-rate, a reasonably current index and margin must be used.
- The period of time during which each simple annual rate of interest will apply.
- The APR for the loan.

Payment Amount. If the advertisement states the amount of any payment, it must also disclose—with equal prominence and in close proximity to the payment—this information:

- The amount of each payment that will apply over the term of the loan, including any balloon payment; if a variable-rate, a reasonably current index and margin must be used.
- The period of time during which each payment will apply.

> ◇ **Note:** When the ad for a first lien mortgage loan states the amount of any payment, it must also state prominently (but not with equal prominence) and in close proximity to the advertised payment that the payments do **not** include amounts for taxes and insurance, if applicable, and that the actual payment amount will be higher.

Payment and Rate Comparisons. Advertisements may not compare actual or hypothetical payments or rates and a "teaser" payment or simple annual rate that will be available for the advertised product unless the ad includes a clear and conspicuous comparison to the terms required to be disclosed (APR, term, payments, etc.). If it is a variable rate transaction where the advertised payment or simple annual rate is based on the index and margin used to make subsequent rate or payment adjustments, the advertisement must include an equally prominent statement in close proximity that the payment or rate is subject to adjustment as well as the time period when the first adjustment will occur.

Use of the Term "Fixed." TILA (§ 1026.24) also indicates that if an advertisement for closed-end credit references a **variable rate** loan, the phrase "adjustable rate mortgage," "variable rate mortgage," or "ARM" must appear before the first use of "fixed" and must be at least as conspicuous as the word "fixed." In addition, the ad must clearly indicate the time period for which the rate or payment is fixed, and the fact that the rate may vary or the payment may increase after that period.

If the ad references a **non-variable rate** loan where the payment will increase, the use of the word "fixed" to refer to a payment must state the time period for which the payment is fixed and the fact that the payment will increase after that period.

If an advertisement references **both variable and non-variable rate** loans, the phrases "adjustable rate mortgage," "variable rate mortgage," or "ARM" must appear with equal prominence as any use of the term "fixed" or "fixed rate mortgage." Also, the term "fixed" must clearly refer *only* to the transactions with fixed rates. If referring to a payment or to a variable rate, it must also include the time period for which the rate or payment is fixed and a statement that the rate may vary or the payment may increase after that period.

Advertising Open-End Credit

Regulation Z was amended to comply with the Mortgage Disclosure Improvement Act of 2009 (12 C.F.R. § 1026.16), to address the unique challenges in advertising open-end credit plans secured by the borrower's dwelling. Remember, **open-end** refers to a loan where credit is extended to the borrower during the term and the lender may impose a finance charge on the outstanding unpaid balance, such as a home equity line of credit (HELOC). It's critical that ads for these loans not use misleading terms, such as "free money." These loans are also subject to disclosure provisions previously discussed as well as these additional provisions:

Additional Disclosures. If any of the triggering terms are used or the payment terms of the plan are set forth, affirmatively or negatively, in an advertisement, the ad must also clearly and conspicuously state the following:

- Any **loan fee** that is a percentage of the credit limit under the plan and an estimate of any other fees imposed for opening the plan expressed as a single dollar amount or a reasonable range
- Any **periodic rate** used to compute the finance charge expressed as an annual percentage rate
- The **maximum annual percentage rate** that may be imposed in a variable-rate plan

Further, if an advertisement states an initial annual percentage rate that is *not* based on the index and margin used to make later rate adjustments in a variable-rate plan, the ad must also clearly indicate the period of time such initial rate will be in effect and a reasonably current APR that would have been in effect using the index and margin.

Balloon Payments. In an ad that states a minimum payment, if it's possible that a balloon payment would result if only that minimum periodic payment is made, that fact must be stated with equal prominence and close proximity.

Promotional Rates and Payment. If a HELOC advertisement (other than broadcast advertisements) states a promotional rate and/or a promotional payment, the ad must disclose—in a clear and conspicuous manner and with equal prominence and in close proximity to each listing of the promotional rate or payment—each of these facts:

- The period of time during which the promotional rate or payment will apply.
- If a promotional rate, any APR that will apply (if a variable rate, the APR must be disclosed within established accuracy standards).
- If a promotional payment, the amounts and time periods of any payments that will apply under the plan (if the payment will be based on the application of a variable index and margin, it must be disclosed based on a reasonable current index and margin).

◇ **Note:** These provisions do **not** apply to an envelope in which an application or solicitation is mailed, nor to a banner advertisement or pop-up advertisement linked to an application or solicitation provided electronically.

CLEAR AND CONSPICUOUS STANDARD (REGULATION Z 1026.24 (b)(5))

When considering **oral advertisements** for credit secured by a dwelling, including alternative disclosures as provided for by § 1026.24(g), a clear and conspicuous disclosure, whether by radio, television, or other medium, means that the required disclosures are given at a speed and volume sufficient for a consumer to hear and comprehend them. For example, information stated very rapidly at a low volume in a radio or television advertisement would not meet the clear and conspicuous standard if consumers cannot hear and comprehend the information required to be disclosed.

Other Advertising Provisions

Any ad stating tax implications—such as whether or not interest is tax-deductible—cannot be misleading; consumers must be advised to consult a tax adviser.

TV and radio ads may provide a toll-free number to allow consumers to obtain more information.

Misrepresentations are prohibited; for example:

- Loan product being endorsed or sponsored by any federal, state, or local government.
- Misleading use of the current lender's name, unless the advertisement also discloses with equal prominence the name of the person or creditor making the advertisement and includes a clear and conspicuous statement that the person making the advertisement is not associated with, or acting on behalf of, the consumer's current lender.
- Misleading claims of debt elimination; making any misleading claim in an advertisement that the mortgage product offered will eliminate debt or result in a waiver or forgiveness of a consumer's existing loan terms with, or obligations to, another creditor if the product advertised would merely replace one debt obligation with another.
- Prohibits use of "counselor" to reference for-profit mortgage broker or mortgage creditor, its employees, or persons working for the broker or creditor that are involved in offering, originating, or selling mortgages.
- In foreign language ads, prohibits making some required disclosures, such as initial rate or payment, only in a foreign language but providing other information, such as a fully-indexed rate or fully amortizing payment, only in English in the same advertisement.

Advertising Case Study

Frank is a state licensed mortgage loan originator. His employer, ABC Mortgage, expects him to close at least four loans a month. To drum up business, Frank takes out the following ad in his local newspaper:

> # Find Your Dream House?
> # Need Money to Buy?
> # Call Frank Jones Now!
> ## I can get you a
> ## FIXED RATE 4%
> ## mortgage * with NO POINTS!
> ## Close in a week!
> ## 1-800-CLL-FRNK
> ** first two years*

Discuss ways in which this advertisement violates TILA.

_____

_____

_____

_____

_____

_____

_____

Real Estate Settlement Procedures Act (RESPA)

The **Real Estate Settlement Procedures Act (RESPA)** of 1974 requires mortgage lenders, mortgage brokers, or servicers of home loans to *provide borrowers with pertinent and timely disclosures of the nature and costs of the real estate settlement process.* Its purpose is to regulate settlement and closing procedures and to protect borrowers. The Act does *not* apply to loans used to finance the purchase of 25 acres or more, vacant land, or transactions where the buyer assumes, or takes subject to, an existing loan. The U.S. Department of **Housing and Urban Development** (HUD) promulgated **Regulation X**, which is implemented and enforced by the Consumer Financial Protection Bureau as of July 2011.

Although RESPA was covered in detail in Chapter 1, here are some important points to remember. RESPA:

- Prohibits kickbacks and fees for services not performed during closing (while allowing payment for *"services performed during closing"*).

- Requires an information booklet be given to buyers explaining RESPA.

- Requires a **Good Faith Estimate** of Closing Costs (GFE) be given to the buyer within **three (3) business days** of a completed loan application.

- The only fee that may be collected prior to mandated disclosures, such as the GFE and TIL, is a fee for a **credit report**.

- Requires use of the **HUD-1 Settlement Statement** for all federally-related residential loans. The HUD-1 shows how much was paid, to what companies or parties, and for what purpose.
- Gives the buyer the right to inspect the HUD-1 Settlement Statement **one (1) business day** before closing.
- Requires brokers and lenders to disclose **affiliated business relationships** without obligating parties to use suggested referrals.
- Sets limits on the amount of **escrow reserves** a lender can hold or require a buyer to deposit in advance to cover real estate taxes, real estate insurance premiums, and other similar costs.
- Requires lenders to make full disclosure to borrowers about the possibility and likelihood that the loan will be **sold or transferred** by the lender to another entity or secondary market investor, as well as the lender's transfer practices and requirements.
- Requires lenders to provide borrowers with a **Servicing Transfer Statement** if the loan servicer sells or assigns the servicing rights to a borrower's loan to another loan servicer; generally required fifteen (15) days before the effective date of the loan transfer.

RESPA violations can result in **criminal penalties** and **triple damages** for the cost of title insurance if the buyer is required to use a title company at the seller's insistence, and / or a **$10,000 fine** per incident of paying or receiving a kickback.

RESPA Scenarios

Section 8 of the Real Estate Settlement Procedures Act specifically prohibits kickbacks and unearned fees. Read through these scenarios and consider who—if anyone—is in violation of RESPA, then discuss with your class.

Scenario 1. XYZ Mortgage encourages borrowers who receive federally-related mortgage loans from them to employ attorney Bob to perform title searches and related settlement services in connection with their transaction. XYZ and Bob have an understanding that in return for the referral of this business, Bob provides legal services to XYZ's officers or employees at abnormally low rates or for no charge.

Since the borrower is not required to use the attorney, is anyone in violation of RESPA?

_____

_____

_____

_____

Scenario 2. ABC Credit Reporting Bureau places a full-feature computer in the office of TOP Mortgage so that TOP can easily transmit requests for credit reports and ABC can respond. ABC supplies the computer for free to any mortgage office that orders a specific number of credit reports each month.

Is anyone in violation of RESPA?

_____

_____

_____

_____

Consumer Protection: Gramm-Leach-Bliley Act

The **Gramm-Leach-Bliley Act**, which was covered in Chapter 1, includes the following consumer protection provisions. Let's briefly review them.

Financial Privacy Rule

- Prohibits financial institutions from disclosing—other than to a consumer reporting agency—access codes or account numbers to any nonaffiliated third party for use in telemarketing, direct mail marketing, or other marketing through electronic mail.

- Requires a **Consumer Privacy Policy** notice that explains the lender's information collection and information sharing practices be provided to **consumers before** the company discloses personal information. **Customers** must receive this notice **annually** during the financial relationship.

- Allows consumers to **opt out** of having private information shared.

Safeguards Rule

The Safeguards Rule requires all financial institutions and institutions that receive consumer's financial information to design, implement, and maintain safeguards to protect customer information while it is in the custody and control of the institution and its agents.

A written Safeguards Policy must include provisions that:

- Ensure the security and confidentiality of customer records.

- Protect against any anticipated threats or hazards to the security of such records.

- Protect against the unauthorized access or use of such records or information in ways that could result in substantial harm or inconvenience to customers.

Pretexting Provisions

- Protects consumers from individuals and companies that obtain their personal financial information under false, fictitious, or fraudulent pretenses.

Illegal Discrimination

Fair and equitable treatment in housing and real estate transactions is a right by law. The **Equal Credit Opportunity Act** (ECOA), which was covered in Chapter 1, is a federal law that ensures that all consumers are given an equal chance to obtain credit. ECOA, implemented as **Regulation B**, specifically prohibits illegal discrimination in granting credit to people. Fair and equitable treatment in housing and real estate transactions is a right by law. In fact, under the Equal Credit Opportunity Act, **no borrower may be discouraged** from making a formal loan application because of his or her membership in a protected class.

Two other federal anti-discrimination statutes that have the greatest impact on real estate transactions are the **Civil Rights Act of 1866** and Title VIII of the Civil Rights Act of 1968, commonly referred to as the **Fair Housing Act**.

Civil Rights Act of 1866

- Prohibits public and private **racial discrimination** in any property transaction in the United States.

- Applies to all property—real or personal, residential or commercial, improved or unimproved.

- Also prohibits any discrimination based on **ancestry**.

- Allows someone who has been unlawfully discriminated against under the 1866 Act to sue in federal district court.

- Remedies may include **injunctions** (court orders requiring the defendant to do or refrain from doing a particular act), **compensatory damages** (reimbursement for expenses caused by the discrimination and/or for emotional distress), and **punitive damages** (to punish the wrongdoer if the acts are deliberate or egregious).
- Codified in Title 42, Section 1981(a) of the U.S. Code.

Fair Housing Act

Title VIII of the Civil Rights Act of 1968 is commonly called the **Fair Housing Act.** It prohibits discrimination of protected classes in the sale or lease of residential property, including vacant land intended for residential housing.

A person who has been discriminated against in violation of the Fair Housing Act may file a written complaint to the nearest HUD office within one year of the alleged violation (42 U.S.C. § 3610).

Protected Classes: Fair Housing Act	Protected Classes: Equal Credit Opportunity Act
Race	Sex
Color	Age
Religion	Marital status
Sex	Race
National origin	Color
Disability	Religion
Familial status	National origin
	Receipt of public assistance
	Exercised rights under the Consumer Credit Protection Act

Prohibited Practices

The Fair Housing Act (42 U.S.C. § 3604-3605) also prohibits the following actions if they are based on a person's membership in a protected class:

- Refusing to make a mortgage loan
- Refusing to provide information regarding loans
- Imposing **different terms** or conditions on a loan, such as different interest rates, points, or fees
- Discriminating in the appraisal of property
- Refusing to **purchase** a loan or setting different terms or conditions for purchasing a loan; for example, a bank charging a higher interest rate to a creditworthy borrower who wants to buy a house in a minority neighborhood than is charged for an equally creditworthy borrower in a different neighborhood
- **Blockbusting** – trying to induce owners to sell their homes by suggesting that the ethnic or racial composition of the neighborhood is changing, with the implication that property values will decline
- **Steering** – channeling prospective real estate buyers or tenants to particular neighborhoods based on their race, religion, or ethnic background

The Fair Housing Act also prohibits discrimination when **advertising** lending and other services associated with residential transactions, requiring lenders to:

- Include the "equal housing lender" slogan in any broadcast advertisement,
- Display the Equal Housing Opportunity poster in every branch where mortgage loans are made, and
- Display the Equal Housing Opportunity logo on all printed promotional material.

Redlining

Redlining is the *refusal to make loans on property located in a particular neighborhood for discriminatory reasons*. Discrimination in mortgage lending is specifically prohibited by the Fair Housing Act (42 U.S.C. § 3604). To combat redlining, the **Community Reinvestment Act (CRA)** was enacted by Congress in 1977 to reduce discriminatory credit practices against low-income neighborhoods (12 U.S.C. § 2901).

The CRA:

* Encourages financial institutions to help meet the credit needs of the communities in which they operate.

* Requires periodic evaluation of an insured depository institution's record.

* Is under the supervision of the Board of Governors of the Federal Reserve System (FRB), the Federal Deposit Insurance Corporation (FDIC), the Office of the Comptroller of the Currency (OCC), and the Office of Thrift Supervision (OTS).

The prohibition against redlining is further enforced by the **Home Mortgage Disclosure Act** of 1975 (12 U.S.C. § 2801-2810), which requires the following lenders to file reports of all loans made during that year:

* Institutional depository lenders with assets in excess of $39 million

* For profit non-depository lenders with assets in excess of $10 million or who originate 100 or more

The loans are categorized according to the locations of the various properties so that cases of redlining can be discovered more easily.

Mortgage Fraud

Fraud is the *misrepresentation, concealment, or omission of material facts*. Fraud falls into two categories:

* **Actual Fraud.** Misrepresentation or concealment of a material fact with the intent to deceive.

* **Constructive Fraud.** Unintentional misrepresentation or concealment of a material fact as the result of carelessness or negligence.

Mortgage fraud involves any misrepresentation or concealment used in an effort to obtain a mortgage loan. This is a serious federal crime when done for any federally related loan (which includes most loans, since HUD, Fannie Mae, or a federally chartered bank are involved at some point in the process).

Mortgage Fraud Perpetrators

Everyone involved in the mortgage transaction can also play a role in a fraud scheme; for example:

* **Borrowers.** Borrower involvement generally falls into two main categories:
  * Lying on applications or supplying false documents.
  * Acting as an illegal **straw buyer**, which is someone who allows his name and personal details to be used to obtain a mortgage loan for a property he has no intention of inhabiting.

* **Mortgage Loan Originators and Lenders.** Ignoring derogatory information to get a loan approved, creating phantom documents for verification, concealing the true nature of a borrower's down payment, falsifying documents, making loans to straw buyers, illegally flipping properties, making loans to unqualified buyers and then selling them to the secondary market as quickly as possible.

* **Appraisers.** Inflating property values to "hit a number" provided by a borrower or lender, using inappropriate comparables.

* **Attorneys.** Preparing bogus deeds and getting them duly recorded on public records with the participation of government workers.

* **Accountants.** Falsifying tax returns, profit and loss statements, and other documentation required by lenders to qualify loans.

* **Title Companies.** Charging borrowers fees for services never provided at the closing or completing incorrect title reports that omit valid liens or that create false chains of title.

* **Government Workers.** Falsifying deeds and other records.

- **Real Estate Agents.** Preparing false documentation such as sales contracts or property inspections, finding straw buyers for the property, raising listing prices of homes after a deal is put together to make the over-inflated appraisal value appear valid, steering borrowers to a specific lender in exchange for a kickback or other consideration.

- **Rehabbers** and **FSBO (For Sale By Owner) Flippers.** Using sub-par material, removing materials or fixtures after an appraisal, providing straw buyers, improperly influencing appraisers or mortgage loan originators.

Typical Fraud Schemes

Sadly, someone determined to act illegally can dream up any number of schemes. For example:

- **Air Loan.** Involves non-existent loans and no-collateral loans. For example, a broker enlists or creates a straw buyer, identifies fictional properties, opens accounts for payments, and maintains custodial accounts for escrow payments.

- **Deed Scam.** The seller's signature on the deed is forged, meaning the real homeowner is not even aware the property is being fraudulently transferred. The deed is recorded; the thief mortgages the property with cash-out refinancing, then takes the money and walks away from the mortgage without making a payment.

- **Double Sold Loans.** May involve the primary mortgage holder who sells the loan to a fraudulent company for servicing, or a borrower who signs multiple copies of the same application/documents that the loan originator submits to different lenders. When approved by more than one lender, the loan originator forges the closing documents for one loan and then makes off with the excess proceeds.

- **Unrecorded or Silent Second.** A buyer gives a seller a second mortgage without informing the lender, who thinks that the borrower's equity in the property is greater. Also, the lender may be aware of the second lien but there is an outside agreement between the parties that no payments on the junior lien are ever going to be paid, or expected. Even if borrower intends to pay the second mortgage, it puts the seller at risk in case of default.

Illegal Flipping

While flipping property—buying property, fixing it up, and selling it for a profit—may be legitimate, **illegal flipping** is one of the most common and well-known mortgage fraud schemes. Illegal flipping:

- Occurs when a property is purchased at a low price, appraised at an inflated value without any valid reason for the increase, and then resold at a much higher price.

- May involve a series of sales and quick re-sales, with one property and a group of sellers and buyers changing ownership among them.

- Generally requires collusion between the seller, appraiser, and lender/broker. Often, it is the unsuspecting buyer who purchases the flipped property who is the victim of such as scheme.

- Is more prevalent in mixed value areas where higher-priced homes are located near lower-priced homes in poor repair, and home values fluctuate extremely.

- May use out-of-town entities to handle the loan so that underwriters who review the loans are unfamiliar with the property and neighborhood.

Illegal flipping is addressed by the Federal Housing Administration, who imposes additional requirements on FHA loans for resales ranging from **91-180 days**:

- The seller must be the owner of record.

- There must be a second appraisal that matches a resale threshold percentage established by HUD.

Furthermore, appraisers are required to investigate the transfer history of a property for the **past three (3) years.** This, too, can assist in identifying potential flipping schemes.

THE IMPORTANCE OF ACCURATE APPRAISALS

Appraisals are a critical aspect of mortgage lending. An appraisal with inaccurate information—whether completed because of fraud or negligence—can have a serious impact. An **inflated appraisal** scheme occurs *when a property is intentionally appraised with a higher-than-market value by an appraiser acting in collusion with a real estate agent or lender*. Lenders hiring these appraisers use only those who agree to "hit the number," "push the value," or "work with us on the number" regardless of its relationship to actual market value. If the mortgages are part of sales transactions, continued inflation of values in the same neighborhood (with inflated sale prices) can result in continued appraisals at higher-than-market values that appear justified. Even unsuspecting appraisers are caught in this when they unknowingly use the inflated sale prices as comparables.

This issue is addressed by an interim final rule on **Valuation Independence** amending Regulation Z (12 C.F.R. § 1026.42) released by the Federal Reserve Board of Governors in October 2010, effective April, 2011. The rule, which applies to any consumer credit transaction secured by a consumer's primary dwelling, requires creditors and their agents to provide customary and reasonable compensation to fee appraisers. It prohibits **coercion** in connection with a covered transaction in any way (including extortion, inducement, bribery, intimidation of, compensation of, or instruction to) of a person who prepares valuations or performs valuation management functions. The rule also prohibits an appraiser from **materially misrepresenting** the value of the consumer's principal dwelling and prohibits someone performing a valuation from having a direct or indirect **conflict of interest**, financial or otherwise, in the property. The rule prohibits creditors from extending credit based on appraisals if they know beforehand of violations involving appraiser coercion or conflicts of interest unless the creditor documents that it has acted with reasonable diligence to determine that the valuation does not materially misstate or misrepresent the value of the consumer's principal dwelling. The rule also mandates that creditors or settlement service providers who have information about appraiser misconduct file a report with the appropriate state licensing authorities.

Red Flags of Mortgage Fraud

The **Federal Financial Institutions Examination Council** (FFIEC) introduces several mortgage fraud red flags in their white paper titled *The Detection, Investigation, and Deterrence of Mortgage Fraud Involving Third Parties*. These include the following:

- **Steering Buyers to a Specific Lender.** If a transaction will close only if a certain lender is used, it is possibly a scam

- **Stated Income.** No doc or low doc loans that require minimal documentation have great potential for fraud. Most lenders will not offer these programs any longer

- **No Money Due at Closing.** If a buyer is not required to pay anything at closing, the sales price may have been inflated to cover the down payment and closing costs

- **Sale Subject to the Seller Acquiring Title.** If the seller on the purchase contract is not the owner of record, participants should verify that the transaction is legitimate

- **Difference in Sale Price.** The sales contract is supposed to guide the title agency or closing agent to the terms of the HUD-1 settlement statement, and there should be no discrepancies

- **Sale Price Changes to Fit Appraisal.** The sales contract is altered after an appraiser comes back with a higher-than-expected appraisal

- **Related Parties Involved.** While there is no law against selling property to a relative, even at a discounted price, mortgage fraud scams often involve family members. Full disclosure is imperative

- **Funds Paid to Undisclosed Third Parties.** When unknown third parties, who appear to have no relevance to the transaction, are paid out of the funds received at the closing, there may be debt not revealed in the closing statements. A closing statement that is not followed to the letter is a red flag to the borrower
- **Cash Paid to Seller Outside of Escrow.** The seller receives cash from the sale of the property; however, it is not stated in closing statements or in the purchase contract
- **Cash Paid to Borrower.** Although seller-paid costs are becoming more typical in today's economy, schemes in which the buyer receives money from the transaction are not

Mortgage Fraud Detection and Prevention

The Federal Bureau of Investigation (FBI) compiles data on mortgage fraud through **Suspicious Activity Reports** (SARs) filed by financial institutions with knowledge or suspicion of fraud, and from reports from the Department of Housing and Urban Development's Office of the Inspector General. The FBI also receives complaints from the mortgage industry at large.

Private subscription services, such as the **Mortgage Asset Research Institute** (MARI), give members access to a database of all fraud and suspected fraud as reported by its members and state and federal regulatory agencies, as well as the actions taken. The service allows those in the industry to check credentials of companies and individuals with whom they work.

There are also many free websites that document various mortgage fraud scams and the consequences to the participants. It would be a good practice to bookmark some of those sites and make a point of visiting them regularly.

Predatory Lending

Predatory lending involves loans that take advantage of ill-informed consumers through excessively high fees, misrepresented loan terms, frequent refinancing that does not benefit the borrower, and other prohibited acts. Predatory lending targets borrowers with little knowledge of, or defense against, these practices. The goal of a predatory lender is to take the property or strip its equity, or to profit from the exorbitant fees charged.

Statement on Subprime Mortgage Lending

The federal financial regulatory agencies occasionally issue guidelines, recommendations, and policy statements for their member institutions. One example is the 2007 Statement on Subprime Mortgage Lending. It was jointly published by the following agencies:

- The Office of the Comptroller of the Currency (OCC)
- The Board of Governors of the Federal Reserve System (Board)
- The Federal Deposit Insurance Corporation (FDIC)
- The Office of Thrift Supervision (OTS)
- The National Credit Union Administration (NCUA)

The final version of this statement reflects the comments and input from financial institutions, trade associations, consumer and community organizations, state and financial regulatory organizations, and other members of the public.

The purpose of this interagency statement was to promote consumer protection standards that lenders should follow to ensure that borrowers only obtain loans that they can afford to repay. The Statement on Subprime Mortgage Lending defines predatory lending as a loan involving at least one of the following elements:

- Making loans based predominantly on the foreclosure or liquidation value of a borrower's collateral rather than on the borrower's ability to repay the mortgage according to its terms
- Inducing a borrower to repeatedly refinance a loan in order to charge high points and fees each time the loan is refinanced (known as "loan flipping" or "equity skimming")

- Engaging in fraud or deception to conceal the true nature of the mortgage loan obligation, or ancillary products, from an unsuspecting or unsophisticated borrower

Note that legitimate subprime lenders offer loans to low-income and risky borrowers, and must charge higher interest rates to accommodate the risk. The higher-than-typical closing and processing fees allow them to take on that risk. While many instances of predatory lending involve subprime loans, it's certainly not reasonable to say that all subprime lenders are predatory lenders.

The Statement includes guidelines for defining predatory lending, underwriting standards, establishing control systems, and consumer protection. In particular, the standards are concerned with certain adjustable rate mortgage (ARM) products, typically offered to subprime borrowers that have one or more of the following characteristics:

- Low initial payments based on a fixed introductory rate that expires after a short period and then adjusts to a variable index rate plus a margin for the remaining term of the loan

- Very high or no limits on how much the payment amount or the interest rate may increase ("payment or rate caps") on reset date

- Limited or no documentation of borrowers' income

- Product features likely to result in frequent refinancing to maintain an affordable monthly payment

- Substantial prepayment penalties and/or prepayment penalties that extend beyond the initial fixed interest rate period

Consumer Cautions

The Statement urges lenders to give consumers the facts necessary to understand material terms, costs, and risks of loan products while the consumer is selecting a loan product and before a loan is closed. According to the Statement, consumers should be informed of:

- **Payment Shock.** Potential payment increases, including how the new payment will be calculated when the introductory fixed rate expires.

- **Prepayment Penalties.** The existence of any prepayment penalty, how it will be calculated, and when it may be imposed.

- **Balloon Payments.** The existence of any balloon payment.

- **Cost of Reduced Documentation Loans.** Whether there is a pricing premium attached to a reduced documentation or stated income loan program.

- **Responsibility for Taxes and Insurance.** The requirement to make payments for real estate taxes and insurance in addition to their loan payments, if not escrowed, and the fact that taxes and insurance costs can be substantial.

Typical Predatory Lending Practices

- **Excessive Fees.** There may be a dozen or more such fees, under a variety of names, alleging services that were done on the borrower's behalf. These are often referred to as **junk fees**. Total fees greater than 4–5% of the loan amount are usually too much. Some scams have involved fees of 10–20% or more of the loan amount.

- **Excessive Prepayment Penalties.** These may lock borrowers into abusive loans that cannot be easily refinanced when credit scores improve. They discourage payoff of the highly profitable loan.

- **Extreme Lending.** Targeting borrowers with extremely high debt in relationship to income, which puts them at great risk.

- **Equity Skimming.** The most common practice is offering to assist homeowners facing foreclosure through buying their home and then selling it back to them, usually at rates and on terms guaranteed to result in default and loss of all equity. Another scheme is where the buyer refinances the home after the sale, taking out all of the equity. Yet another type of equity skimming is when the "rescuing" buyer takes out the new mortgage for the homeowner, who promises to pay; once the homeowner fails to make a payment, the buyer evicts.

- **Loan Flipping.** Refinancing the lender's own high-cost loan with another fee-rich loan (unless a lender can show that the new loan benefits the borrower).

Indicators of Predatory Lending

According to the Mortgage Bankers Association, the following are the 12 indicators of predatory lending:

1. Steering borrowers to high-rate programs
2. Falsely identifying loans as lines of credit or open mortgages
3. Structuring high-cost loans with unaffordable payments
4. Falsifying loan documents
5. Making loans to mentally incapacitated homeowners
6. Forging signatures on loan documents
7. Changing loan terms at closing
8. Requiring credit insurance
9. Increasing interest rates for late payments
10. Charging excessive prepayment penalties
11. Failing to report good payment history on a borrower's credit report
12. Failing to provide the accurate loan balance and payoff information

Predatory Lending Scenarios

Read through the following scenarios and decide if they are examples of predatory lending. Discuss the rationale for your conclusions with your class.

Scenario 1: Allen faces possible foreclosure, and contacts a mortgage lender whose ad promises to save his home. At closing, Allen sees that the lender changed the terms of the loan that they had agreed to, but he felt he had no choice but to go ahead with the loan or lose the house.

_____

_____

_____

_____

_____

_____

_____

_____

Scenario 2: Bill takes an application for a cash-out loan from a woman on a fixed income so that she can pay her past-due real estate taxes. Bill does not tell her that she can make sure the new loan collects for real estate taxes, hoping in a few years she will need to get a new loan for the same reason.

_____

_____

_____

_____

_____

_____

_____

Scenario 3: Kara has some credit issues, trying to bounce back from a recent bankruptcy. Still, she is interested in buying a home. She finds a mortgage broker who can secure a loan for her, but only if she will pay 20% down and consent to an interest rate that is higher than that offered to consumers with perfect credit.

_____

_____

_____

_____

_____

_____

_____

_____

Anti-Predatory Lending Laws

To review, the **Home Ownership and Equity Protection Act (HOEPA)** amended the Truth in Lending Act in 1994 (12 C.F.R. § 1026.32) and prohibits equity stripping due to excessive fees and other abusive lending practices related to a "high-cost" loan—also known as a Section 32 loan—which is one that meets one of these triggers:

- For a first mortgage, the annual percentage rate (APR) exceeds the rates in Treasury securities of comparable maturity by **more than eight (8) percentage points**.
- For a second mortgage, the APR exceeds the rates in Treasury securities of comparable maturity by **more than ten (10) percentage points**.
- The total points and fees paid by the consumer exceed **eight (8) percent of the loan amount.**
- The total dollar amount of the finance charge exceeds a specified trigger as adjusted annually by the Federal Reserve Board. The total dollar fee trigger for 2011, based on the annual percentage change reflected in the Consumer Price Index, is **$592, ($611 for 2012)**.

Recall that triggers for HOEPA loans will be lower when relevant provisions of the Dodd-Frank Wall Street Reform and Consumer Protection Act are implemented.

HOEPA provides the following consumer protections for loans identified as "high cost" loans by prohibiting these loan terms:

- **Balloon Payments.** Prohibited on HOEPA loans with terms of less than five years.
- **Negative Amortization.** Prohibits loans having any kind of interest or payment adjustment that could result in negative amortization. Payments must, at a minimum, pay off interest and should also reduce principal.
- **Pressure Tactics.** Requires lenders to include text in the disclosure stating the consumer is not required to complete the credit transaction.
- **Loan Pricing.** Cannot include more than two advance payments from the loan proceeds.
- **Acceleration Clauses.** Prohibits increasing interest rates if the customer is in default.
- **Prepayment Penalties.** Places limitations on prepayment penalties so consumers are not locked into loans that may not be, or are no longer, in their best interest.
- **Loan Flipping.** Prohibits refinancing a HOEPA loan within a one-year period unless it is clearly in the borrower's best interest.
- **Demand Clauses.** Prohibits any provision that would enable the creditor to call the loan before maturity (except in instances of fraud, material misrepresentation, default, or damage to the property).

HOEPA also imposes **income verification** provisions that require lenders to compile written income verification and create a written record of ratios, such as debt to income or cash flow analysis.

Mortgage Assistance Relief Services (MARS) Rule

In October of 2010, the Federal Trade Commission issued a final rule that, according to the FTC, addresses many mortgage relief scams that have sprung up recently that take advantages of distressed homeowners. The following are among the provisions of the final rule (16 C.F.R. Part 322):

- A ban on those who provide mortgage foreclosure rescue and loan modification services from collecting fees until homeowners have a written offer from their lender or servicer that they decide is acceptable.
- A requirement that mortgage relief companies disclose key information to consumers to protect them from being misled and to help them make better informed purchasing decisions, for example, the company's fee, the fact that the company is not associated with the government, and that the consumer has the right to discontinue doing business with the company at any time.
- A prohibition against making any false or misleading claims about their services, for example, any guarantees or the amount of money the consumer will save.
- A prohibition barring mortgage relief companies from advising consumers to discontinue communication with their lenders.

See: http://www.ftc.gov/opa/2010/11/mars.shtm

Case Study and Discussion

To conclude this chapter, read the following consumer complaint letter, review the mortgage loan oiriginator's notes, and then discuss the ethical considerations of this scenario with your class.

January 18, 2011

State Commissioner, Division of Banks

Anytown, USA 10001

Dear Commissioner,

On December 1, 2010 I telephoned the ABCDFG Mortgage Company of Anytown, USA. I spoke to John Doe. On that day, Mr. Doe advised me that his company was one of the most competitive and respected in the state. He informed me that he could refinance my present mortgage for 15 years at 6.625% with 0 points. He also told me that based upon the information I had given him and my credit report, this would be an easy loan and I would have no problem at all.

A sudden death in my family made it impossible for me to meet with Mr. Doe until December 14. On that morning, I called Mr. Doe to confirm our appointment for later in the day and also to confirm that the rate of 6.625% with no points was still in place. He confirmed this. That evening when Mr. Doe arrived at my home, he informed me that the market changed and the rate would now be 6.75%. We proceeded to complete the application at the 6.75% rate.

Mr. Doe completed the mortgage application, had me sign some documents and disclosures, and assured me that copies would be made for my records of the signed disclosures. He also told me that his processor would mail back my original documents along with some other mortgage papers I would need to sign.

On December 28, I called and emailed John Doe for a status of my mortgage application. He returned my call and said everything was "fine." I had read that interest rates had increased but did not worry because my rate had been locked in for 30 days. I asked Mr. Doe when I would be hearing from the appraiser, and he told me that the appraisal had been ordered but the appraisers were busy. He told me not to worry; he would take care of everything.

On January 15, John Doe called me to let me know my interest rate would be 7.375%. I told him that this was not the rate we had agreed to and wanted my money back. He said that my application fee was already "spent," my interest rate was "floating," and he would forward me a copy of my appraisal. He told me I was not entitled to any refund.

I am enclosing copies of the papers given to me at application. I am disappointed over how my mortgage application was handled—the increase in the interest rate and the loss of my application fee. Because of current interest rates, I have lost the ability to refinance and lower my current interest rate. Is there anything you can do to assist me?

Sincerely,

Jane Consumer

Loan Application Log

ABCDFG Mortgage Company of Anytown

Borrower:	Jane Consumer	Loan #:	123456-78
Address:	123 Elm St.	LO/Proc.:	John Doe / Sue Smith
	Anytown, USA 10001		

12-14-10	Notes to Processor:
	Copy attached original documents and return to borrower. Open file and send GFE, TIL and mortgage disclosures. Lock loan at Investor A at 6.625% with 0 points. (JD)
12-15-10	Opened file, ordered appraisal, sent originals back to borrower. (SS)
12-18-10	Sue – lock in fax confirmation to Investor A shows busy, called Stan in secondary marketing dept., he shows NO LOCK!!!! Rates have moved... will have to float. Notice we didn't send the GFE/TIL/disclosures ... backdate disclosures but do not send lock conf. (JD)
12-28-10	Sue – borrower called on appraisal. What is the status? (JD)
12-28-10	John – called appraiser. They let their clerical person go because of mistakes, couldn't find order. Will send out appraiser ASAP and will RUSH. Rates are rising and loan is still not locked. (SS)
1-5-11	Loan submitted to investor. (SS)
1-7-11	Loan approved by investor – rate is floating, need to send commitment letter. (SS)
1-7-11	Send approval out dated January 8 at original rate with 0 points. Will advise borrower that we are unable to close... don't see rate lock in file. (JD)
1-12-11	Advised borrower that investor needed 48 hours notice to close, also that loan had to fund within three-day rescission period. Told the borrower the only option is to wait until original "lock" expires, then get best market price. Will call borrower on 1-15-11. (JD)

1. *If you were the Commissioner of Banks who received that letter from Jane Consumer, what would be your impression of the ABCDFG Mortgage Company?*

_____

_____

_____

_____

2. *Were the mortgage loan originator's actions:*

        ETHICAL   UNETHICAL   DEBATABLE

3. *Discuss what bothers you about the actions taken by the MLO.*

_____

_____

_____

_____

KEY TERM REVIEW

Blockbusting The illegal practice of inducing owners to sell their homes (often at a deflated price) by suggesting that the ethnic or racial composition of the neighborhood is changing, with implication that property values will decline as a result. Also called **panic selling.**

Ethics The study of standards of conduct and moral judgment; the system of morals of a particular person or group.

Flipping Defined by Fannie Mae as the process of purchasing existing properties with the intention of immediately reselling them for a profit.

Flipping, Illegal Property purchased at a low price, appraised at a high value without valid reason, and resold at the higher price.

Fraud An intentional or negligent misrepresentation or concealment of a material fact; making statements that a person knows, or should realize, are false or misleading.

Fraud, Actual Intentional misrepresentation or concealment of a material fact; when a person actively conceals material information or makes statements known to be false or misleading. Also called **Deceit.**

Fraud, Constructive A negligent misrepresentation or concealment of a material fact; when a person carelessly fails to disclose material information, or makes false or misleading statements. Also called **Negligent Misrepresentation.**

HOEPA Loan A loan that is defined by the Home Ownership and Equity Protection Act (HOEPA) as a "high cost" loan by meeting certain triggers related to APR and total finance charges. A HOEPA loan requires additional disclosure and regulations as a means of eliminating equity stripping and other abusive practices. Also called a **Section 32 loan.**

Junk Fees Charges assessed to a borrower by a loan originator that serve little, if any, function and are often hidden in mortgage documents.

Kickbacks Fees or other compensation given for services not performed, but as a means of undisclosed commission for business referrals. Kickbacks are prohibited by RESPA.

Negligence Unintentional breach of a legal duty. It's a tort if it causes harm.

Predatory Lending Loans that take advantage of ill-informed consumers through excessively high fees, misrepresented loan terms, frequent refinancing that does not benefit the borrower, and other prohibited acts.

Redlining When a lender refuses to make loans secured by property in a certain neighborhood because of the racial or ethnic composition of the neighborhood.

Steering Illegal activity of channeling prospective buyers or tenants to particular neighborhoods based on their race, religion, national origin, or ancestry.

Straw Buyer A person who receives payment from the use of that person's name and credit history to apply for a loan—or is unaware that their information is used—generally as part of a mortgage fraud scheme.

Suspicious Activity Reports (SARs) Reports of mortgage fraud activity that are filed with the Federal Bureau of Investigation (FBI) from data filed by financial institutions and from the Department of Housing and Urban Development's Office of the Inspector General.

CHAPTER 3 QUIZ

1. *A lender who refuses to make loans on property in certain neighborhoods is demonstrating the discriminatory practice of*

   A. blockbusting.
   B. redlining.
   C. servicing.
   D. steering.

2. *At closing, the buyer realizes that the terms of the loan were different from those he agreed to. Since his furniture was already on the moving truck, the buyer felt he had to go through with the loan. This could be an example of*

   A. affinity marketing.
   B. loan flipping.
   C. negative amortization.
   D. predatory lending.

3. *Under RESPA, who would be subject to fines and penalties if a kickback is paid?*

   A. all parties paying or receiving a kickback
   B. the person who initiated the kickback arrangement
   C. the person who received the kickback
   D. no one, assuming that it was paid for services actually rendered

4. *Which will trigger the required disclosures of the Truth in Lending Act if included in an advertisement for credit?*

   A. "Affordable financing"
   B. "Easy monthly payments"
   C. "FHA financing available"
   D. "Only 10% down"

5. *If any triggering terms are used in an ad, which fact is EXEMPT from the disclosure requirement?*

   A. amount or percentage of down payment
   B. APR
   C. terms of repayment
   D. total closing costs

6. *What law is violated if a mortgage loan originator discourages a minority from applying for a mortgage?*

   A. CRA
   B. ECOA
   C. HMDA
   D. This would not be a violation of any law.

7. *Which of these is NOT included as a protected class by the federal Fair Housing Act?*

   A. national origin
   B. race
   C. religion
   D. sexual orientation

8. *In order to ensure a loan closes, a mortgage loan originator conceals the fact that the down payment is made with borrowed funds. This could be considered*

   A. actual fraud.
   B. constructive fraud.
   C. good business.
   D. negligent misrepresentation.

9. *Which is an example of steering?*

   A. A real estate agent tells homeowners that their property values will drop when an Asian family moves in.
   B. A mortgage banker refuses to make loans for a particular inner city neighborhood.
   C. A property manager suggests that an applicant would be happier in a more diverse building.
   D. A seller tells his listing agent to find only Muslim buyer prospects.

10. *Which is LEAST LIKELY to be an indicator of predatory lending?*

    A. changing loan terms at the closing
    B. charging excessive prepayment penalties
    C. increasing interest charges on late loan payments
    D. requiring mortgage insurance

11. *A for-profit MLO who claims to be a "counselor" in an ad about loan modification would be in violation of what law?*

    A. Fair and Accurate Credit Transaction Act
    B. Fair Lending Act
    C. Home Ownership and Equity Protection Act
    D. Truth in Lending Act

12. *Which regulation ensures that some borrowers have the right of rescission for three business days after a loan contract is signed?*

    A. Regulation B
    B. Regulation X
    C. Regulation Z
    D. Title VIII

13. *To address the problem of property flipping, appraisers must analyze the transfer history of a property for the previous*

   A. three months.
   B. one year.
   C. eighteen months.
   D. three years.

14. *The Civil Rights Act of 1866 prohibits discrimination based on*

   A. age.
   B. race.
   C. religion.
   D. sex.

15. *What type of scam entails homeowners who are encouraged to refinance their property over and over until little or no equity remains?*

   A. double sold loan
   B. loan flipping
   C. property skimming
   D. reverse equity

16. *What federal legislation requires the term "equal housing lender" to be used in any advertisement that is broadcast over the airwaves?*

   A. Equal Credit Opportunity Act
   B. Fair Credit Reporting Act
   C. Fair Housing Act
   D. Truth in Lending Act

17. *Which class IS specifically protected by the Fair Housing Act but IS NOT protected by the Equal Credit Opportunity Act?*

   A. disability
   B. marital status
   C. religion
   D. sex

18. *A mortgage loan originator realizes that his customer will not qualify for the loan, so he convinces her to apply using her mother's identity and financial data. Even though the mother does not know that her information was used, she could be considered a*

   A. co-mortgagor.
   B. mock purchaser.
   C. secret signer.
   D. straw buyer.

19. *Which federal law was intended to provide some remedy for the illegal practice of redlining?*

   A. Community Reinvestment Act
   B. Fair and Accurate Credit Transaction Act
   C. Financial Services Modernization Act
   D. Homeowners Protection Act

20. *If you tell your mortgage loan applicant that his monthly check from public assistance is not an acceptable source of income, you will be in violation of*

   A. the Civil Rights Act of 1866.
   B. the ECOA.
   C. the Fair Housing Act.
   D. no federal law.

Chapter 4

Mortgage Loan Origination Activities Review

Module Introduction

Origination is the process of making or initiating a new loan. It may involve tasks such as being the initial contact to a consumer and taking a loan application to ordering a credit report and assembling all of the other forms and documents required by the person or company who is underwriting the loan. Next, a **loan processor** is typically responsible for verifying the information contained in the file assembled by the originator, such as sending out employment verification forms, and coordinating the various aspects of the loan (such as working with the title company). **Underwriting** is *the process of evaluating and deciding whether to make a new loan*. This is done by the funding source (lender), never by a mortgage broker. Underwriting involves evaluating all of the information in the file, including income, credit scores, credit history, appraisals, job history, and other measures of strength or weakness in the borrower and the collateral. **Servicing** is the continued maintenance of a loan after the loan has closed.

This chapter provides a quick review of loan origination activities and some related terminology.

Key Terms

Assumption
Automated Underwriting
Closing
Co-Mortgagor
Credit History
Loan-to-Value Ratio (LTV)
Mortgage Insurance Premium (MIP)
Origination
Origination Fee
PITI
Points
Pre-Approval
Pre-Qualification
Principal
Private Mortgage Insurance (PMI)
Processing
Rate Protection
Reserves
Seller-Paid Items
Servicing
Underwriter

Application Information and Requirements

The uniform **loan application** (Fannie Mae **Form 1003** or Freddie Mac **Form 65**) is a form lenders require potential borrowers to complete, which allows them to collect pertinent information about the borrower and the property. Information required to complete the application includes:

- Type of mortgage and terms of the loan

- Property information and purpose of the loan, including property address, whether the loan is for purchase or refinance, source of down payment, etc.

- Borrower information, such as name, address, Social Security number, age, schooling, marital status, dependents, etc.

- Employment information for the past two years, including position, years on the job, self-employment information, etc.

- Monthly income from primary employment and other sources

- Assets and liabilities

- Details of the transaction, including purchase price, prepaid items, estimated closing costs, mortgage insurance, secondary financing, etc.

- Information for government monitoring purposes to show compliance with the Equal Credit Opportunity Act and for HDMA reporting

Application is defined by RESPA (Sec. 3500.2) as *the submission of a borrower's financial information in anticipation of a credit decision which includes the borrower's name, monthly income, and Social Security number to obtain a credit report; the property address and estimate of value; and the loan amount.* The receipt of all of that information constitutes a completed application and triggers mandated disclosures.

If the loan has a balloon payment, the lender must insert a special notice about the features of the balloon payment on Form 1003 or in a separate attachment.

Application Accuracy and Truthfulness

Each borrower must declare that the information in the application is truthful and whether the borrower:

- Is obligated to pay alimony or child support,

- Has any outstanding judgments, bankruptcies, foreclosures, etc.,

- Has borrowed any part of the down payment,

- Is a co-signer on any other debt,

- Is a U.S. citizen or permanent resident, and

- Intends to occupy the property as a primary residence.

The borrower and co-borrower must date and sign the application to acknowledge that they have answered everything truthfully and that they understand and agree to be bound by the terms of the loan, if granted. Additionally, borrowers are obligated to update any material changes to income or assets after signing the initial application and prior to closing.

Mortgage loan originators also have an obligation for accuracy and truthfulness because they are required to assist borrowers with completion of the application.

Verification and Documentation

A borrower's **net worth** is determined by subtracting liabilities from total assets. In other words, it's the value of all property (real and personal) a person has accumulated after subtracting all debts or obligations owed. Underwriters want to confirm the borrower has:

- Sufficient assets and personal money to make the **down payment** on the property and to pay closing costs, without having to borrow them.

- Adequate **reserves** to cover two months of PITI mortgage payments after making a down payment and paying closing costs.

- Other **assets**, showing an ability to manage money and a resource, if needed, to handle emergencies and make mortgage payments.

For the down payment, lenders:

- Will want to know the **source** of the buyer's down payment (which usually cannot be borrowed funds or gifts) for the first 5% for conventional loans.

- May require **two months** of bank statements and/or a **Verification of Deposit** (VOD) form.

- **Gift letter** signed by the donor to confirm the money does not need to be repaid and donor bank statement showing that the gift funds are available.

Employment Documentation

- Self-employed borrowers will need to provide personal and corporate tax returns (all schedules) for a **minimum of two years** to verify this income.

- As a general rule, a borrower should have continuous employment for at least **two years** in the same field, demonstrated by:

  - Appropriate W-2 forms.

  - Original pay stub for the previous 30-day period.

  - May require **Verification of Employment** (VOE) forms.

- Employment changes for advancement or special education and training can mitigate the two-year requirement.

Qualification: Processing and Underwriting

Once an application has been properly completed, the lender can begin gathering other pertinent information, which includes:

- Borrower analysis, including income and credit

- Property analysis, including appraisals and title reports

- Required insurances

Loan Processing

Processing the loan application involves:

1. Reviewing the information it contains and verifying items as necessary.

2. Assembling a **loan package** that includes the credit report, income and asset documentation, verification forms, preliminary title report, appraisal, and loan disclosures.

3. Giving the package to an **underwriter**, who evaluates a loan application to determine its risk level for the lender. The underwriter is usually the final decision maker on a borrower's loan application. The underwriting process can be automated, where all information is fed into a computer, or done by an individual who works for the lender. **Automated underwriting** is popular with many lenders because it can reduce the time and costs necessary to close a loan.

   - Fannie Mae's automated underwriting system is **Desktop Underwriter®** (DU®).

   - Freddie Mac's direct electronic underwriting system is called **Loan Prospector®** (LP®).

Borrower Analysis

Qualifying a buyer simply means evaluating a borrower's creditworthiness. In reviewing the borrower's loan application to determine whether to make the loan, the lender considers the applicant's credit, capacity, collateral, and cash by looking specifically at the following:

- Assets
- Liabilities
- Income
- Credit report
- Qualifying ratios

The primary concern throughout the loan underwriting process is determining the degree of **risk** a loan represents. The underwriter attempts to answer two fundamental questions:

1. Is there sufficient value in the property pledged as **collateral** to assure recovery of the loan amount in the event of default?

2. Does the borrower's overall financial situation—which is comprised of income, credit history, and net worth—indicate he can reasonably be expected to make the proposed monthly loan payments in a timely manner?

Assets and Liabilities

Loan applicants must provide a list of assets and all liabilities:

- **Assets** are *items of value owned by the borrower*, such as cash on hand, checking or savings accounts, stocks, bonds, insurance policies, real estate, retirement funds, automobiles, and personal property.

- **Liabilities** are *financial obligations or debts owed by a borrower*. **Debts** are *any recurring monetary obligation that cannot be cancelled.* The distinction is that liabilities are any amount of money owed; debts specifically refer to recurring obligations (e.g., monthly bills). Generally, the lender will not consider installment loan debt with **less than ten payments** remaining.

Income

Stable monthly income, the monthly income that can reasonably be expected to continue in the future, is generally meant to include the gross base income of the borrower(s) from primary jobs, plus earnings from acceptable secondary sources that's considered reliable and likely to endure.

Secondary sources of income include, but are not limited to the following:

- Bonuses (if consistent and verifiable)
- Commissions above base salary
- Part-time earnings
- Overtime (if consistent)
- Disability payments (if permanent)
- Social Security (if permanent)
- Pensions
- Retirement payments
- Rental income (if stable)
- Interest-yielding investments (if sound and consistent)
- Alimony
- Child support (if verifiable and will continue for a minimum of 3 years)
- Maintenance
- Unemployment/Welfare (if extended pattern received during certain times, such as seasonal work)

Other Income Considerations

- Bonuses and commissions, if consistent and verifiable, may be considered durable income but should be averaged.

- Alimony, child support, and/or maintenance do *not* need to be listed as sources of income if a borrower does not want them considered as income for the loan.

z 125%!

- Income that is tax free may be "grossed up" by 1.25%.

- Lenders cannot discriminate because of the source of stable monthly income, according to the Equal Credit Opportunity Act (15 U.S.C. § 1691).

- Generally, only the earnings of the head(s) of household are considered when calculating a borrower's stable monthly income unless there is a co-mortgagor. Support income from other family members may *not* be considered, although income from a non-occupying co-mortgagor is acceptable when considering debt ratio.

- Income from rental properties should be counted only at 75%; this allows for vacancy losses.

- To convert a person's hourly wages to monthly earnings:

  1. Multiply the hourly wage by 40 (hours in a work week).

  2. Multiply by 52 (weeks in a year).

  3. Divide by 12 (months in a year).

IRS Form 4506-T

Underwriters require the lender to obtain a completed and signed **Form 4506-T** from all borrowers at both application and closing. This form gives the lender permission to request electronic transcripts of federal tax returns from the IRS when documenting the borrower's income. Under current requirements, the lender determines if and when to submit the form to the IRS (or designee) to obtain the tax information. These transcripts are used to verify the borrower's income with the intention of helping to reduce instances of mortgage fraud.

Credit Report

The loan originator will order a **credit report** from one or all of the credit bureaus in order to review the applicant's credit history. This is a record of debt repayment, detailing how a person paid credit accounts in the past as a guide to whether he is likely to pay accounts on time and as agreed in the future. The **Fair Credit Reporting Act** (§ 605) indicates that consumer reporting agencies may maintain bankruptcy information on a consumer's credit report for no more than 10 years from the date of entry of the order for relief or the date of adjudication, whichever the case may be. Generally speaking, however:

- Chapter 7 bankruptcy (liquidation) remains on a credit report for **ten (10) years.**

- Chapter 13 bankruptcy (wage earner plan) remains on a credit report for **seven (7) years.**

Credit scoring is:

- An objective means of determining creditworthiness of potential borrowers based on a number system.

- A numeric representation of the borrower's credit profile compiled by assigning specified numerical values to different aspects of the borrower. These numbers are adjusted up and down based on the strengths and weaknesses of particular qualifications.

- Calculated differently by all credit bureaus, although credit scores range from about **300 to 850.** The three most familiar credit bureaus are:

  - Experian.

  - Equifax.

  - TransUnion.

Qualifying Ratios

Lenders look at a number of ratios to evaluate the borrower and the property. The key ones follow:

Loan-to-Value Ratio (LTV)

The amount of money borrowed (the loan amount of a first mortgage) compared to the value of the property. Lenders use LTV to determine how much they are willing to loan on a given property based on its value. The lender will always use **the lower of the appraised value or the sale price** in order to protect its interest. The lower the LTV, the higher the borrower's down payment, which means the loan is more secure.

Loan Amount ÷ Lesser of Sale Price or Appraised Value = LTV

Conventional loan programs can be classified by the LTV. The lower the LTV, the higher the borrower's down payment, which means the loan is more secure. An **80% conventional loan** does *not* need private mortgage insurance (PMI).

Qualifying standards for LTVs above 80% may be more stringent, and lenders adhere to those standards more strictly even if the loan is insured through private mortgage insurance (PMI). These loans may also have a higher interest rate, call for higher loan origination fees, or impose additional conditions and standards.

Housing Expense Ratio

Also known as the front end ratio, this indicates the relationship of the borrower's total monthly housing expense (**PITI**=principal, interest, taxes, and insurances) to income, expressed as a percentage:

Total Housing Expense (PITI) ÷ Gross Monthly Income = Housing Expense Ratio %

Total Debt to Income Ratio

Also known as the back end ratio, this indicates the relationship of the borrower's total monthly debt obligations (including PITI housing and long-term debts with more than ten payments left) to income, expressed as a percentage:

Total Debt ÷ Gross Monthly Income = Total Debt to Income Ratio %

The borrower must qualify under **both** the housing expense ratio and the total debt to income ratio. The total debt to income ratio is a more realistic measure of the borrower's ability to support the loan payments because it considers all of the borrower's recurring financial obligations.

	Housing Expense Ratio	Total Debt to Income Ratio
Conventional Loans	28%	36%
FHA Loans	31%	43%
VA Loans	Not used	41%

Note that Fannie Mae focuses on the back end ratio, where their benchmark is 36%.

Appraisals

An **appraisal** is:

- An opinion of market value (most probably selling price) as of a certain date that is supported by objective data.

- Only an estimate or opinion; it is not a guarantee of value.

- Only valid as of its effective date, which establishes terms, conditions, and economic circumstances upon which the value is estimated.

Appraisers value properties using three different approaches. Each approach is independent of the others and is performed separately to arrive at an opinion of value.

Sales Comparison Approach

- Compares the property being appraised, the **subject property**, with other similar properties, called **comparables** or comps, which have sold recently in the same market area as the subject property (usually within six months).

- Comps that are missing or have additional significant features are adjusted in relation to the subject property. The subject property is never adjusted.

- Considered the most useful and accurate of the three appraisal methods because it's rooted in actual market activity.

- Typically uses three to five comparables, but a **minimum of three** is required by most secondary market lenders to ensure an accurate appraisal from sufficient data.

- Appraiser reconciles the values of the comparables to reflect an opinion of value for the subject, considering each comp and giving the most weight to the one that is most similar to the subject property as indicated by the fewest adjustments. The final values are never averaged.

- Most useful for residential property.

Cost Approach

- Calculates the cost of the land, site improvements, and the cost to build the structure on the land.

- Most useful for unusual properties, special purpose, or non-income producing commercial property such as churches, schools, etc.

Income Approach

- Analyzes the revenue, or income, the property currently generates or could generate.

- Sometimes called the capitalization approach.

- Most useful for income-producing commercial/investment property.

Insurance

An **insurance policy** is *a contract in which one party agrees to compensate another party for a loss that occurs as a result of a designated hazard.* Providing funds to a borrower to purchase a home carries with it a great deal of financial risk for the lender, who is said to have an **insurable interest** in the property. Lenders, therefore, normally require different types of insurance:

- Homeowner's hazard insurance.
- Flood insurance (if applicable).
- Mortgage insurance (if the LTV is greater than 80%).

Homeowner's Hazard Insurance

Insurance that covers loss or damage to the home or property in the event of fire or other disaster such as tornado, snow, and hail damage. Lenders generally:

- Require the policy to be sufficient to replace the home or reimburse the mortgage amount with the lender being named on the actual policy.

- Have the right to place insurance on the property to cover its interest (the loan value) in the event of a loss if the customer does not comply with the lender's insurance requirements.

- Require buyers to pay the first year's insurance premium in full *prior* to closing.

- Incorporate the annual insurance cost (along with current property taxes) into an **escrow account,** which is prorated over the next 12 months to determine a monthly insurance and property tax payment amount. This is added to the monthly principal and interest due for loan repayment. Upon payment each month, the insurance and taxes are deposited into the client's escrow account. When property taxes and insurance become due, the lender forwards the payment to the respective recipients on behalf of the property owner.

Flood Insurance

Homeowner's hazard insurance does *not* cover damage caused by the peril of flood. When a property is located in a designated flood zone, the lender will likely require a flood insurance policy in addition to homeowner's hazard insurance. Flood insurance must be purchased from the **National Flood Insurance Program (NFIP)** or from an insurer participating in the Write Your Own program. In order to buy flood insurance, the property must be in a community that participates in the NFIP.

Private Mortgage Insurance (PMI)

Private mortgage insurance (PMI) is offered by private insurance companies to insure a lender against default on a loan by a borrower. In the event of default and foreclosure, lenders can make a claim for reimbursement of actual losses (if any) up to the face amount of the policy after foreclosing and selling the property.

- Conforming loans require third-party mortgage insurance on home loans with less than 20% down on a first mortgage. The mortgage insurance company insures only the upper portion of the loan that exceeds the standard 80% LTV.

- Many private mortgage companies have guidelines related to underwriting mortgage insurance in so-called declining markets.

- Premiums may be paid a number of ways:
  - Fee at closing and a renewal premium.
  - One-time mortgage insurance premium.
  - Lender Paid Mortgage Insurance, which is an interest rate adjustment made at closing in exchange for the lender "insuring" the loan themselves and is not cancelable at any LTV; even if the lender cancels it, the borrower will not receive a reduction in the monthly payment.

- The **Homeowners Protection Act of 1998 (HPA)** requires lenders to cancel mortgage insurance:
  - Automatically, when a home has been paid down to **78%** of its original value.
  - At the buyer's request and with mortgage/deed holder's permission, when LTV reaches **80%** according to a new appraisal, and the mortgage payments are current.

◇ **Note:** See the new FHA rules related to cancellation eligibility in the New FHA Rules section.

New FHA Rules

As of April 1, 2013, the FHA increased mortgage insurance fees and the length of time a borrower must pay them.

Prior to April 2013, FHA had two tiers of MI:

(1) Upfront MI was 1% of loan amount. It can be added to closing costs, or you can finance it by adding it to the loan amount.

(2) Annual MI was 1.1% of loan amount if your down payment is 5% or more, or 1.15% of loan amount if your down payment is less than 5% (you can go as low as 3.5% down with FHA). These annual fees are paid monthly. The calculation is loan amount x MI rate / 12mo = monthly MI payment.

Effective April 1, 2013, the two tiers of FHA MI changed as follows:

(1) Upfront MI for loans up $729,750: Will be 1.75% of loan amount

(2a) Annual MI for loans up to $729,750: Will be 1.2% of loan amount if your down payment is 5% or more, or 1.25% of loan amount if your down payment is less than 5%.

(2b) Annual MI for loans $625,501 to 729,750: Will be 1.45% of loan amount if your down payment is 5% or more, or 1.5% of loan amount if your down payment is less than 5%.

Note that FHA loans go up to $729,750 and the Fannie/Freddie (non-FHA) limits are only $625,500.

This is why FHA is implementing higher annual MI fees for those higher tier loans as of June 1. FHA mortgage insurance for loans to $625,500 will remain at the level discussed in 2a after June 1.

Increases to FHA MI Premiums (Effective April 1, 2013)

The following chart shows increases to FHA MI premiums under the new FHA rules:

Loan Terms > 15 Years					
Base Loan	LTV	Effective	Previous MIP	New MIP	Up Front Premium
≤ $625,500	>95%	4/1/2013	1.25	**1.35**	1.75 (Stays the same)
≤ $625,500	≤95%	4/1/2013	1.20	**1.30**	
> $625,500	>95%	4/1/2013	1.50	**1.55**	
> $625,500	≤95%	4/1/2013	1.45	**1.50**	
Loan Terms ≤ 15 Years					
≤ $625,500	78 - 90%	4/1/2013	.35	**.45**	1.75 (Stays the same)
≤ $625,500	>90%	4/1/2013	.60	**.70**	
> $625,500	78 - 90%	4/1/2013	.60	**.70**	
> $625,500	>90%	4/1/2013	.85	**.95**	
All Loan Amounts	≤78%	6/3/2013	0	**.45**	

Streamline Refinances (Stays the same)			
Base Loan	Endorsed By[1]	Annual MIP (Monthly)	Up Front Premium
All Loan Amounts	On or Before May 31, 2009[2]	.55	.01

[1]The endorsement date can be found on the Case Query screen in FHA Connection. Request to restore the case number to see the endorsement dat.

[2]Loans endorsed after May 31, 2009 will follow the premium charts for the loan term stated above and must meet the 5% Net Tangible Benefit.

Changes to FHA MI Cancellation Eligibility (Effective June 3, 2013)

The following chart shows changes to FHA MI cancellation eligibility under the new FHA rules:

Term	LTV(%)	Previous	New
≤ 15 Years	≤ 78	No Annual MIP	**11 Years**
≤ 15 Years	> 78 - 90	Cancelled at 78% LTV	**11 Years**
≤ 15 Years	> 90	Cancelled at 78% LTV	**Loan Term**
> 15 Years	≤ 78	5 Years	**11 Years**
> 15 Years	> 78 - 90	Cancelled at 78% LTV & 5 Years	**11 Years**
> 15 Years	> 90	Cancelled at 78% LTV & 5 Years	**Loan Term**

Loan Program Guidelines

In additional to conventional, conforming loans, lenders and government agencies offer multiple mortgage loan programs in order to meet the varied needs of borrowers; for example:

- **FHA Loans**. Federal Housing Administration (FHA) loans are **insured** by the federal government. Lenders approved by the FHA either submit applications from prospective borrowers to one of the regional HUD Homeownership Centers for approval or may act as **Direct Endorsers** (DEs), which are lenders authorized to underwrite their own FHA loan applications.

- **VA Loans.** VA loans are guaranteed by the federal government through the Veterans Benefits Administration, which is part of the **Department of Veterans Affairs**. The VA rarely loans money directly to borrowers, but may do so in isolated rural areas where financing isn't readily available. Lenders approved by the VA to make loans either submit applications from prospective borrowers to the VA for approval or they may act as VA **Automatic Endorsers.**

- **USDA Rural Development Loans.** U.S. Department of Agriculture (USDA) **Rural Development** administers the **Housing and Community Facilities Programs** (HCFP), which offers loan assistance in rural communities. "Rural" may include small towns up to 20,000 people. Rural Development **Section 502** loan programs for single-family homes either **guarantees** loans made by approved private lenders or **makes direct loans** if no local lender is available.

	Conforming	FHA	VA	USDA
Eligible Borrower	Any borrower who meets Fannie Mae/Freddie Mac standards so selling on secondary market	Anyone who is a U.S. citizen or lawful permanent resident; FHA loans can be made to non-permanent resident if: • Property will be borrower's principal residence move in within 60 days of close; remain for 12 months) • Borrower has a valid SSN • Borrower is eligible to work in the U.S	Veteran of the U.S. armed forces, based on a person's length of continuous active service; requires: • DD-214 (commonly called Discharge Papers or Report of Separation) issued by the Department of Defense • Certificate of Eligibility (COE) issued by the VA; required by a lender to establish the amount and status of the veteran's eligibility under the VA loan guarantee program; $104,250 max. guaranty amount	Any qualified buyer who meets certain income requirements based on area median income (AMI)
Borrower Qualifying Standards	Housing Expense Ratio 28% Total DTI Ratio 36%	Housing Expense Ratio 31% (33% for those who qualify under FHA's Energy Efficient Homes, (EEH) Total DTI Ratio 43% (Ratios exceeding these limits may be acceptable only if significant compensating factors are documented and recorded.)	Residual Income guidelines based on family size Total DTI Ratio 41%	GRH – income up to 115% AMI Direct – between 50-80% AMI
Maximum Loan (Cannot exceed appraisal)	$417,000 (higher in designated high-cost areas)	Lesser of the statutory loan limit for the area-typically a county, or metropolitan statistical area (MSA)--or applicable LTV limit, applied to the lesser of the sales price, or the appraised value	None	None
Down Payment	Traditionally, at least 5%, though 10% is more common; 2 months reserves on deposit	3.5% (FICO 580 or above) or 10% minimum (FICO 500-579)	None required if VA loan guaranty is equal to at least 25% of the loan amount	None
Fee/ Insurance	Mortgage insurance if LTV is greater than 80%	Non-refundable UFMIP: 1.75% of loan amount 30-year loans: 95% LTV or less MIP is 1.20% annually; more than 95% LTV MIP is 1.25% annually 15-year loans: 90% LTV or less MIP is 0.35 annually; more than 90% LTV, MIP is 0.60% annually	Non-refundable funding fee: 1.25% to 3.30%; no funding fee if disabled No mortgage insurance required	GRH made by approved lenders may require non-refundable upfront guarantee fee of 2% Effective October 1, 2011, there will be an annual guarantee fee of 0.03%, based on the remaining balance.

Loan Consummation

Loan consummation, also known as **closing** or **settlement**, is the process by which the terms of the loan agreement are fulfilled, the appropriate parties sign the paperwork, and funds may be disbursed. On a purchase loan, closing is also when ownership of real property transfers from seller to buyer, according to the terms and conditions in the sales contract or escrow agreement. Closing procedures may be different from state to state.

Closing Agent

A **closing agent**, sometimes called an escrow agent, is the person responsible for the mechanics of closing. This could be an attorney or someone from the lender's in-house escrow department, an independent escrow company, or a title insurance company. The closing agent:

- Simultaneously follows the instructions of both buyer and seller in a sales transaction, as per the sales contract, agreement, or a separate set of escrow instructions.

- Gathers all necessary documents (e.g., promissory note, mortgage, deed) and makes certain they're properly signed.

- Documents the various adjustments and fees charged to each party:

  - **Debits** (like debts) are sums of money owed. A debit is charged to a particular party to represent money that must be paid out.

  - **Credits** are sums of money received. A credit is given to a particular party to represent money that is paid by another party or that has already been paid. The mortgage amount shows up as a **credit** to the borrower, since it is the lender who brings that money to closing.

- Calculates the various **prorations**, which is the division of expenses between buyer and seller in proportion to the actual usage of the item represented by a particular expense as of the **day the loan is funded.**

- Completes the **HUD-1 Settlement Statement** to comply with RESPA.

- Compares the Good Faith Estimate of closing costs to the HUD Settlement Statement to verify the proper tolerance with disclosed fees.

Title and Title Insurance

- When conveying real property, the seller is generally expected to deliver a **marketable title**, a title that is free and clear from undisclosed encumbrances or other defects that would expose a purchaser to litigation or impede a purchaser's ability to enjoy the property or to later sell the property easily.

- A **title search** of the public records, also known as a title examination, is necessary to determine ownership and the quality of the title prior to conveyance. If a marketable title cannot be produced, a closing may have to be postponed.

- The **chain of title** is a clear and unbroken chronological record of the ownership of a specific piece of property. Tracing the chain of title simply means tracing the successive conveyances of title, starting with the current deed and going back a suitable number of years.

- A gap in the chain of title creates uncertainty, which is referred to as a **cloud on the title.**

- **Color of title** is the appearance of having title to personal or real property by some evidence, but in reality, there is either no title or a vital defect in the title. One might show a title document to real property, but in reality, someone may have deeded property to another person and not be the true titled owner.

- A **suit to quiet title**, also called a quiet title action, may be required to close any missing links and remove the cloud on the title. This is a lawsuit filed to determine and resolve problems of instruments conveying a particular piece of land.

- **Title insurance** protects lenders (and sometimes property owners) against loss due to disputes over ownership of a property and defects in the title not found in the search of the public record. The existence of a mortgagee's policy helps facilitate the sale of the mortgage to the secondary market.

- A mortgagee title insurance policy, generally paid for with a one-time premium, is for the loan amount outstanding at the time a claim is paid. Coverage runs from the time of purchase for as long as the policyholder owns the property, usually with no additional premium.

Explanation of Fees

There are many fees associated with processing a real estate loan. Some early expenses incurred by lenders must be paid even if the loan doesn't close. For loans that actually close, lenders charge a loan **origination fee** (also called a loan service fee) to cover the administrative costs of making and servicing the loan. This fee is usually based on a percentage of the loan amount (**1% = 1 point**), and paid out of closing funds.

Some lenders may take all fees out of closing funds, while others have buyers pay some fees up front and give them a credit back at closing. The **Real Estate Settlement Procedures Act** (RESPA) guidelines prohibit the collection of any fee unless it was properly disclosed to the borrower on the Good Faith Estimate (GFE) of closing costs (Sec. 3500.7). Note that:

- No fee may be charged for completing mandated disclosures, such as the TIL and the GFE.
- The only fee that may be charged before these mandatory disclosures is one for obtaining a credit report.
- Lender and mortgage broker origination fees are lumped together on the GFE.

Explanation of Closing Documents

The primary documents at closing include:

Promissory Note

The evidence of a promise to pay a specific amount of money to a specific person within a specific time frame. The one promising to pay the money is called the **maker** of the note, usually the homebuyer. The one to whom payment is promised is called the **payee**, usually the lender, which could also be the seller. A typical promissory note includes:

- Date
- Names of the parties
- Amount of the debt
- How and when the money is to be paid
- What happens in the event of default
- Prepayment penalties, if any
- Signature of the maker

Mortgage (or Deed of Trust)

A security instrument that creates a voluntary lien giving a creditor the right to have the collateral sold to satisfy the debt if the debtor fails to pay according to the terms of the agreement. The concept of **hypothecation** means a debtor can pledge property as security for a debt without giving up possession of it. This serves as security for the creditor and motivation for the debtor to make sure that the terms of the note are fulfilled and the note is repaid as agreed. Failure to do so could result in loss of possession. Hypothecation is a voluntary act.

Funding the Loan

Conditional approval usually requires additional items, such as closing statement from the sale of the buyer's previous home, final inspection report, and/or commitment for private mortgage insurance (often mortgage insurance is a condition for approving conventional loans with less than 20% down).

The lender issues a **clear to close** when the loan is approved, all conditions are met, and the loan papers are ready to be signed. Loan funds are then disbursed to the proper parties, according to the sales contract or escrow instructions (**funding** the loan), assuming the three (3) business-day right of rescission has passed for specific loans:

- Refinance loans secured by a primary residence.
- Section 32 loans (high-cost loans) as designated by the Home Ownership and Equity Protection Act (HOEPA).

KEY TERM REVIEW

Assumption A financing strategy where one party takes over the responsibility for the loan of another party and the terms of the loan or note remain unchanged. (Usually lender approval is needed. Also, a release is needed or original party remains secondarily liable for the loan.)

Automated Underwriting Process where loan applicant information is entered into a computer and an evaluation comes back within minutes advising the lender to accept the loan, or refers the loan application for further review.

Closing The final stage in a real estate transaction where ownership of real property is transferred from seller to buyer according to the terms and conditions set forth in a sales contract or escrow agreement.

Co-Mortgagor A person who signs a mortgage with the primary mortgagor and thus accepts a joint obligation to repay the loan. Also called Co-Borrower or Co-Signer.

Credit History A person's record of debt repayment detailing how a person paid credit accounts in the past. Credit history is used as a guide to how likely the borrower is to pay accounts on time and as agreed in the future.

Loan-to-Value Ratio (LTV) The amount of money borrowed compared to the value or price of the property.

Mortgage Insurance Premium (MIP) Non-refundable fee charged for FHA mortgage insurance coverage; initial premium (upfront mortgage insurance premium or UFMIP) can be financed and there may be a renewal premium.

Origination The process of making or initiating a new loan.

Origination Fee An upfront fee charged by some lenders, usually expressed as a percent of the loan amount.

PITI A typical mortgage payment that includes Principle, Interest, Taxes, and Insurance.

Points One percent of the loan amount. Points are charged for any reason, but are often used for buydowns (where they may also be called discount points).

Pre-Approval Process by which a lender determines if potential borrowers can be financed through the lender, and for what amount of money. Requires borrower to complete a loan application and supply documentation necessary to make a credit determination.

Pre-Qualification Process by which a mortgage loan originator estimates the amount of loan for which a borrower might be approved; this is non-binding.

Principal With regard to a loan, the amount originally borrowed or the outstanding balance subsequently.

Private Mortgage Insurance (PMI) Insurance offered by private companies to insure a lender against default on a loan by a borrower.

Processing Compiling and maintaining the file of information about a mortgage transaction, including the credit report, appraisal, verification of employment and assets, and so on.

Rate Protection Protection for a borrower against the danger that rates will rise between the time the borrower applies for a loan and the time the loan closes. This protection can take the form of a "lock" where the rate and points are frozen at their initial levels until the loan closes; or a "float-down" where the rates and points cannot rise from their initial levels but they can decline if market rates decline.

Reserves Cash on deposit or other highly liquid assets a borrower must have in order to cover two months of PITI mortgage payments, after they make the cash down payment and pays all closing costs.

Seller-Paid Items Closing costs paid by the seller instead of the buyer. This usually refers to items normally paid by the buyer, but in some instances are paid by the seller to help close the sale. FHA and VA loans limit this.

Servicing The process of collecting payments, keeping records, and handling defaults for loans.

Underwriter The individual who evaluates a loan application to determine its risk level for a lender or investor. The underwriter is usually the final decision maker on a borrower's loan application.

CHAPTER 4 QUIZ

1. *The lender usually does NOT allow the source of a borrower's down payment to be*
   A. borrowed funds.
   B. a gift from a relative.
   C. proceeds from the sale of a house.
   D. savings.

2. *When calculating the debt ratio, the calculation that best represents the front ratio is monthly*
   A. debt divided by gross monthly income.
   B. debt divided by net monthly income.
   C. housing debt divided by gross monthly income.
   D. housing debt divided by net monthly income.

3. *A unique property, such as a geodesic home, being purchased as a primary residence would most logically employ what method of appraisal?*
   A. cost approach
   B. income approach
   C. salability approach
   D. sales comparison approach

4. *What is the loan-to-value if the loan amount is $118,000, the appraised value is $131,000, and the sales price is $135,000?*
   A. 88%
   B. 90%
   C. 95%
   D. 100%

5. *Market value can best be defined as a property's*
   A. appraised value for property tax purposes.
   B. listing price.
   C. most probable selling price.
   D. most recent selling price.

6. *A borrower with a gross income of $3,000 per month would qualify for a housing payment of what amount—including taxes and insurance—using the housing expense ratio for a conventional mortgage?*
   A. $840
   B. $870
   C. $1,080
   D. $1,230

7. *What is the correct calculation used to determine gross monthly income, for a borrower paid by the hour?*
   A. hourly rate x hours worked weekly x 4
   B. hourly rate x hours worked weekly x 4.33
   C. hourly rate x hours worked weekly x 4 x 52 ÷ 12
   D. hourly rate x hours worked weekly x 52 ÷ 12

8. *What is the minimum number of comps required by most secondary lenders to ensure an accurate estimate of value when performing the sales comparison approach?*
   A. two
   B. three
   C. four
   D. five

9. *When qualifying a borrower, an installment debt does not need to be included in the debt to income ratio when the balance of the term of repayment is less than how many months?*
   A. 5
   B. 10
   C. 15
   D. 20

10. *Qualifying guidelines on an FHA loan are*
    A. 28% housing ratio and 36% total debt to income ratio.
    B. 29% housing ratio and 41% total debt to income ratio.
    C. 31% housing ratio and 43% total debt to income ratio.
    D. 36% housing ratio and 41% total debt to income ratio.

11. *Section 502 loans are a program of which government entity?*
    A. Federal Housing Administration
    B. Housing and Urban Development
    C. USDA Rural Development
    D. Veterans Administration

12. *A borrower offers $105,000 for a house that was appraised for $112,000. If the seller accepts the offer, what is the minimum down payment required for an FHA loan (assuming a FICO score of at least 580)?*

    A. $3,675
    B. $3,920
    C. $5,250
    D. $5,600

13. *A Chapter 7 bankruptcy could show on a credit report for a maximum of how many years?*

    A. five
    B. seven
    C. eight
    D. ten

14. *Susan is purchasing a house for $200,000. It was appraised for $220,000. In order to avoid paying PMI on this conventional loan, how much should Susan put down on this house?*

    A. $7,700
    B. $20,000
    C. $22,000
    D. $40,000

15. *A closing agent is responsible for all of these tasks EXCEPT*

    A. following instructions according to the sales contract.
    B. gathering all necessary documentation to close.
    C. issuing the final loan approval.
    D. preparing the settlement statement.

16. *What is the maximum LTV allowed for VA loans?*

    A. 100%
    B. 96.5%
    C. 90%
    D. 80%

17. *A borrower is buying a house for $150,000 at 6.5%. He provides a down payment of $15,000. How much would he have to pay for three discount points?*

    A. $2,925
    B. $3,000
    C. $4,050
    D. $4,500

18. *The UFMIP is charged on what type of mortgage loans?*

    A. conforming loans sold to GNMA
    B. FHA loans
    C. subprime loans sold to FNMA
    D. VA loans

19. *In a loan closing, hypothecation occurs. This is described as*

    A. assigning the mortgage from the broker to the lender.
    B. the seller transferring appliance warranties to the buyer.
    C. the transfer of title through the deed.
    D. using property as collateral without surrendering use or possession of it.

20. *A borrower is purchasing a home for $120,000 and closing costs total 4% of the purchase price. The seller has agreed to contribute 2% of the purchase price toward the buyer's closing costs. How much cash would the borrower need at closing in order to obtain an LTV of 85%?*

    A. $18,360
    B. $18,720
    C. $20,400
    D. $20,800

Chapter 5

SAFE ACT and UST Content Update

Introduction

On April 1, 2013, the NMLS launched the Uniform State Test or UST. This is the first major change to SAFE Mortgage Loan Originator (MLO) Test requirements since the SAFE MLO Tests were launched in July 2009.

The UST content is a new section in the MLO National Test. This new section includes 25 questions on high-level state content, which brings the length of the National Test Component to 125 questions; of which, 115 are scored and ten are unscored.

As of January 2013, there are 24 states or agencies that have indicated they will adopt the UST either on April 1 or July 1, 2013. Twenty adopted the UST on April 1, 2013 and the remaining four will adopt it on July 1, 2013. For a current list of state adoptions, log on to the NMLS Resource Center (http://mortgage.nationwidelicensingsystem.org/Pages/default.aspx), click on "Professional Standards," then "Testing." On the right side of the page, under "Related Links," click on the "UST Implementation Information "link, and then again click on "UST Adoption Table."

For persons who have already passed the National Test component, who may wish to pursue licensing in a state that has adopted the UST for its state licensure testing requirement, there will be a Standalone UST component available for some interim period. This Standalone UST component will consist of 25 scored questions.

The old National Test has been retired. Going forward, all candidates, regardless of the state in which they intend to get licensed, are required to take and pass the SAFE MLO National Test Component with UST.

Key Terms

Administrative or Clerical Tasks

American Association of Residential Mortgage Regulators (AARMR)

Application

Bureau

Clerical or Support Duties

Conference of State Bank Supervisors

Consumer Financial Protection Bureau (CFPB)

Director

Dodd-Frank Wall Street Reform and Consumer Protection Act

Employee

Farm Credit Administration

Independent Contractor

Loan Processor or Underwriter

Nationwide Mortgage Licensing System and Registry (NMLS)

Nontraditional Mortgage Product

Origination of a Residential Mortgage Loan

Real Estate Brokerage Activities

Residential Mortgage Loan

Secure and Fair Enforcement for Mortgage Licensing Act of 2008 (SAFE Act)

State

Unique Identifier

National Component with UST Content Outline

This is the published content outline for the **SAFE Mortgage Loan Originator Test – National Component with Uniform State Test:**

I. Federal mortgage-related laws (24-25%)

A. RESPA

B. Equal Credit Opportunity Act (Reg. B)

C. Truth-in-Lending Act (Reg. Z and HOEPA)

D. Other Federal laws and guidelines

   1. Home Mortgage Disclosure Act (HMDA)

   2. Fair Credit Reporting Act

   3. Privacy protection / Do Not Call

   4. FTC Red Flag (Fair and Accurate Credit Transactions Act of 2003)

   5. Dodd-Frank

   6. Mortgage Assistance Relief Services (MARS)

   7. FTC Safeguard Rules

   8. Bank Secrecy Act/Anti-Money Laundering (BSA/AML)

   9. Gramm-Leach-Bliley Act

II. General mortgage knowledge (19-20%)

A. Mortgage programs

   1. Conventional/conforming

   2. Government (FHA, VA, USDA)

   3. Conventional/nonconforming (Jumbo, Alt-A, etc.)

      a. Statement on Subprime Lending

      b. Guidance on Nontraditional Mortgage Product Risk

B. Mortgage loan products

   1. Fixed

   2. Adjustable

   3. Balloon

   4. Reverse mortgage

   5. Other (home equity [fixed and line of credit], construction mortgage, interest-only, bridge financing)

C. Terms used in the operation of the mortgage market

   1. Loan terms

   2. Disclosure terms

   3. Financial terms

   4. General terms

III. Mortgage loan origination activities (19-20%)

A. Application information and requirements

   1. Application accuracy and required information (e.g., 1003)

      a. Customer

      b. Loan originator

      c. Verification and documentation

   2. Suitability of products and programs

   3. Disclosures

      a. Accuracy

      b. Timing

B. Qualification: processing and underwriting

   1. Borrower analysis

      a. Assets

      b. Liabilities

      c. Income

      d. Credit report

      e. Qualifying ratios (e.g. housing, debt-to-income, loan-to-value)

   2. Appraisals

   3. Title report

   4. Insurance: hazard, flood, and mortgage

C. Specific program guidelines

   1. VA, FHA, USDA, HECM

   2. Fannie Mae, Freddie Mac

   3. Other (e.g. Private mortgage insurance, flood)

D. Closing

   1. Title and title insurance

   2. Settlement/Closing agent

   3. Explanation of Fees

   4. Explanation of Documents

   5. Funding

E. Financial calculations used in mortgage lending

   1. Periodic interest

   2. Payments (principal, interest, taxes, and insurance; mortgage insurance, if applicable)

   3. Down payment

   4. Loan-to-value (loan-to-value, combined loan-to-value, total loan-to-value)

   5. Debt-to-income Ratios

   6. Temporary and Fixed interest rate buy-down (discount points)

7. Closing costs and prepaid items

8. ARMs (eg., fully indexed rate)

IV. Ethics (14-15%)

A. RESPA

B. Gramm-Leach-Bliley Act

C. Truth-in-Lending Act

D. Equal Credit Opportunity Act

E. Appraisal

F. Fraud detection, reporting, and prevention (e.g. BSA/AML)

G. Ethical behavior

1. Consumers

2. Appraisers

3. Underwriters

4. Investors

5. Real estate professionals

6. Settlement/Closing agents

7. Employers

8. Mortgage Loan Originators

V. Uniform State Content (20-22%)

A. Department of Financial Institutions or Mortgage Regulatory Commission

1. Regulatory authority

2. Responsibilities and limitations

B. State Law and Regulation Definitions

C. License Law and Regulation

1. Persons required to be licensed

2. Licensee qualifications and application process

3. Grounds for denying a license

4. License maintenance

D. Compliance

1. Prohibited conduct and practices

2. Required conduct

3. Advertising

Note: The Standalone Uniform State Test content outline is identical to the content outline provided for the new Section V on Uniform State Content, which makes up 20-22% of the National Test with UST.

UST Content References and Resources

A number of references and resources have been used to develop the Standalone Uniform State Test (UST).

Note: The following list is intended to be used as a guide to assist test candidates to prepare for the Standalone Uniform State Test (UST). It is *not* intended to be an all-inclusive list.

- Title V—S.A.F.E. Mortgage Licensing Act
- State Model Language for Implementation of Public Law 110-289, Title V—S.A.F.E. Mortgage Licensing Act
- 12 CFR 1008—S.A.F.E. MORTGAGE LICENSING ACT—STATE COMPLIANCE AND BUREAU REGISTRATION SYSTEM (REGULATION H)

A. STATE REGULATORY AUTHORITY

The SAFE Act

Title V: "Secure and Fair Enforcement for Mortgage Licensing Act of 2008" or "S.A.F.E. Mortgage Licensing Act of 2008":

- Is a key component of the **Housing and Economic Recovery Act of 2008 (HERA)** (Pub.L. 110-289).
- Requires all states to implement a SAFE-compliant mortgage loan originator (MLO) licensing process that meets certain *minimum* standards through the **Nationwide Mortgage Licensing System & Registry (NMLS).**

The effective date of this Act was July 31, 2009.

> **Note:** For this Refresher text, we will use the shortened term: **SAFE Act.**

SAFE Act Objectives

The SAFE Act is designed to enhance consumer protection and reduce fraud by encouraging states to establish *minimum* standards for the licensing and registration of state-licensed mortgage loan originators (MLOs) and for the **Conference of State Bank Supervisors (CSBS)** and the **American Association of Residential Mortgage Regulators (AARMR)** to establish and maintain a nationwide mortgage licensing system and registry for the residential mortgage industry. (*http://www.hud.gov/offices/hsg/ramh/safe/smlicact.cfm*)

Let's review some of the SAFE Act's objectives:

- Provide uniform license applications and reporting requirements for state-licensed mortgage loan originators.
- Provide a comprehensive licensing and supervisory database.
- Aggregate and improve flow of information to and between regulators.
- Provide increased accountability and tracking of mortgage loan originators.
- Streamline the licensing process and reduce regulatory burden.
- Enhance consumer protections and support anti-fraud measures.
- Provide consumers with easily accessible information, offered at no charge, utilizing electronic media, including the Internet, regarding the employment history, and public disciplinary and enforcement actions against mortgage loan originators.
- Establish a means by which residential mortgage loan originators would be required, to the greatest extent possible, to act in the best interests of the consumer.
- Facilitate responsible behavior in the subprime mortgage marketplace.
- Provide comprehensive training and examination requirements related to nontraditional mortgage products.
- Facilitate the collection and disbursement of consumer complaints.

State Regulatory Authority Agencies

The regulatory authority agency for each state may be referred to by a name similar to one of the following examples:

- Department of Financial Institutions
- Mortgage Regulatory Commission
- Division of Banking

State Regulatory Authority Responsibilities

Let's review *minimum* requirements for each state mortgage loan originator regulatory authority under the SAFE Act:

- Must provide effective supervision and enforcement of the law, including the suspension, termination, or nonrenewal of a license for a violation of any state or federal law.

- Must ensure that all state-licensed mortgage loan originators operating in the state are registered with the Nationwide Mortgage Licensing System and Registry (NMLS).

- Must regularly report violations, as well as enforcement actions and other relevant information, to the NMLS.

- Must have a process in place for challenging information contained in the NMLS.

- Must have an established mechanism to assess civil money penalties for individuals acting as mortgage loan originators in their state without a valid license or registration.

- Must have one of these protection options in place: An established *minimum* net worth or surety bonding requirement that reflects the dollar amount of loans originated by a residential mortgage loan originator, or have an established recovery fund paid into by mortgage loan originators.

Enforcement Authorities of the CFPB

As of July 2011, the **Consumer Financial Protection Bureau (CFPB)** is responsible for enforcement of the SAFE Act at the federal level.

The **CFPB** has the authority to:

- Examine any books, papers, records, or other data of any mortgage loan originator operating at any time, in any state, to investigate compliance with the SAFE Act.

- Summon any mortgage loan originator or any person having possession, custody, or care of the reports and records relating to such mortgage loan originator in any state, under the SAFE Act, to appear before the Bureau at a time and place named in the summons.

- Compel any mortgage loan originator or any person from any state, subject to the SAFE Act, to produce such books, papers, records, or other relevant data.

- Order any mortgage loan originator from any state to give testimony, under oath, as may be relevant or material to an investigation of such mortgage loan originator for compliance with the requirements of the SAFE Act.

CFPB Examiners

Any appointed examiner shall have power, on behalf of the Bureau, to make any examination of any mortgage loan originator, operating at any time, in any state, which is subject to a licensing system established by the Bureau, whenever the Bureau determines that an examination of any mortgage loan originator is necessary to determine the compliance by the mortgage loan originator with *minimum* requirements of the SAFE Act.

Each Bureau examiner shall make a full and detailed report to the Bureau of examination of any mortgage loan originator examined.

Administration of Oaths

In connection with examinations of mortgage loan originators operating in any state, the Bureau and the examiners appointed by the Bureau may administer oaths and affirmations, and examine and take and preserve testimony under oath, as to any matter in respect to the affairs of any such mortgage loan originator.

Assessments

The cost of conducting any examination of any mortgage loan originator operating in any state shall be assessed by the Bureau against the mortgage loan originator, or the mortgage company, or both, to meet the expenses in carrying out such examination.

Fees

CSBS, AARMR, or the Bureau, as applicable, may charge reasonable fees to cover the costs of maintaining and providing access to information from the Nationwide Mortgage Licensing System and Registry (NMLS). Fees *shall not* be charged to consumers for access to such system and registry. If the Bureau determines to charge fees, the fees to be charged shall be issued by notice with the opportunity for comment prior to any fees being charged.

State System of Supervision and Enforcement

The SAFE Act requires that each state implement an effective system of supervision and enforcement of the mortgage lending industry, including the authority to:

- Issue licenses to conduct business under the Act, including the authority to write rules or regulations or adopt procedures necessary to the licensing of persons covered under the Act.
- Deny, suspend, condition, or revoke licenses issued under the Act.
- Examine, investigate, and conduct enforcement actions as necessary to carry out the intended purposes of the Act, including the authority to subpoena witnesses and documents, enter orders (including cease and desist orders, order restitution and monetary penalties), and order the removal and ban of individuals from office or employment.

Broad Administrative Authority

The state regulatory authority must have a broad administrative authority to administer, interpret, and enforce the SAFE Act, and promulgate rules or regulations implementing the Act, in order to carry out the intentions of the Legislature.

State Examination Authority

In addition to any authority allowed under state law, a state-licensing agency must have the authority to conduct investigations and examinations.

For the purposes of investigating violations or complaints arising under the SAFE Act, or for the purposes of examination, the state regulatory authority may review, investigate, or examine any mortgage loan originator licensed, or required to be licensed, under the Act, or licensed mortgage company, as often as necessary in order to carry out the purposes of this Act.

Access to Books and Records

Each mortgage loan originator must make available upon request to the state regulatory authority the books and records relating to the operations of that originator. The state regulatory authority may have access to such books and records and interview the officers, principals, mortgage loan originators, employees, independent contractors, agents, and customers of the licensee concerning their business.

In addition, no person subject to investigation or examination under this Act may knowingly withhold, abstract, remove, mutilate, destroy, or secrete any books, records, computer records, or other information.

Authority to Access Information

For purposes of initial licensing, license renewal, license suspension, license conditioning, license revocation or termination, or general or specific inquiry or investigation to determine compliance with the SAFE Act, the state regulatory authority shall have the authority to access, receive and use any books, accounts, records, files, documents, information, or evidence, including but *not* limited to:

- Criminal, civil and administrative history information, including non-conviction data as specified in state criminal code.
- Personal history and experience information, including independent credit reports obtained from a consumer reporting agency described in section 603(p) of the Fair Credit Reporting Act.
- Any other documents, information, or evidence the Commissioner deems relevant to the inquiry or investigation, regardless of the location, possession, control, or custody of such documents, information, or evidence.

Investigation, Examination and Subpoena Authority

For the purposes of investigating violations or complaints arising under this Act, or for the purposes of examination, the state regulatory authority may review, investigate, or examine any licensee, individual, or person subject to the SAFE Act, as often as necessary in order to carry out the purposes of the Act.

The state regulatory authority may direct, subpoena, or order the attendance of and examine under oath all persons whose testimony may be required about the loans, or the business, or subject matter of any such examination or investigation; and may direct, subpoena, or order any such person to produce books, accounts, records, files, and any other documents the regulatory agency deems relevant to the inquiry.

Availability of Books and Records

Each licensee, individual, or person subject to the SAFE Act shall make available to the state regulatory authority, upon request, the books and records relating to the operations of such licensee, individual, or person subject to the Act.

The state regulatory authority shall have access to such books and records and interview the officers, principals, mortgage loan originators, employees, independent contractors, agents, and customers of the licensee, individual, or person subject to this Act concerning their business.

No licensee, individual, or person subject to investigation or examination under this section of the SAFE Act may knowingly withhold, abstract, remove, mutilate, destroy, or secrete any books, records, computer records, or other information.

Reports and Other Information

Each licensee, individual, or person subject to the SAFE Act shall make or compile reports or prepare other information as directed by state regulatory authority in order to carry out the purposes of the Act, including but *not* limited to:

- Accounting compilations.
- Information lists and data concerning loan transactions in a format prescribed by the state regulatory authority.
- Such other information deemed necessary to carry out the purposes of this Act.

Mortgage Call Reports

Each mortgage licensee shall submit to the Nationwide Mortgage Licensing System and Registry (NMLS) reports of condition, which shall be in such form and shall contain such information as the NMLS may require.

Control of and Access to Records

In making any examination or investigation authorized by the SAFE Act, the state regulatory authority may control access to any documents and records of the licensee or person under examination or investigation.

An examiner may take possession of the documents and records or place a person in exclusive charge of the documents and records in the place where they are usually kept. During the period of control, no individual, or person shall remove or attempt to remove any of the documents and records; except pursuant to a court order, or with the consent of the state regulatory authority.

Unless the state regulatory authority has reasonable grounds to believe the documents or records of the licensee have been, or are at risk of being altered or destroyed for purposes of concealing a violation of the SAFE Act, the licensee, or owner of the documents and records, shall have access to the documents or records as necessary to conduct its ordinary business affairs.

Additional Authority

In order to carry out the purposes of the SAFE Act, the state regulatory authority may:

- Retain attorneys, accountants, or other professionals and specialists as examiners, auditors, or investigators to conduct or assist in the conduct of examinations or investigations.

- Enter into agreements or relationships with other government officials or regulatory associations in order to improve efficiencies and reduce regulatory burden by sharing resources, standardized or uniform methods or procedures, and documents, records, information, or evidence obtained under this section of the SAFE Act.
- Use, hire, contract, or employ public or privately available analytical systems, methods, or software to examine or investigate the licensee, individual, or person subject to the SAFE Act.
- Accept and rely on examination or investigation reports made by other government officials, within or outside of this state.
- Accept audit reports made by an independent certified public accountant for the licensee, individual, or person subject to the SAFE Act in the course of that part of the examination, covering the same general subject matter as the audit and may incorporate the audit report in the report of the examination, report of investigation, or other writing of the state regulatory authority.

Supervision and Enforcement

In order to ensure effective supervision and enforcement, the state regulatory authority may:

- Deny, suspend, revoke, condition, or decline to renew a license for a violation of the SAFE Act, rules or regulations issued under the Act, or order or directive entered under the Act.
- Deny, suspend, revoke, condition, or decline to renew a license if an applicant or licensee fails at any time to meet the requirements of MSL XX.XXX.060 or MSL XX.XXX.090, or withholds information or makes a material misstatement in an application for a license or renewal of a license.
- Order restitution against persons subject to the SAFE Act for violations of this Act.
- Impose fines on persons subject to the SAFE Act.

Orders or Directives

In order to ensure effective supervision and enforcement, the state regulatory authority may issue orders or directives as follows:

- Order or direct persons subject to the SAFE Act to cease and desist from conducting business, including immediate temporary orders to cease and desist.
- Order or direct persons subject to the SAFE Act to cease any harmful activities or violations of this Act, including immediate temporary orders to cease and desist.
- Enter immediate temporary orders to cease business under a license or interim license issued pursuant to the authority granted under MSL XX.XXX.040(5) if the state regulatory authority determines that such license was erroneously granted or the licensee is currently in violation of the SAFE Act.
- Order or direct such other affirmative action as the state regulatory authority deems necessary.

Penalties

The state regulatory authority may impose a civil penalty on a mortgage loan originator or person subject to the SAFE Act, if the state regulatory authority finds, after notice and opportunity for hearing, that such mortgage loan originator or person subject to this Act, has violated or failed to comply with any requirement of this Act, or any regulation prescribed by the state regulatory authority under this Act, or order issued under authority of this Act.

The **maximum** amount of penalty for each act or omission shall be **$25,000**.

Each violation or failure to comply with any directive or order of the state regulatory authority is a **separate and distinct** violation or failure.

One of Three Protection Options

Pursuant to PL 110-289, Title V, Section 1508(d)(6), each state must choose one of the following options:

- Required **Surety Bond**
- Required **Minimum Net Worth**
- Required **State Fund**

Option One: Surety Bond

Under this option, each mortgage loan originator must be covered by a **surety bond**. In the event that the mortgage loan originator is an employee or exclusive agent of a person subject to the SAFE Act, the surety bond of such person, subject to this Act, can be used in lieu of the mortgage loan originator's surety bond requirement.

The surety bond must provide coverage for each mortgage loan originator in an amount and form as prescribed by the state regulatory authority. The state regulatory authority may promulgate rules or regulations with respect to the requirements for such surety bonds as are necessary to accomplish the purposes of the SAFE Act.

The penal sum of the surety bond must be maintained in an amount that reflects the dollar amount of loans originated as determined by the state regulatory authority.

When an action is commenced on a licensee's bond, the state regulatory authority may require the filing of a new bond. Immediately upon recovery upon any action on the bond, the licensee must file a new bond.

Option Two: Minimum Net Worth

A *minimum* net worth must be continuously maintained for mortgage loan originators. In the event that the mortgage loan originator is an employee or exclusive agent of a person subject to the SAFE Act, the net worth of such person subject to this Act can be used in lieu of the mortgage loan originator's *minimum* net worth requirement.

Minimum **net worth** must be continuously maintained in an amount that reflects the dollar amount of loans originated as determined by the state regulatory authority. The state regulatory authority may promulgate rules or regulations with respect to the requirements for *minimum* net worth as are necessary to accomplish the purposes of this Act.

Option Three: State Fund

Each state choosing this option must draft unique language establishing a **state recovery fund**. The fund is paid into by the state-licensed mortgage loan originator and the state-licensed mortgage entity at the time of state mortgage license application and annual state license renewal.

Challenges

The state regulatory authority must establish a process whereby mortgage loan originators may challenge information entered into the NMLS.

Fees

Fees to apply for or renew licenses may be remitted through the Nationwide Mortgage Licensing System and Registry (NMLS).

Setting Dates

The state regulatory authority may be responsible for the setting or resetting as necessary of renewal or reporting dates.

License Surrender

The state regulatory must establish requirements for amending, transferring, or surrendering a license or any other license status change the state regulatory authority deems necessary for participation in the Nationwide Mortgage Licensing System and Registry (NMLS).

Regulatory Authority Limitations

State and federal regulating authorities do *not* have the authority, nor are they empowered, to impose a prison sentence.

At this time, mortgage loan originators, processors, and underwriters employed by credit unions and depository institutions (local, state, and federal banks, and savings associations) are *not* required to be state licensed under the SAFE Act. The exception requires that the employees of these institutions be registered through the Nationwide Mortgage Licensing System and Registry and have an NMLS Unique Identifier.

B. STATE LAW AND REGULATION DEFINITIONS

State Model

With the enactment of the SAFE Act, the **Conference of State Bank Supervisors (CSBS)** and the **American Association of Residential Mortgage Regulators (AARMR)** worked with the **Department of Housing and Urban Development (HUD)** to fulfill the mandates of the SAFE Act, including the requirements that states establish *minimum* standards for the licensing or registration of all mortgage loan originators.

To that end, CSBS and AARMR developed a model state law that met the *minimum* standards for the SAFE Act, including definitions, education and testing requirements, and financial responsibility and criminal background standards for mortgage loan originators. HUD reviewed the model legislation and determined that it did indeed meet the requirements of the SAFE Act.

Therefore, any state legislation that follows the model state law will also have met the applicable *minimum* requirements of the SAFE Act.

Definitions

Let's review some of the standard definitions included in the state laws that follow the model.

Depository Institution

The term **depository institution** means any **bank** or **savings association** (the same meaning as in Section 3 of the Federal Deposit Insurance Act), and includes any **credit union**.

Federal Banking Agencies

The term **Federal Banking Agencies** refers to any of the following:

- The Board of Governors of the Federal Reserve System
- The Comptroller of the Currency
- The Director of the Office of Thrift Supervision
- The National Credit Union Administration
- The Federal Deposit Insurance Corporation

Immediate Family Member

The term **immediate family member** includes:

- Spouse
- Child
- Sibling
- Parent
- Grandparent
- Grandchild

◇ **Note:** This term also includes: **Step** (stepparents, stepchildren, stepsiblings) and **adoptive** relationships.

Individual

The term **individual** means a natural person.

Loan Processor or Underwriter

~~In general, the term **loan processor** or **underwriter** means:~~

- ~~An individual who performs clerical or support duties as an employee at the direction of and subject to the supervision and instruction of a person licensed, or exempt from licensing under state mortgage licensing laws.~~

Clerical or Support Duties

The term **clerical or support duties** may include subsequent to the receipt of an application:

(i) The receipt, collection, distribution, and analysis of information common for the processing or underwriting of a residential mortgage loan

(ii) ommunicating with a consumer to obtain the information necessary for the processing or underwriting of a loan, to the extent that such communication does *not* include offering or negotiating loan rates or terms, or counseling consumers about residential mortgage loan rates or terms

Representations to the Public

An individual engaging solely in loan processor or underwriter activities shall *not* represent to the public, through advertising or other means of communicating or providing information, including the use of business cards, stationery, brochures, signs, rate lists, or other promotional items, that such individual can or will perform any of the activities of a mortgage loan originator.

Mortgage Loan Originator

In general, the term **mortgage loan originator** means (i) an individual who for compensation or gain, or in the expectation of compensation or gain:

(A) **Takes a residential mortgage loan application**; or

(B) **Offers or negotiates terms** of a residential mortgage loan.

Exemptions

The term **mortgage loan originator** does *not* include:

(ii) An individual engaged solely as a loan processor or underwriter working as an employee paid on a W-2, except as otherwise provided in MSL XX.XXX.040(4);

(iii) A person or entity that only performs real estate brokerage activities and is licensed or registered in accordance with state law, unless the person or entity is compensated by a lender, a mortgage broker, or other mortgage loan originator or by any agent of such lender, mortgage broker, or other mortgage loan originator; and

(iv) A person or entity solely involved in extensions of credit relating to timeshare plans, as that term is defined in section 101(53D) of title 11, United States Code.

Real Estate Brokerage Activity

For purposes of the SAFE Act, the term **real estate brokerage activity** means any activity that involves offering or providing real estate brokerage services to the public, including:

(i) Acting as a real estate agent or real estate broker for a buyer, seller, lessor, or lessee of real property;

(ii) Bringing together parties interested in the sale, purchase, lease, rental, or exchange of real property;

(iii) Negotiating, on behalf of any party, any portion of a contract relating to the sale, purchase, lease, rental, or exchange of real property (other than in connection with providing financing with respect to any such transaction);

(iv) Engaging in any activity for which a person engaged in the activity is required to be registered or licensed as a real estate agent or real estate broker under any applicable law; and

(v) Offering to engage in any activity, or act in any capacity, described in subsections (i), (ii), (iii), or (iv) of this section.

Nationwide Mortgage Licensing System and Registry

The term **Nationwide Mortgage Licensing System and Registry** means a mortgage licensing system developed and maintained by the Conference of State Bank Supervisors and the American Association of Residential Mortgage Regulators for the licensing and registration of licensed mortgage loan originators.

Nontraditional Mortgage Product

The term **nontraditional mortgage product** means any mortgage product *other than* a 30-year fixed rate mortgage.

Person

The term **person** refers to any of the following:

- Natural person
- Corporation
- Company
- Limited liability company
- Partnership
- Association

Registered Mortgage Loan Originator

The term **registered** mortgage loan originator means any individual who

(a) meets the definition of mortgage loan originator and is an employee of:

- (i) A **depository institution**;
- (ii) A **subsidiary** that is (A) *owned and controlled* by a depository institution; and (B) *regulated* by a Federal Banking Agency; or
- (iii) An **institution** *regulated* by the Farm Credit Administration

(b) Is registered with, and maintains a **unique identifier** through the Nationwide Mortgage Licensing System and Registry (NMLS).

Residential Mortgage Loan (SAFE Act)

According to the SAFE Act, the term **residential mortgage loan** means any loan primarily for personal, family, or household use that is secured by a mortgage, deed of trust, or other equivalent consensual security interest on a dwelling (as defined in section 103(v) of the Truth in Lending Act) or residential real estate upon which is constructed or intended to be constructed a dwelling (also as defined by TILA).

Dwelling

TILA Section 103(v) defines **dwelling** as:

- A residential structure or mobile home which contains one-to-four-family housing units, or individual units of condominiums or cooperatives.

Examples

A "residential mortgage loan" is a dwelling-secured consumer credit transaction, which can include:

- A home purchase, refinancing, or home equity loan
- A loan secured by a first lien or a subordinate lien on a dwelling
- A loan secured by a dwelling that is a principal residence, second home, or vacation home (other than a timeshare residence)
- A loan secured by a one-to-four unit residence, condominium, cooperative, mobile home, or manufactured home

Residential Mortgage Loan (Dodd-Frank)

According to Dodd-Frank, Subtitle A—Residential Mortgage Loan Origination Standards, Section 1401 definitions, the term **residential mortgage loan** means any consumer credit transaction that is secured by a mortgage, deed of trust, or other equivalent consensual security interest on a dwelling or on residential real property that includes a dwelling, other than a consumer credit transaction under an open end credit plan or, for purposes of sections 129B and 129C and section 128(a) (16), (17), (18), and (19), and sections 128(f) and 130(k), and any regulations promulgated thereunder, an extension of credit relating to a plan described in section 101(53D) of title 11, United States Code.

Exemptions

- Open-end loans, such as home-equity lines of credit (HELOCs).
- Timeshare plans—the cross-reference to plans under 11 U.S.C. 101(53D).

Residential Real Estate

The term **residential real estate** means any real property located in the state upon which is constructed or intended to be constructed a dwelling (as defined under TILA).

Unique Identifier

The term **unique identifier** means a number (or other identifier) assigned by protocols established by the Nationwide Mortgage Licensing System and Registry (NMLS).

C. LICENSE LAW AND REGULATION

Persons Required to Be Licensed

An individual required to be licensed under the SAFE Act is an individual who is engaged in the "business of a mortgage loan originator"; that is, an individual who acts as a residential mortgage loan originator with respect to financing that is provided in a commercial context and with some degree of **habitualness** or **repetition**.

Mortgage Loan Originator: Definition

Let's briefly review the definition. The SAFE Act defines a mortgage loan originator as an individual who for compensation or gain or in the expectation of compensation or gain:

(A) **Takes a residential mortgage loan application,** or

(B) **Offers** or **negotiates terms** of a **residential mortgage loan**.

Tasks That Require Licensees

An individual "**assists a consumer in obtaining or applying to obtain a residential mortgage loan**" by among other things:

 Advising on loan terms (including rates, fees, and other costs).

 Preparing loan packages.

 Collecting information on behalf of the consumer with regard to a residential mortgage loan.

Exemptions

Under the SAFE Act, the definition of a mortgage loan originator does *not* include:

- Any individual who performs purely **administrative or clerical tasks** on behalf of a licensee.

- A person or entity that only performs **real estate brokerage activities** and is licensed or registered in accordance with applicable state law, unless the person or entity is compensated by a lender, a mortgage broker, or other mortgage loan originator or by any agent of such lender, mortgage broker, or other mortgage loan originator.

- A person or entity solely involved in extensions of credit relating to **timeshare plans**.

- **A loan processor or underwriter** who does *not* represent to the public, through advertising or other means of communicating or providing information (including the use of business cards, stationery, brochures, signs, rate lists, or other promotional items), that he or she can or will perform any of the activities of a mortgage loan originator shall *not* be required to be a state-licensed mortgage loan originator.

Independent Contractors

In compliance with the SAFE Act, an **independent contractor** may *not* engage in residential mortgage loan origination activities as a loan processor or underwriter *unless* such independent contractor is a **state-licensed mortgage loan originator**.

Registered Mortgage Loan Originator

A **registered mortgage loan originator** is any individual who meets the definition of mortgage loan originator and is an employee of a **depository institution** or a subsidiary that is (a) owned and controlled by a depository institution; and (b) regulated by a federal banking agency; or (c) an institution regulated by the **Farm Credit Administration**; and who is registered with, and maintains a **unique identifier** through, the Nationwide Mortgage Licensing System and Registry.

A State-Licensed Mortgage Loan Originator

A **state-licensed mortgage loan originator** is any individual who is a mortgage loan originator; is *not* an employee of a depository institution or a subsidiary that is (a) owned and controlled by a depository institution; and (b) regulated by a Federal banking agency; or (c) an institution regulated by the Farm Credit Administration; and who is licensed by a state or by the state regulatory authority under section 1508 and registered as a mortgage loan originator with, and maintains a unique identifier through, the Nationwide Mortgage Licensing System and Registry.

Unique Identifier

The SAFE Act requires all residential mortgage loan originators to be identified by a unique NMLS identifier number as either:

- **Federally registered mortgage loan originators**—Any mortgage loan originator employed by a depository institution, a subsidiary that is owned and controlled by a depository institution and regulated by a federal banking agency, or an institution regulated by the Farm Credit Administration.

- **State-licensed mortgage loan originators**—All other mortgage loan originators, *without exception*.

About the Unique Identifier

The unique identifier:

- Permanently identifies a mortgage loan originator.

- Is assigned by protocols established by the NMLS and the Federal Banking Agencies to facilitate electronic tracking of mortgage loan originators and uniform identification of, and public access to, the employment history of, and the publicly adjudicated disciplinary and enforcement actions against mortgage loan originators.

- Shall *not* be used for purposes other than those set forth under the SAFE Act.

Required on All Marketing Materials

The NMLS unique identifier is required on *all* **marketing materials**, applications, required disclosures, and business cards. If the marketing materials are referencing the company only, the company's unique identifier must be used. If the marketing materials and business cards are issued in the name of the mortgage loan originator, then the marketing materials and business cards require the MLO's unique identifier. All disclosures require the MLO's unique identifier.

License Qualifications

Applicants for a state mortgage loan originator license, working for a mortgage broker or mortgage banker, must:

- Submit to a background check (including fingerprints, state and national criminal check).
- Provide personal history and experience.
- Provide authorization to obtain an independent credit report and information relative to any administrative, civil or criminal findings.
- *Never* have had a mortgage loan originator license revoked in any government jurisdiction (a subsequent formal vacation of such revocation is not considered a revocation).
- *Not* have been convicted of or pled guilty or *nolo contendere* to, a felony in a domestic, foreign, or military court during **the seven-year period preceding** the date of the application for licensing and registration or at **any time preceding** such date of application, if such felony involved an act of fraud, dishonesty, or a breach of trust, or money laundering (any pardon of a conviction is *not* considered a conviction).

Character and Fitness

The model state language of the SAFE Act indicates that an applicant must demonstrate **financial responsibility, character, and general fitness** such as to command the confidence of the community and to warrant a determination that the mortgage loan originator will operate honestly, fairly, and efficiently within the purposes of the Act.

A person has shown that he or she is *not* financially responsible when he or she has shown a disregard in the management of his or her own financial condition. A determination that an individual has *not* shown financial responsibility may include, but *not* be limited to:

- Current outstanding judgments, except judgments solely as a result of medical expenses.
- Current outstanding tax liens or other government liens and filings.
- Foreclosures within the past three years.
- A pattern of seriously delinquent accounts within the past three years.

Prelicensing Education Requirements

To become a state-licensed mortgage loan originator, applicants must complete *at least* **twenty (20) hours** of NMLS-approved prelicensing education, which includes these national topics:

- Federal law and regulation (3 hours)
- Ethics, including fraud, consumer protection, and fair lending (3 hours)
- Lending standards for nontraditional mortgage products (2 hours)
- Electives (12 hours)

States/territories may also require jurisdiction-specific topics.

> **Note:** On April 1, 2013, the NMLS will launch the Uniform State Test or UST. The new UST material will test applicants on their knowledge of **high level state-related content** that is based on the SAFE Act and the CSBS/AARMR Model State Law (MSL), which many states used to implement the SAFE Act. The UST will become a new domain or section of the National Test Component. In addition, a short version of the UST, called the Standalone UST, will be introduced on an interim basis for mortgage loan originators who have already passed the national component and wish to be licensed in a state which has adopted the UST component as their state licensing test requirement.

Approved Courses and Course Providers

Prelicensing education courses shall be reviewed, and approved by the NMLS based upon reasonable standards. Review and approval of a prelicensing education course includes review and approval of the course provider.

Employer and Affiliate Educational Courses

Nothing in the SAFE Act shall preclude any pre-licensing education course, as approved by the Nationwide Mortgage Licensing System and Registry that is provided by the employer of the applicant or an entity which is affiliated with the applicant by an agency contract, or any subsidiary or affiliate of such employer or entity.

Educational Offerings

Prelicensing education may be offered either in a classroom, online, or by any other means approved by the NMLS.

Reciprocity of Education

Prelicensing education requirements approved by the NMLS for any one state shall be accepted as credit towards completion of prelicensing education requirements in any other state.

Relicensing Education Requirements

A person previously licensed under the SAFE Act (subsequent to the effective date of the Act) applying to be licensed again must prove that he has completed **all of the continuing education requirements for the year in which the license was last held**.

Mortgage Loan Originator Exam

In order to meet the written test requirement referred to in MSL XX.XXX.060(5), an individual must pass, in accordance with the standards established under this subsection, a qualified written test developed by the NMLS and administered by a test provider approved by the NMLS based upon reasonable standards.

After April 1, 2013, all state-licensed mortgage loan originators must pass the NMLS MLO National Test Component with UST licensing exam that includes a national component and a UST component.

This new state component will include 25 questions which will bring the length of the National Test to 125 questions, of which, 115 will be scored and ten will be unscored.

The national component covers these topics:

- Federal mortgage-related laws (24-25%)
- General mortgage knowledge (19-20%)
- Mortgage loan origination activities (19-20%)
- Ethics (14-15%)

The new UST material will test applicants on their knowledge of high level state-related content that is based on the SAFE Act and the CSBS/AARMR Model State Law (MSL), which many states used to implement the SAFE Act.

The state component covers these topics:

- Uniform State Content (20-22%)

  A. Department of Financial Institutions or Mortgage Regulatory Commission

  B. State Law and Regulation Definitions

  C. License Law and Regulation

  D. Compliance

Minimum Competence

An individual shall *not* be considered to have passed a qualified written test unless the individual achieves a test score of *not* less than **75 percent** correct answers to questions.

Retaking the Exam

According to the U.S. Department of Housing and Urban Development (HUD) final rule implementing the SAFE Act, any candidate for licensure who enrolls to take a test on or after August 29, 2011, may only take and fail the national or a state component of the SAFE MLO Test three consecutive times. After the third failure, that candidate must wait at least six (6) months before taking the test again.

Timeframes for Retesting

Let's review these key timeframes related to retesting:

- **Initial Retests:** An individual may retake a test 3 consecutive times with each consecutive taking occurring at least 30 days after the preceding test.
- **Subsequent Retests:** After failing 3 consecutive tests, an individual shall wait at least 6 months before taking the test again.
- **Retest after Lapse of License**: A licensed mortgage loan originator who fails to maintain a valid license for a period of 5 years or longer shall retake the test, *not* taking into account any time during which such individual is a registered mortgage loan originator.

License Maintenance Requirements

The *minimum* standards for license renewal for mortgage loan originators shall include the following:

- The mortgage loan originator continues to meet the *minimum* standards for license issuance under MSL XX.XXX.060(1)-(6)
- The mortgage loan originator has satisfied the annual continuing education requirements described in MSL XX.XXX.100
- The mortgage loan originator has paid all required fees for renewal of the license

Failure to Satisfy Minimum Standards

The license of a mortgage loan originator failing to satisfy the *minimum* standards for license renewal shall expire. The state regulatory agency may adopt procedures for the reinstatement of expired licenses consistent with the standards established by the NMLS.

Continuing Education for Mortgage Loan Originators

State-licensed mortgage loan originators must complete **at least eight (8) hours** of continuing education every year, including these topics:

- Federal law and regulation (3 hours)
- Ethics, including fraud, consumer protection, and fair lending (2 hours)
- Nontraditional mortgage products (2 hours)
- Elective (1 hour)

Each jurisdiction may impose additional continuing education requirements. Mortgage loan originators *cannot* get credit for the same continuing education class twice in consecutive years.

Approved Courses

Continuing education courses shall be reviewed, and approved by the NMLS based upon reasonable standards. Review and approval of a continuing education course shall include review and approval of the course provider.

Employer and Affiliate Educational Courses

Nothing in the SAFE Act shall preclude any education course, as approved by the NMLS, which is provided by the employer of the mortgage loan originator, or an entity which is affiliated with the mortgage loan originator, by an agency contract, or any subsidiary or affiliate of such employer or entity.

Educational Offerings

Continuing education may be offered either in a classroom, online, or by any other means approved by the NMLS.

Continuing Education Credits

A licensed mortgage loan originator may only receive credit for a continuing education course in the year in which the course is taken; and may *not* take the same approved course in the same or successive years to meet the annual requirements for continuing education. This is known as the **Successive Year Rule.**

Instructor Credit

A licensed mortgage loan originator who is an approved instructor of an approved continuing education course may receive credit for the licensed mortgage loan originator's own annual continuing education requirement at the rate of 2 hours credit for every 1 hour taught.

Reciprocity of Education

A person having successfully completed the education requirements approved by the Nationwide Mortgage Licensing System and Registry in subsections (1)(a), (b) and (c) of this section for any state shall be accepted as credit towards completion of continuing education requirements in any other state.

Lapse in License

 A licensed mortgage loan originator who subsequently becomes unlicensed must complete the continuing education requirements for the last year in which the license was held prior to issuance of a new or renewed license.

Make Up of Continuing Education

A person meeting the requirements of MSL XX.XXX.090(1)(a) and (c) may make up any deficiency in continuing education as established by rule or regulation of the state regulatory authority.

License Application Process

Applicants for a license shall apply in a form as prescribed by the state regulatory authority. Each such form shall contain content as set forth by rule, regulation, instruction, or procedure of the state regulatory agency and may be changed or updated as necessary in order to carry out the purposes of the SAFE Act.

Background Checks

In connection with an application for licensing as a mortgage loan originator, the applicant shall, at a *minimum*, furnish to the NMLS information concerning the applicant's identity, including:

* Fingerprints for submission to the Federal Bureau of Investigation (FBI), and any governmental agency or entity authorized to receive such information for a state, national, and international criminal history background check.
* Personal history and experience in a form prescribed by the NMLS.
* Authorization for the NMLS and the state regulatory authority to obtain an independent credit report obtained from a consumer reporting agency described in section 603(p) of the Fair Credit Reporting Act (FCRA).
* Records related to any administrative, civil, or criminal findings by any governmental jurisdiction.
* Any other information deemed necessary by the NMLS or state regulatory authority.

Issuance of License

The *minimum* standards for licensing and registration as a state-licensed mortgage loan originator shall include the following:

- The applicant has *never* had a mortgage loan originator license revoked in any governmental jurisdiction.
- The applicant has *not* been convicted of, or pled guilty or nolo contendere, to a felony in a domestic, foreign, or military court during the 7-year period preceding the date of the application for licensing and registration; or at any time preceding such date of application, if such felony involved an act of fraud, dishonesty, or a breach of trust, or money laundering.
- The applicant has demonstrated financial responsibility, character, and general fitness such as to command the confidence of the community and to warrant a determination that the mortgage loan originator will operate honestly, fairly, and efficiently within the purposes of this Act.
- The applicant has completed the prelicensing education requirement.
- The applicant has passed a written test that meets the test requirement.
- The applicant has met the protection options required by the state regulatory authority; either a net worth or surety bond requirement, or paid into a state recovery fund.

Grounds for Denying a License

The state regulatory authority shall *not* issue a mortgage loan originator license if the applicant meets any of the following, at *minimum*:

- Has had a mortgage loan originator license revoked in any governmental jurisdiction, except that a subsequent formal vacation of such revocation shall *not* be deemed a revocation.
- Has been convicted of, or pled guilty or nolo contendere to, a felony in a domestic, foreign, or military court (a) during the 7-year period preceding the date of the application for licensing and registration; or (b) at any time preceding such date of application, if such felony involved an act of fraud, dishonesty, or a breach of trust, or money laundering; provided that any pardon of a conviction shall *not* be deemed a conviction.
- The applicant has *not* demonstrated financial responsibility, character, and general fitness such as to command the confidence of the community and to warrant a determination that the mortgage loan originator will operate honestly, fairly, and efficiently within the purposes of this Act.

Not Financially Responsible

A person has shown that he or she is *not* financially responsible when he or she has shown a disregard in the management of his or her own financial condition.

A determination that an individual has *not* shown financial responsibility may include, but is *not* limited to:

- Current outstanding judgments, *except judgments solely as a result of medical expenses.*
- Current outstanding tax liens or other government liens and filings.
- Foreclosures within the past three years.
- A pattern of seriously delinquent accounts within the past three years.

State regulatory agencies do have the option of allowing the applicant the opportunity to submit a detailed explanation of their financial circumstance or appeal to the state licensing authority.

D. COMPLIANCE

Prohibited Conduct and Practices

It is a violation of the SAFE Act for a person or individual subject to the SAFE Act to:

- Directly or indirectly employ any scheme, device, or artifice to defraud or mislead borrowers or lenders or to defraud any person.
- Engage in any unfair or deceptive practice toward any person.
- Obtain property by fraud or misrepresentation.
- Solicit or enter into a contract with a borrower that provides in substance that the person or individual subject to this Act may earn a fee or commission through "best efforts" to obtain a loan, even though no loan is actually obtained for the borrower.
- Solicit, advertise, or enter into a contract for specific interest rates, points, or other financing terms, unless the terms are actually available at the time of soliciting, advertising, or contracting.
- Conduct any business covered by the SAFE Act without holding a valid license as required under the Act, or assist or aide and abet any person in the conduct of business under the SAFE Act without a valid license as required under the Act.
- Fail to make disclosures as required by the SAFE Act and any other applicable state or federal law, including regulations thereunder.
- Fail to comply with the rules or regulations promulgated under the SAFE Act, or fail to comply with any other state or federal law, including the rules and regulations thereunder, applicable to any business authorized or conducted under the SAFE Act.
- Make, in any manner, any false or deceptive statement or representation, or optional add-on, including, with regard to the rates, points, or other financing terms or conditions for a residential mortgage loan, or engage in bait and switch advertising.
- Negligently make any false statement or knowingly and willfully make any omission of material fact in connection with any information or reports filed with a governmental agency or the Nationwide Mortgage Licensing System and Registry or in connection with any investigation conducted by the Commissioner or another governmental agency.
- Make any payment, threat or promise, directly or indirectly, to any person for the purposes of influencing the independent judgment of the person in connection with a residential mortgage loan, or make any payment threat or promise, directly or indirectly, to any appraiser of a property, for the purposes of influencing the independent judgment of the appraiser with respect to the value of the property.
- Collect, charge, attempt to collect or charge or use or propose any agreement purporting to collect or charge any fee prohibited by the SAFE Act.
- Cause or require a borrower to obtain property insurance coverage in an amount that exceeds the replacement cost of the improvements as established by the property insurer.
- Fail to truthfully account for monies belonging to a party to a residential mortgage loan transaction.

Required Conduct

Let's review some of the activities performed by mortgage loan originators. The following conduct and activities would require an individual to be licensed as a mortgage loan originator through the Secure and Fair Enforcement for Licensing Act of 2008 (SAFE Act).

Taking a Loan Application

Taking a residential mortgage loan application, within the meaning of Section 1008.103(c)(1), means:

- Receipt by an individual, for the purpose of facilitating a decision whether to extend an offer of loan terms to a borrower or prospective borrower, of an application as defined in Section 1008.23 (a request in any form for an offer, or a response to a solicitation of an offer, of residential mortgage loan terms, and the information about the borrower or prospective borrower that is customary or necessary in a decision whether to make such an offer).

Example 1

An individual "**takes a residential mortgage loan application**," even if the individual:

- Has received the borrower or prospective borrower's request or information **indirectly**. Section 1008.103(c)(1) provides that an individual takes an application, whether he or she receives it "**directly or indirectly**" from the borrower or prospective borrower.

This means that an individual who **offers or negotiates residential mortgage loan terms for compensation or gain** cannot avoid licensing requirements simply by having another person *physically* receive the application from the prospective borrower and then pass the application to the individual.

Example 2

An individual "**takes a residential mortgage loan application**," even if the individual:

- Is *not* responsible for **verifying** information. The fact that an individual who takes application information from a borrower or prospective borrower is *not* responsible for verifying that information.

This example highlights the fact that just because an individual is a **mortgage broker,** who collects and sends information to a lender who makes the ultimate lending decision; that does *not* mean that the individual who receives the information is *not* taking an application.

Example 3

An individual "**takes a residential mortgage loan application**," even if the individual:

- **Only inputs** the information into an online application or other automated system; or
- Is *not* **involved in approval of the loan**, including determining whether the consumer qualifies for the loan.

Similar to an individual who is *not* responsible for verification, an individual can still "take a residential mortgage loan application" even if he or she is *not* ultimately responsible for approving the loan. **A mortgage broker, for example, can "take a residential mortgage loan application,"** even though it is passed on to a lender for a decision on whether the borrower qualifies for the loan and for the ultimate loan approval.

Exempt Activities

Let's compare some examples of activities that do *not* constitute "taking a loan application" and would *not* require a mortgage loan originator to be state licensed:

Not Taking a Loan Application

An individual does *not* take a loan application merely because the individual:

- Receives a loan application through the mail and forwards it, without review, to loan approval personnel.

    Note: The **Consumer Financial Protection Bureau** (CFPB) interprets the term "takes a residential mortgage loan application" to exclude an individual whose only role with respect to the application is physically handling a completed application form; or transmitting a completed form to a lender on behalf of a borrower or prospective borrower. This interpretation is consistent with the definition of "mortgage loan originator" in section 1503(3) of the SAFE Act.

Not Taking a Loan Application: Other Examples

An individual does *not* take a loan application merely because the individual assists a borrower, or prospective borrower, who is filling out an application by:

- **Explaining the contents** of the application and where particular borrower information is to be provided on the application.
- **Generally describing** the loan application process without a discussion of particular loan products.

An individual also does *not* take a loan application merely because the individual

- **Responds to an inquiry** regarding a prequalified offer that a borrower, or prospective borrower, has received from a lender.
- **Collects only basic identifying information** about the borrower or prospective borrower on behalf of that lender.

Required Conduct: Offering or Negotiating the Terms of a Loan

The following examples are designed to illustrate when an individual **offers or negotiates terms of a loan** within the meaning of Section 1008.103(c)(2): and **would require** state licensing.

Presenting Particular Loan Terms: Example 1

Offering or negotiating the terms of a loan includes:

Presenting for consideration by a borrower or prospective borrower particular loan terms, whether verbally, in writing, or otherwise, even if:

- Further verification of information is necessary.
- The offer is conditional.
- Other individuals must complete the loan process.
- The individual lacks authority to negotiate the interest rate or other loan terms.
- The individual lacks authority to bind the person that is the source of the prospective financing.

Communicating a Mutual Understanding of Terms: Example 2

Communicating directly or indirectly with a borrower or prospective borrower for the purpose of reaching a mutual understanding about prospective residential mortgage loan terms, including responding to a borrower or prospective borrower's request for a different rate or different fees on a pending loan application by presenting to the borrower or prospective borrower a revised loan offer, even if a mutual understanding is *not* subsequently achieved.

Exempt Activities Not Requiring State Licensure

The following examples are designed to illustrate what does *not* constitute offering or negotiating terms of a loan within the meaning of Section 1008.103(c)(2):

- Providing general explanations or descriptions in response to consumer queries, such as explaining loan terminology (*e.g.,* debt-to-income ratio) or lending policies (*e.g.,* the loan-to-value ratio policy of the lender), or describing product-related services.
- Arranging the loan closing or other aspects of the loan process, including by communicating with a borrower or prospective borrower about those arrangements, provided that any communication that includes a discussion about loan terms only verifies terms already agreed to by the borrower or prospective borrower.
- Providing a borrower or prospective borrower with information unrelated to loan terms, such as the best days of the month for scheduling loan closings at the bank.
- Making an underwriting decision about whether the borrower or prospective borrower qualifies for a loan.
- Explaining or describing the steps that a borrower or prospective borrower would need to take in order to obtain a loan offer, including providing general guidance about qualifications or criteria that would need to be met that is *not* specific to that borrower or prospective borrower's circumstances.
- Communicating on behalf of a mortgage loan originator that a written offer has been sent to a borrower or prospective borrower without providing any details of that offer.
- Offering or negotiating loan terms solely through a third-party licensed mortgage loan originator, so long as the non-licensed individual does *not* represent to the public that he or she can or will perform covered activities and does *not* communicate with the borrower or potential borrower.

Examples

- A seller who provides financing to a purchaser of a dwelling owned by that seller in which the offer and negotiation of loan terms with the borrower, or prospective borrower, is conducted exclusively by a third-party licensed mortgage loan originator.

- An individual who works solely for a lender, when the individual offers loan terms exclusively to third-party licensed mortgage loan originators and *not* to borrowers or potential borrowers.

Required Conduct: For Compensation or Gain

An individual acts **"for compensation or gain"** within the meaning of Section 1008.103(c)(2)(ii) if the individual receives or expects to receive, in connection with the individual's activities, **anything of value,** including, but *not* limited to, payment of a salary, bonus, or commission. The concept "anything of value" is interpreted broadly and is *not* limited only to payments that are contingent upon the closing of a loan.

Exempt Activities: Not For Compensation or Gain

An individual does *not* act "for compensation or gain" if the individual acts as a volunteer, without receiving, or expecting to receive, anything of value in connection with the individual's activities.

Required Conduct: Engaging in the Business of a Mortgage loan originator

An individual who acts (or holds himself or herself out as acting) as a mortgage loan originator in a **commercial context** and with some degree of **habitualness** or **repetition** is considered to be "engaged in the business of a mortgage loan originator."

Commercial Context

An individual who acts as a mortgage loan originator does so in a **commercial context** if the individual acts for the purpose of obtaining anything of value for himself or herself, or for an entity, or individual.

Habitualness or Repetition

The **habitualness** or **repetition** of the origination activities that is needed to "engage in the business of a mortgage loan originator" may be met either if the individual who acts as a mortgage loan originator does so with a degree of habitualness or repetition, or if the source of the prospective financing provides mortgage financing or performs other origination activities with a degree of habitualness or repetition.

Exempt Activities: Not Requiring Licensure

The following examples illustrate when an individual generally does *not* "engage in the business of a mortgage loan originator":

(1) An individual who acts as a mortgage loan originator in providing financing for the sale of that individual's own residence, provided that the individual does *not* act as a mortgage loan originator or provide financing for such sales so frequently and under such circumstances that it constitutes a habitual and commercial activity.

(2) An individual who acts as a mortgage loan originator in providing financing for the sale of a property owned by that individual, provided that such individual does not engage in such activity with habitualness.

(3) A parent who acts as a mortgage loan originator in providing loan financing to his or her child.

(4) An employee of a government entity who acts as a mortgage loan originator only pursuant to his or her official duties as an employee of that government entity, if all applicable conditions in Section 1008.103(e)(6) of this part are met.

(5) If all applicable conditions in Section 1008.103(e)(7) of this part are met, an employee of a nonprofit organization that has been determined to be a bona fide nonprofit organization by the state supervisory

authority, when the employee acts as a mortgage loan originator pursuant to his or her duties as an employee of that organization.

(6) An individual who does *not* act as a mortgage loan originator habitually or repeatedly, provided that the source of prospective financing does *not* provide mortgage financing or perform other loan origination activities habitually or repeatedly.

Loan Processing/Underwriting Activities that Require Licensing

An individual who is a **loan processor** or **underwriter** that must obtain and maintain a state mortgage loan originator license includes:

- Any individual who **engages in the business of a mortgage loan originator** as defined in the SAFE Act.

- Any individual who performs clerical or support duties and who is an **independent contractor**, as those terms are defined in the SAFE Act.

- Any individual who collects, receives, distributes, or analyzes information in connection with the making of a credit decision and who is an **independent contractor**, as that term is defined in the SAFE Act.

- Any individual who communicates with a consumer to obtain information necessary for making a credit decision and who is an **independent contractor**, as that term is defined in the SAFE Act.

Loan Processing/Underwriting Activities that Do Not Require Licensing

A state is *not* required to impose SAFE Act licensing requirements on any individual loan processor or underwriter who:

- Performs *only* clerical or support duties (i.e., the loan processor's or underwriter's activities *do not* include, e.g., offering or negotiating loan rates or terms, or counseling borrowers or prospective borrowers about loan rates or terms), and who performs those clerical or support duties at the direction of and subject to the supervision and instruction of an individual who either: Is licensed and registered in accordance with Section 1008.103(a) (state licensing of mortgage loan originators); or is *not* required to be licensed because he or she is excluded from the licensing requirement pursuant to Section 1008.103(e)(2) (time-share exclusion), (e)(5)(federally registered mortgage loan originator), (e)(6) (government employees exclusion), or (e)(7) (nonprofit exclusion).

- Performs only clerical or support duties as an employee of a mortgage lender or mortgage brokerage firm, and who performs those duties at the direction of and subject to the supervision and instruction of an individual who is employed by the same employer and who is licensed in accordance with Section 1008.103(a) (state licensing of mortgage loan originators).

- Is an employee of a loan processing or underwriting company that provides loan processing or underwriting services to one or more mortgage lenders or mortgage brokerage firms under a contract between the loan processing or underwriting company and the mortgage lenders or mortgage brokerage firms, provided the employee performs only clerical or support duties and performs those duties only at the direction of and subject to the supervision and instruction of a licensed mortgage loan originator employee of the same loan processing and underwriting company.

- Is an individual who does *not* otherwise perform the activities of a mortgage loan originator and is *not* involved in the receipt, collection, distribution, or analysis of information common for the processing or underwriting of a residential mortgage loan, nor is in communication with the consumer to obtain such information.

Actual Nexus

In order to conclude that an individual who performs clerical or support duties is doing so at the direction of and subject to the supervision and instruction of a mortgage loan originator who is licensed or registered in accordance with Section 1008.103 (or, as applicable, an individual who is excluded from the licensing and registration requirements under Section 1008.103(e)(2), (e)(6), or (e)(7)), there must be an **actual nexus** between the licensed or registered mortgage loan originator's (or excluded individual's) direction, supervision, and instruction and the loan processor or underwriter's activities.

This actual nexus must be more than a nominal relationship on an organizational chart. For example, there is an actual nexus when:

(1) The supervisory licensed or registered mortgage loan originator assigns, authorizes, and monitors the loan processor or underwriter employee's performance of clerical and support duties.

(2) The supervisory licensed or registered mortgage loan originator exercises traditional supervisory responsibilities, including, but *not* limited to, the training, mentoring, and evaluation of the loan processor or underwriter employee.

Other Circumstances That Require a State Mortgage Loan Originator License

SAFE Act compliant licensing is required for a licensed attorney if the individual is engaged in the business of a mortgage loan originator as defined in the SAFE Act.

Other Circumstances That Do Not Require a State Mortgage Loan Originator License

SAFE Act-compliant licensing is *not* required for a licensed attorney performing activities that come within the definition of a mortgage loan originator. The attorney is *not* required to be licensed, provided that such activities are:

- Considered by the state's court of last resort (or other state governing body responsible for regulating the practice of law) to be part of the authorized practice of law within the state.
- Carried out within an attorney-client relationship.
- Accomplished by the attorney in compliance with all applicable laws, rules, ethics, and standards.

Advertising

The unique identifier of any person originating a residential mortgage loan shall be clearly shown on **all** residential mortgage loan application forms, solicitations or advertisements, including business cards or websites, and any other documents as established by rule, regulation or order of the state regulatory authority.

Prohibited Advertising Practices

It is prohibited for a mortgage loan originator to:

- Solicit, advertise, or enter into a contract for specific interest rates, points, or other financing terms unless the terms are actually available at the time of soliciting, advertising, or contracting.
- Make, in any manner, any false or deceptive statement or representation, or optional add on, including, with regard to the rates, points, or other financing terms or conditions for a residential mortgage loan, or engage in bait and switch advertising.

KEY TERM REVIEW

Administrative or Clerical Tasks The receipt, collection, and distribution of information common for the processing or underwriting of a loan in the mortgage industry and communication with a consumer to obtain information necessary for the processing or underwriting of a residential mortgage loan.

American Association of Residential Mortgage Regulators (AARMR) The national association of executives and employees of the various states who are charged with the responsibility for administration and regulation of residential mortgage lending, servicing, and brokering, and dedicated to the goals described at *www.aarmr.org.*

Application A request, in any form, for an offer (or a response to a solicitation of an offer) of residential mortgage loan terms, and the information about the borrower or prospective borrower that is customary or necessary in a decision on whether to make such an offer.

Bureau The Consumer Financial Protection Bureau.

Clerical or Support Duties: (1) Includes: (i) The receipt, collection, distribution, and analysis of information common for the processing or underwriting of a residential mortgage loan; and (ii) Communicating with a consumer to obtain the information necessary for the processing or underwriting of a loan, to the extent that such communication does not include offering or negotiating loan rates or terms, or counseling consumers about residential mortgage loan rates or terms; and (2) Does not include: (i) Taking a residential mortgage loan application; or (ii) Offering or negotiating terms of a residential mortgage loan.

Conference of State Bank Supervisors (CSBS) The national organization composed of state bank supervisors dedicated to maintaining the state banking system and state regulation of financial services in accordance with the CSBS statement of principles described at www.csbs.org.

Consumer Financial Protection Bureau (CFPB) The Dodd-Frank Wall Street Reform and Consumer Protection Act of 2010 (Dodd-Frank Act) established the CFPB. The CFPB consolidates most Federal consumer financial protection authority in one place. The Consumer Bureau is focused on one goal: Watching out for American consumers in the market for consumer financial products and services.

Director The Director of the Consumer Financial Protection Bureau. In January of 2012, President Barack Obama appointed Rich Cordray to be the first Director of the CFPB.

Dodd-Frank Wall Street Reform and Consumer Protection Act In 2010, the US Congress passed the largest financial regulation overhaul since the 1930s. The two titles of the Dodd-Frank Wall Street Reform and Consumer Protection Act of 2010 with the greatest impact on the mortgage industry are Title X, designated as the **Consumer Financial Protection Act**, and Title XIV, designated as the **Mortgage Reform and Anti-Predatory Lending Act**.

Employee An individual: (1) Whose manner and means of performance of work are subject to the right of control of, or are controlled by, a person, and (2) Whose compensation for Federal income tax purposes is reported, or required to be reported, on a W-2 form issued by the controlling person.

Farm Credit Administration The independent federal agency, authorized by the Farm Credit Act of 1971 that examines and regulates the Farm Credit System.

Independent Contractor An individual who performs his or her duties other than at the direction of and subject to the supervision and instruction of an individual who is licensed and registered in accordance with § 1008.103(a), or is not required to be licensed, in accordance with § 1008.103(e)(5), (6), or (7).

Loan Processor or Underwriter An individual who, with respect to the origination of a residential mortgage loan, performs clerical or support duties at the direction of and subject to the supervision and instruction of: (1) A state-licensed mortgage loan originator; or (2) A registered mortgage loan originator.

Nationwide Mortgage Licensing System and Registry (NMLS) The mortgage licensing system developed and maintained by the Conference of State Bank Supervisors and the American Association of Residential Mortgage Regulators for the licensing and registration of mortgage loan originators and the registration of registered mortgage loan originators or any system established by the Director, as provided in subpart D of this part.

Nontraditional Mortgage Product Any mortgage product other than a 30-year fixed-rate mortgage.

Origination of a Residential Mortgage Loan (*For purposes of the definition of loan processor or underwriter*) All residential mortgage loan-related activities from the taking of a residential mortgage loan application through the completion of all required loan closing documents and funding of the residential mortgage loan.

Real Estate Brokerage Activities Any activity that involves offering or providing real estate brokerage services to the public including— (1) Acting as a real estate agent or real estate broker for a buyer, seller, lessor, or lessee of real property; (2) Bringing together parties interested in the sale, purchase, lease, rental, or exchange of real property; (3) Negotiating, on behalf of any party, any portion of a contract relating to the sale, purchase, lease, rental, or exchange of real property (other than in connection with providing financing with respect to any such transaction); (4) Engaging in any activity for which a person engaged in the activity is required to be registered as a real estate agent or real estate broker under any applicable law; and (5) Offering to engage in any activity, or act in any capacity, described in paragraphs (1), (2), (3), or (4) of this definition.

Residential Mortgage Loan Any loan primarily for personal, family, or household use that is secured by a mortgage, deed of trust, or other equivalent consensual security interest on a dwelling (as defined in section 103(w) of the Truth in Lending Act) or residential real estate upon which is constructed or intended to be constructed a dwelling (as so defined).

Secure and Fair Enforcement for Mortgage Licensing Act (SAFE Act) A key element of the Housing and Economic Recovery Act of 2008 (HERA) designed to enhance consumer protection and reduce fraud by requiring states to establish minimum standards for the licensing and registration of mortgage loan originators.

State Any state of the United States, the District of Columbia, any territory of the United States, Puerto Rico, Guam, American Samoa, the Virgin Islands, and the Commonwealth of the Northern Mariana Islands.

Unique Identifier A number or other identifier that: (1) Permanently identifies a mortgage loan originator; (2) Is assigned by protocols established by the Nationwide Mortgage Licensing System and Registry and the Bureau to facilitate electronic tracking of mortgage loan originators and uniform identification of, and public access to, the employment history of and the publicly adjudicated disciplinary and enforcement actions against mortgage loan originators; and (3) Shall *not* be used for purposes other than those set forth under the SAFE Act.

UST Content Quiz

1. *The state regulatory authority may suspend or revoke an MLO license for failure to*

   A. consider opening an additional location in a low-income area.
   B. display a unique NMLS identifier for each branch office.
   C. provide proper disclosures to a borrower.
   D. request a copy of the annual report.

2. *Performing which task requires licensing?*

   A. analyzing a loan application that is received from a consumer
   B. communicating details of a loan closing arrangement
   C. making an underwriting decision
   D. offering or negotiating loan terms

3. *Which fact about a borrower may an underwriter take into consideration when approving a mortgage loan application?*

   A. ancestry
   B. likelihood of continued income
   C. marital status
   D. receipt of public assistance

4. *Who is exempt from licensing under the SAFE Act?*

   A. Bradford, a registered mortgage loan originator who is an independent contractor
   B. Lavinia, an administrative assistant who negotiates the terms of a residential mortgage loan on behalf of the mortgage loan originator while he is on vacation
   C. Rachael, who negotiates the terms of a residential mortgage loan on behalf her best friend
   D. Trace, who negotiates the terms of a residential mortgage loan on behalf of his sister

   FAMILY

5. *Which is an example of "offering or negotiating the terms of a loan"?*

   A. communicating details of loan closing arrangements
   B. communicating directly or indirectly with a borrower in order to reach a mutual understanding about prospective residential mortgage loan terms
   C. describing the steps that a borrower or prospective borrower would need to take in order to obtain a loan offer
   D. providing general explanations or responses to consumer inquiries about loan programs

6. *All of these are required of the state regulatory authority EXCEPT to*

   A. approve or deny mortgage loan originator license applications.
   B. approve prelicensing and continuing educational course offerings and course providers.
   C. establish procedures for appropriate enforcement and/or disciplinary actions.
   D. examine or investigate licensees in a systematic manner based on identified risk factors or on a periodic schedule.

7. *The SAFE Act made it the responsibility of states to use unique identifiers instead of*

   A. drivers license numbers.
   B. federal tax id numbers.
   C. Social Security numbers.
   D. telephone numbers.

8. *David is a loan processor who is exempt from licensure as a mortgage loan originator. Which of the following acts would constitute a violation under the SAFE Act?*

   A. David calls a consumer directly to obtain some basic information that was cut-off when the loan application form was faxed.

   B. David circulates a business card that indicates he provides loan origination services.

   C. David distributes loan application information received from the consumer to the underwriter for further analysis.

   D. David inputs loan application information into the computer system to prepare for analysis.

9. *Who would be subject to fines and penalties if a kickback is paid?*

   A. all parties paying or receiving a kickback

   B. the person who initiated the kickback arrangement

   C. the person who received the kickback

   D. no one, assuming that it was paid for services actually rendered

10. *A mortgage loan originator is NOT required to provide a GFE or a TIL if the borrower*

    A. applies for loans from multiple lenders.

    B. s unlikely to be approved for a loan.

    C. refuses to provide the government monitoring data required in the application.

    D. withdraws the application within 3 business days.

11. *All of these examples illustrate an individual NOT engaged in the business of a mortgage loan originator EXCEPT*

    A. Helen provides the financing for the sale of her own residence.

    B. Ivan provides mortgage loan financing for his child, Ivan Jr.

    C. Jennifer acts as a mortgage loan originator fulfilling her duties as an employee of a non-profit organization.

    D. Kirk provides financing for the sale of multiple properties he owns repeatedly and with habitualness.

12. *George is starting his own business in this state. Previously, George was a director, employed by a mortgage lending company in Massachusetts whose principal's lending license was revoked for violations associated with making improper disclosures and misleading statements to borrowers. George was NOT personally convicted. Will George likely be granted a mortgage loan originator license in this state?*

    A. It is likely he may be granted a license since George was *not* personally convicted of the crime in another state.

    B. It is likely he may be granted a license since the license revocation did *not* occur in this state.

    C. It is likely he may be granted a license since the violation that resulted in revocation did *not* involve fraud.

    D. It is *not* likely that he will be granted a license since George served as a director for a mortgage lending company whose license was revoked in another state.

13. *A mortgage broker rents office space from a title company at a discount in exchange for referring customers for settlement services. Which law does this arrangement violate?*

    A. RESPA

    B. SAFE Act

    C. TILA

    D. It does not violate any law

14. *Which of these situations would NOT violate ECOA?*

    A. While looking at your customer's loan application and check stubs, you notice that support payments are being made and ask, "Do you pay monthly child support, alimony, or separate maintenance?"

    B. Your customer's income information includes aid to dependent children from the state. You ask, "Are you sure you want to include this as part of your income on this application? It won't look good."

    C. Your customer's last name is Singh and you observe, "That's Indian, right?"

    D. Your very pregnant customer is sitting at your desk while two more little ones who came in with her are running around your office. You ask her, "Do you think this is your last child?"

15. **According to the SAFE Act definition, a nontraditional mortgage loan is**

    A. any 30-year fixed rate mortgage loan.
    B. any 30-year fixed rate mortgage loan obtained through the FHA or VA.
    C. any 30-year fixed rate mortgage loan that has an escrow account associated with it.
    D. any mortgage loan that is *not* a 30-year fixed rate mortgage loan.

16. **An individual's act is "for compensation or gain" only when that individual**

    A. achieves a profit (capital gain) from the transaction.
    B. has ownership interest in the transaction.
    C. is a W-2 employee.
    D. receives anything of value.

17. **Under the SAFE Act, a state has all of the following authorities EXCEPT**

    A. to deny, suspend, or revoke licenses.
    B. to issue cease and desist orders.
    C. to waive the requirement for fingerprints for an initial license application.
    D. to write rules and regulations.

18. **The state regulatory authority may deny a mortgage loan originator applicant a license if the applicant has**

    A. been convicted of any felony in the last 10 years.
    B. ever been convicted of an act of domestic violence or endangering a minor, unless pardoned.
    C. ever been convicted of an act of fraud, dishonesty, breach of trust, or money laundering, unless pardoned.
    D. ever been convicted of driving under the influence.

19. **Arianna has failed to pass the written test for her MLO license two consecutive times. She can retake the test after waiting**

    A. 10 days.
    B. 30 days.
    C. 6 weeks.
    D. 6 months.

20. **A borrower closed a loan last week with ABC Mortgage Company. Her name is on the National Do Not Call Registry and on ABC's internal Do Not Call list. ABC**

    A. can call her for up to 3 months because they have an established business relationship.
    B. can call her for up to 18 months from the transaction date.
    C. cannot call her because she is on ABC's internal list.
    D. cannot call her because she is on the National Do Not Call Registry.

Practice Exams

Practice Exam #1: MLO National Test with UST

1. *A customer asks his mortgage broker for the name of a good title company. The broker has a list of several companies with whom she has done business in the past. At what point, according to RESPA, must she give the customer an AfBA disclosure?*

   A. at least three days prior to closing
   B. at the closing table
   C. at the same time that she gives the customer the list of title companies
   D. She is not required to give the customer an AfBA disclosure if she has no ownership or other interest in any of the title companies on the list.

2. *Which would NOT be considered a RESPA violation?*

   A. You pay for all the advertising for your favorite real estate agent to keep the referrals coming in.
   B. You refer your borrower client to a title company that you own.
   C. You rent space in a title company office below market value for the convenience of letting them handle your loans.
   D. Your primary lender takes you on a weekend golf trip, all expenses paid, if you close 10 loans in a month with them.

3. *The Real Estate Settlement Procedures Act (RESPA) is implemented under*

   A. Regulation B.
   B. Regulation C.
   C. Regulation X.
   D. Regulation Z.

4. *Which includes the provision that mortgage relief companies may NOT collect any fees until they have provided consumers with a written offer from their lender or servicer that is acceptable?*

   A. Financial Privacy Rule
   B. MARS Rule
   C. Red Flags Rule
   D. Safeguards Rule

5. *What type of loan requires a non-refundable funding fee?*

   A. conventional loan
   B. FHA loan
   C. subprime loan
   D. VA loan

6. *What is a provision in a mortgage enabling the lender to demand full repayment if the borrower sells the mortgaged property or partial interest in a mortgaged property?*

   A. acceleration clause
   B. alienation clause
   C. partial lien release
   D. prepayment penalty clause

7. *When evaluating a Good Faith Estimate, each of these are subject to a 10% tolerance EXCEPT*

   A. government recording charges.
   B. owner's title insurance.
   C. services the borrower can shop for.
   D. transfer taxes.

8. **Which act encourages financial institutions to help meet the credit needs of their communities, including low- and moderate-income neighborhoods, consistent with safe and sound lending practices?**

    A. CRA

    B. HOEPA

    C. RESPA

    D. TILA

9. **Which requires that all financial institutions ensure the security and confidentiality of customer records?**

    A. Bank Secrecy Act

    B. Dodd-Frank Wall Street Reform and Consumer Protection Act

    C. MARS Rule

    D. Safeguards Rule

10. **Conforming loans follow the underwriting guidelines of**

    A. Fannie Mae and Freddie Mac.

    B. FHA and VA.

    C. Freddie Mac and Ginnie Mae.

    D. Ginnie Mae and HUD.

11. **ECOA is a law that ensures**

    A. borrowers are shown how much they will pay for credit in dollars and percentages.

    B. financial institutions provide funding for low-income and moderate-income housing.

    C. lenders make credit available with fairness and without discrimination.

    D. settlement procedures are regulated so buyers can compare the cost of services.

12. **A 65-year-old homeowner does not currently have a mortgage on his home but is in need of funds to make some substantial repairs and is living on a small fixed income. Which mortgage option would best address his need?**

    A. blanket mortgage

    B. equity participation mortgage

    C. reverse mortgage

    D. wraparound mortgage

13. **The borrower knows that his credit is bad, but he really wants to buy a house. He convinces his cousin to apply for a loan, knowing she will be able to get better terms. He promises her that he will pay the full mortgage amount every month. She could be considered a(n)**

    A. identity thief.

    B. investor.

    C. mortgage rescuer.

    D. straw buyer.

14. **An FHA borrower may**

    A. be eligible only if qualified as low-income.

    B. buy a six-unit dwelling.

    C. purchase a home with nothing down.

    D. use a gift for the entire down payment.

15. **The value remaining in property after all liens and debts are considered is its**

    A. assessment.

    B. equity.

    C. surety.

    D. valuation.

16. **A borrower is refinancing his home and signs the loan papers. How much time does Regulation Z give him to change his mind?**

    A. 3 business days

    B. 30 days

    C. 3 years

    D. He has no right of rescission.

17. **An 80/20 combo loan with the sales price of $175,000, a rate of 6% for the 80% first mortgage, and a rate of 8.5% for the 20% second mortgage would have a first mortgage loan amount of what?**

    A. $35,000

    B. $105,000

    C. $140,000

    D. $175,000

18. **A convertible ARM allows a borrower to change**

    A. from an adjustable rate mortgage to a fixed rate mortgage.

    B. the index on which the interest rate is based.

    C. the margin when interest rates rise.

    D. the rate cap when interest rates fall.

19. *The act of redlining may be defined as*

    A. channeling buyers to certain neighborhoods based on their race or ethnic background.

    B. charging a greater rate of interest on a mortgage loan than the law allows.

    C. refusing to make loans, limiting loans, or making loans with less favorable terms on property in certain neighborhoods for discriminatory reasons.

    D. using voluntary reconveyance or friendly forfeiture to avoid judicial foreclosure.

20. *A borrower wants to get a loan to buy a house. When evaluating his credit obligations, which would NOT be considered as debt?*

    A. cable service payment

    B. car payment

    C. child support payments

    D. credit card payments

21. *HOEPA amends what law?*

    A. ECOA

    B. FCRA

    C. RESPA

    D. TILA

22. *The relationship between the cost of borrowing and the total amount financed, represented as a percentage, is known as*

    A. an ARM.

    B. the APR.

    C. a discount point.

    D. the note rate.

23. *While underwriting a loan file, you calculate this formula: PITI divided by gross monthly income. What have you just determined?*

    A. housing expense ratio

    B. loan-to-value ratio

    C. stable monthly income ratio

    D. total debt to income ratio

24. *Which loan characteristic may be used to determine the fee that a mortgage loan originator is paid?*

    A. annual percentage rate charged

    B. interest rate charged

    C. loan-to-value ratio

    D. total loan amount

25. *An opinion of value is also known as*

    A. an appraisal.

    B. a comparable.

    C. market value.

    D. an offer.

26. *TILA requires creditors to maintain records that they complied with the disclosure requirements for how many years?*

    A. one

    B. two

    C. three

    D. four

27. *What is the maximum length of time that collection information can be reported on a credit report according to the Fair Credit Reporting Act?*

    A. indefinitely

    B. 10 years

    C. 7 years

    D. 3 years

28. *A borrower has a stable monthly income of $4,000 and recurring debts of $600. If he's getting an FHA loan, what's the maximum monthly payment for which he would qualify?*

    A. $1,054

    B. $1,120

    C. $1,240

    D. $1,462

29. *Which law allows a consumer who has had her credit card used by an identify thief to place a freeze on her credit report?*

    A. CRA

    B. ECOA

    C. FACTA

    D. SAFE Act

30. *You are pre-qualifying a borrower for a purchase loan. She has debt equaling $950 each month and gross monthly income totaling $5,200 each month. What is the maximum qualifying house payment, including principal, interest, taxes and insurance on a conventional loan?*

    A. $590

    B. $922

    C. $1,000

    D. $1,456

31. **Under the FCRA, consumers do NOT have the right to**

    A. dispute inaccurate information in writing and demand the information be removed from the credit report.
    B. inspect information on their credit reports.
    C. receive a free copy of their credit report even if they have not applied for credit.
    D. require bankruptcies be removed from their credit report after five years, if credit has been reestablished.

32. **Which situation is NOT a red flag that illegal flipping may be taking place?**

    A. a group of sellers and buyers changing ownership of one property among them
    B. an inflated appraisal
    C. purchasing and remodeling a house and selling it for quick profit
    D. a series of sales and quick resales

33. **A borrower closes a loan with ABC Mortgage. His name is NOT on the National Do Not Call Registry nor on ABC's internal do not call list. ABC Mortgage can call the borrower to solicit new business**

    A. for up to 3 months from the transaction date.
    B. for up to 12 months from the transaction date.
    C. for up to 18 months from the transaction date.
    D. indefinitely.

34. **Which loans are NOT covered under HMDA?**

    A. commercial loans
    B. home improvement loans
    C. home purchases for any residential dwelling
    D. refinancing a loan previously covered under RESPA

35. **You are refinancing a $200,000 mortgage with a prepayment penalty of six months of interest at 6.5%. How much is the prepayment penalty?**

    A. $1,083
    B. $2,500
    C. $6,500
    D. $13,000

36. **A borrower reports income of $40,000 from rental properties. How much of that should be considered when applying for a mortgage loan?**

    A. $40,000
    B. $32,000
    C. $30,000
    D. $20,000

37. **Which includes a general definition (essentially an outline) of a qualified mortgage (QM) loan?**

    A. Equal Credit Opportunity Act
    B. Dodd-Frank Act
    C. Gramm-Leach-Bliley Act
    D. Truth in Lending Act

38. **What is the maximum LTV on a Rural Development loan?**

    A. 75%
    B. 80%
    C. 90%
    D. 100%

39. **During the application process, an MLO asks if the borrower is widowed; he is violating which law?**

    A. ECOA
    B. Fair Housing
    C. FCRA
    D. RESPA

40. **Under Regulation Z, which advertisement would require full disclosure of credit terms?**

    A. "Affordable rates available"
    B. "Assume loan at 8% interest"
    C. "Low down payment"
    D. "We'll work with you"

41. **The Privacy Rule of the Gramm-Leach-Bliley Act requires that financial institutions provide the consumer with a Consumer Privacy Policy**

    A. before disclosing information to non-affiliated third parties.
    B. each time the servicing is transferred.
    C. three business days prior to closing.
    D. within three business days of applying for a loan.

42. **A borrower is buying a house with a sales price of $200,000 and an LTV of 75%. If he pays two discount points, what is the total cost of the points?**

    A. $1,500
    B. $2,000
    C. $3,000
    D. $4,000

43. **RESPA's Section 8 prohibits all fees EXCEPT**

    A. earned fees.
    B. giving a referral fee.
    C. receiving a referral fee.
    D. unearned fees.

44. **What is NOT considered a protected class under the Fair Housing Act?**

    A. age
    B. race
    C. religion
    D. sex

45. **HMDA**

    A. applies only to new purchase loans.
    B. establishes a quota for mortgage loans within a certain geographic area.
    C. identifies possible discriminatory lending patterns.
    D. prohibits lenders from considering an applicant's religion.

46. **If an MLO or a real estate agent engages in the practice of soliciting homeowners in a particular community to sell their properties because people of other races, religions, or social status have purchased in the area, they would be guilty of**

    A. blockbusting.
    B. fraud.
    C. redlining.
    D. steering.

47. **Which household does NOT qualify as a protected class under the familial status clause of the Fair Housing Act?**

    A. family with a single parent and children
    B. grandparents raising their grandchildren
    C. pregnant woman
    D. retired couple

48. **A homeowner's house appraises for $125,000. He qualifies for an 85% LTV. He owes $63,000 on his first mortgage and $5,000 on his second mortgage. He would like to refinance his house into one mortgage loan and receive additional cash to pay off other debt. How much cash would be available if his closing costs are $4,200 and are financed in the loan?**

    A. $34,050
    B. $38,250
    C. $43,250
    D. $52,800

49. **A residential lender is EXEMPT from the policies of the federal Civil Rights Act**

    A. at all times; federal civil rights laws apply only to agents who sell property, not to lenders.
    B. when the loan is for less than $50,000.
    C. when the loan is for vacant land.
    D. never; a lender is not exempt from civil rights laws affecting property.

50. **The down payment requirement for a VA loan can be as little as**

    A. 0%.
    B. 3.5%.
    C. 5%.
    D. 10%.

51. **Which mortgage clause allows a lender to declare the entire unpaid balance due on a borrower's default?**

    A. acceleration
    B. escalator
    C. foreclosure
    D. forfeiture

52. **Which two federal acts have the most pertinent disclosure requirements related to loan terms?**

    A. CRA and FCRA
    B. ECOA and FACT Act
    C. ECOA and RESPA
    D. RESPA and TILA

53. **Ralph and Alice are thinking about getting an HECM reverse mortgage. If they choose the tenure payment option, they will receive their money as**

    A. a lump sum.
    B. a line of credit to borrow against as needed.
    C. equal monthly payments for a fixed number of months.
    D. equal monthly payments for as long as they stay in the home.

54. **What risk is PMI intended to cover?**

    A. death of the borrowers
    B. loss by foreclosure
    C. interest rates rising
    D. loss in property value serving as collateral

55. *According to the definition provided by the Consumer Financial Protection Bureau, which is a feature that a qualified mortgage (QM) CANNOT have?*

    A. amortization
    B. balloon payment
    C. buydown
    D. private mortgage insurance

56. *The purpose of using PITI to structure payments in a mortgage is to*

    A. allow the borrower to obtain actual cash from the equity built up in the property.
    B. allow the lender to participate in any earnings, income, or profits generated.
    C. ensure that enough funds are collected to cover taxes and insurance premiums.
    D. include the financing of personal property such as appliances or furnishings.

57. *Provisions in title III of the USA Patriot Act amended which law?*

    A. Bank Secrecy Act/Anti-Money Laundering Act
    B. Dodd-Frank Act
    C. Real Estate Settlement Procedures Act
    D. SAFE Act

58. *What terminology is the only correct way to ask a client about his or her marital status?*

    A. Are you married or divorced?
    B. Are you married, unmarried, or separated?
    C. Are you single, married, or widowed?
    D. You cannot ask this question since marital status is a protected class.

59. *With an ARM, the margin is added to the _____ to determine the _____ .*

    A. APR / cost of funds index
    B. home value / amount borrowed
    C. index / interest rate charged
    D. qualifying ratio / maximum monthly mortgage payment

60. *The interim final rule on Valuation Independence does NOT prohibit an appraiser from*

    A. being instructed to hit a specific property value so that the consumer can get a loan he wants.
    B. being paid a fee by a creditor based on what's customary for that area.
    C. materially misrepresenting the value of the consumer's principal dwelling.
    D. offering an opinion of value on a property for which he or she has only an indirect conflict of interest.

61. *A lender is obligated to provide a borrower with what document one business day prior to the loan closing if requested to do so?*

    A. GFE
    B. HUD-1
    C. mortgage servicing statement
    D. promissory note

62. *The right of rescission is in effect for what type of loan closing?*

    A. owner-occupied purchase
    B. owner-occupied refinance
    C. non-owner-occupied purchase
    D. non-owner-occupied refinance

63. *A borrower with less than perfect credit or other risk factors may qualify most easily for what type of loan?*

    A. conforming
    B. FHA
    C. subprime
    D. VA

64. *During the loan process, you find HMDA government monitoring information on*

    A. a custom form created by your company.
    B. the Good Faith Estimate.
    C. Section X of the Residential Loan Application.
    D. the Truth in Lending statement.

65. *Borrower A has a $100,000 30-year loan at 5%. Borrower B has a $100,000 15-year loan at 5.5%. At the end of their respective loan terms, who will have paid more principal?*

    A. Borrower A
    B. Borrower B
    C. Both borrowers would pay the same amount of principal.
    D. It's impossible to tell since either could pay off the loan sooner.

66. **Funds for FHA loans are provided by**

    A. the Federal Reserve.

    B. the FHA.

    C. HUD.

    D. qualified lending institutions.

67. **With a fixed rate loan,**

    A. a balloon payment is due at the end of the loan term for any unpaid interest.

    B. a lender may increase the interest rate if a borrower misses two payments in a year.

    C. PMI is required if the LTV exceeds 20%.

    D. principal and interest payments must remain constant.

68. **According to the Fair Credit Reporting Act, which of these would NOT have a valid need to information from a consumer credit reporting agency?**

    A. a "buy here, pay here" car lot

    B. an employer looking to hire a sales agent

    C. a landlord thinking of renting a home to someone

    D. a man who wants to know his brother's credit score before starting a business with him

69. **The regulation that prevents a seller from requiring the use of a particular title company is**

    A. Regulation B – Equal Credit Opportunity Act (ECOA)

    B. Regulation C – Home Mortgage Disclosure Act (HMDA)

    C. Regulation X – Real Estate Settlement Procedure Act (RESPA)

    D. Regulation Z – Truth in Lending Act (TILA)

70. **Which law requires notification to a borrower before the servicing of a loan is transferred to someone else?**

    A. ECOA

    B. HOEPA

    C. RESPA

    D. TILA

71. **According to the FCRA, a credit agency must give a consumer a free copy of his credit report**

    A. at time of a loan application.

    B. if the loan application is denied because of information in the report.

    C. never.

    D. whenever he requests it.

72. **A TIL Statement must be provided to the applicant within how many business days of a completed application?**

    A. one

    B. two

    C. three

    D. four

73. **When qualifying for a conventional mortgage loan, which would be LEAST LIKELY to count as allowable income?**

    A. annual bonuses

    B. occasional overtime

    C. retirement income

    D. salary

74. **For which transaction must a lender follow the regulations of the Truth in Lending Act?**

    A. an application to purchase a duplex where the borrower will live in one unit and rent the other

    B. an application to purchase a farm

    C. an application to purchase a warehouse

    D. a corporation's application to purchase a condominium for the use of its contract employees

75. **A borrower who is paid $750 per week has a qualifying monthly income of**

    A. $2,999.

    B. $3,000.

    C. $3,248.

    D. $3,250.

76. **What is the most common appraisal approach used in appraising single-family housing?**

    A. cost approach

    B. highest and best use approach

    C. income approach

    D. sales comparison approach

77. **A higher priced loan is defined by TILA as one that has**

    A. an APR that exceeds the applicable average prime offer rate by at least 1.5% on first liens.

    B. an APR that exceeds the rates on Treasury securities of comparable maturity by more than 8%.

    C. total points and fees greater than 8% of the loan amount.

    D. total points and fees greater than 10% of the loan amount for junior liens.

78. *The Financial Services Modernization Act of 1999 is more commonly known as the*

    A. Community Reinvestment Act.
    B. Gramm-Leach-Bliley Act.
    C. Homeowners Protection Act.
    D. SAFE Act.

79. *Which question would NOT be considered a violation of the ECOA, even if asked very innocently during the loan interview process?*

    A. You look very young; can you provide proof that you're 18?
    B. Your accent is really interesting; where are you from?
    C. Your name is unusual; what nationality is that?
    D. Your necklace is beautiful; is that a crucifix?

80. *Which regulation requires lenders to make full disclosure about APR to borrowers in real estate financial transactions?*

    A. Regulation C
    B. Regulation V
    C. Regulation X
    D. Regulation Z

81. *Which federal act requires that a "Notification of Action Taken" form be delivered to the applicant within 30 days of application?*

    A. ECOA
    B. HMDA
    C. RESPA
    D. TILA

82. *As of July 2011, all these laws are implemented and enforced by the Consumer Financial Protection Bureau (CFPB) EXCEPT the*

    A. Fair Housing Act.
    B. Fair and Accurate Credit Transactions Act.
    C. Fair Credit Reporting Act.
    D. Secure and Fair Enforcement for Mortgage Licensing Act.

83. *A situation where loan balance grows because of deferred due interest is known as _____ amortization.*

    A. adjustable
    B. ballooning
    C. deducting
    D. negative

84. *Which of these actions would indicate that a mortgage loan originator is NOT committed to FACTA compliance?*

    A. erasing electronic records
    B. hiring a document disposal company for weekly pick up
    C. placing locked shredding boxes throughout the office
    D. putting files in an unlocked drawer at the end of each work day

85. *Which statement about loan origination fees on a GFE is FALSE?*

    A. The fee cannot change unless there is a changed circumstance.
    B. The fee includes services performed by or on behalf of the loan originator.
    C. Lender and mortgage broker fees for the same transaction must be itemized.
    D. Origination fees must be expressed as lump sum.

86. *Who is most generally responsible for completing the accurate final HUD-1 once a closing date has been scheduled?*

    A. broker
    B. lender
    C. mortgage loan originator
    D. settlement agent

87. *A minimum of how many hours of approved prelicensing education are required by the SAFE Act for state-licensed mortgage loan originators?*

    A. 8
    B. 12
    C. 20
    D. 24

88. *Disclosing income such as child support and alimony is not required of the borrower. When this type of income is disclosed on the application, what federal act requires that it be considered in the approval process?*

    A. Equal Credit Opportunity Act
    B. Fair Credit Reporting Act
    C. Home Mortgage Disclosure Act
    D. Truth in Lending Act

89. *One purpose of the Truth in Lending Act is to*

    A. allow lenders to order credit reports, appraisals, etc.
    B. enable borrowers to compare credit costs and shop for best credit terms.
    C. inform borrower of a lender's privacy policies.
    D. prevent kickbacks by disclosing business interests.

90. *If Mary pays $695.20 for principal and interest every month for 30 years on her $110,000 loan, how much interest will she pay over the life of the loan?*

    A. $20,856
    B. $110,000
    C. $140,272
    D. $250,272

91. *A mortgage that includes more than one parcel of land is called a*

    A. blanket mortgage.
    B. package mortgage.
    C. purchase money mortgage.
    D. wraparound mortgage.

92. *Which law regulates the activities of consumer reporting agencies and users of consumer credit reports?*

    A. ECOA
    B. FCRA
    C. RESPA
    D. TILA

93. *Lending institutions gather data from Section X (Information for Government Monitoring Purposes) on the Uniform Residential Loan Application to comply with the*

    A. Bank Secrecy Act/Anti-Money Laundering Act.
    B. Equal Credit Opportunity Act.
    C. Fair Credit Reporting Act.
    D. Home Mortgage Disclosure Act.

94. *The SAFE Act is part of what larger law?*

    A. FRCA
    B. HERA
    C. RESPA
    D. TILA

95. *A telemarketer can be fined how much per incident for calling someone registered on the National Do Not Call Registry?*

    A. $5,000
    B. $10,000
    C. $16,000
    D. $20,000

96. *If a loan includes an escrow account, RESPA allows the lender to require a cushion of up to how many months?*

    A. two
    B. four
    C. six
    D. nine

97. *ABC Mortgages makes a loan even though the borrower is unlikely to repay it, anticipating that they'll eventually foreclose on the property and get the equity in the property. This is an example of*

    A. predatory lending.
    B. prime lending.
    C. secondary lending.
    D. subprime lending.

98. *The MARS Rule is intended to protect*

    A. borrowers from high-risk (toxic) loan features.
    B. consumers from companies and individuals from obtaining personal financial information.
    C. consumers from identity theft.
    D. distressed homeowners from mortgage relief scams.

99. *According to the SAFE Act, which would be considered a task that would require someone to be a licensed MLO?*

    A. assisting a borrower in obtaining a mortgage loan by offering to negotiate terms with a lender
    B. calling a mortgage loan applicant and asking him to send in three years worth of tax returns
    C. evaluating a mortgage loan application to determine if all the necessary information has been included
    D. submitting the information in a loan file to the mortgage underwriter for a credit decision

100. *A mortgage broker with 20 years of experience is neither registered nor licensed as a mortgage loan originator. If he continues his loan origination activities, he would be in violation of what law?*

    A. Gramm-Leach-Bliley Act
    B. Real Estate Settlement and Procedures Act
    C. SAFE Act
    D. He is not in violation of any federal law.

101. *Licensed lenders or brokers may be subject to an examination of their affairs, business, premises, and records by*

    A. competitors.
    B. consumers.
    C. NMLS
    D. the state regulatory authority.

102. *When a licensee ceases to engage in business and files a plan for withdrawal with the state regulatory authority, this is referred to as*

    A. cease and desist.
    B. revocation.
    C. surrender.
    D. suspension.

103. *The state regulatory authority may issue an order suspending the license of a mortgage loan originator if the MLO*

    A. applies for a transfer to change affiliation from one originating entity to another.
    B. fails to file a required report with the state regulatory authority.
    C. makes a bona fide clerical error that impacts a borrower.
    D. submits a request to be placed on inactive status.

104. *The state regulatory authority has these authorities, EXCEPT to*

    A. change NMLS testing requirements.
    B. impose a civil penalty or fine.
    C. issue cease and desist orders.
    D. issue subpoenas for witnesses and documents.

105. *Which service is NOT typically provided by the state regulatory authority*

    A. educates communities about financial issues
    B. performs on-site examinations of financial institutions
    C. provides low-interest loans for low-income families
    D. regulates the licensing process of financial institutions

106. *The unique identifier of any person originating a residential mortgage loan must be*

    A. always kept confidential.
    B. changed annually at the time of renewal.
    C. included on all forms of advertising.
    D. issued by the state regulatory authority.

107. *For purposes of licensing, an individual who takes a residential mortgage loan application or negotiates the terms of mortgage loan for compensation is NOT a*

    A. mortgage loan administrator.
    B. mortgage loan originator.
    C. residential mortgage broker.
    D. residential mortgage lender.

108. *Registered mortgage loan originator refers to a*

    A. a mortgage loan originator who is licensed under the state regulatory authority but has an office that is in another state.
    B. a mortgage loan originator who is registered with and maintains a unique identifier through the Nationwide Mortgage Licensing System and Registry.
    C. any licensed mortgage loan originator whose license has been suspended or revoked by the state regulatory authority.
    D. any licensed mortgage loan originator that is employed by a lender licensed under the state regulatory authority.

109. *Of these identify which is considered a third party in a loan transaction?*

    A. borrower
    B. closing agent
    C. mortgage broker
    D. mortgage loan originator

110. *A dwelling is defined as*

A. any residential structure that contains more than four units, whether or not that structure is attached to real property.

B. any residential structure that contains one-to-four units and is attached to real property.

C. any residential structure that contains one-to-four units, whether or not that structure is attached to real property.

D. any residential structure that is attached to real property.

111. *States may require a licensee to satisfy a*

A. net worth minimum.

B. state fund contribution amount.

C. surety bond requirement.

D. all of these choices are possible state requirements.

112. *Who is "taking" a loan application?*

A. Cole receives a loan application through the mail and forwards it on to the lender without review

B. Drew delivers a completed application form to a lender on behalf of a borrower

C. Ellen responds to a borrower's request for a different rate or fees by presenting the borrower with a revised loan offer

D. Fiona collects only basic identifying information about the borrower in response to an inquiry regarding a prequalified offer from the lender

113. *Before getting a state loan originator's license, an applicant must have a unique ID number from*

A. Department of Housing and Urban Development.

B. NMLS.

C. state regulatory authority.

D. National Association of Mortgage Professional.

114. *Tom's initial application for a mortgage broker license was denied. His notification of denial must include a*

A. reason for denial.

B. referral to another licensing agency.

C. refund of his application fee.

D. request for hearing.

115. *Maureen, a licensed mortgage loan originator, retakes the same approved 2-hour online course in nontraditional mortgage products she took the previous year but she cannot count it toward her continuing education requirements for license renewal because*

A. she cannot receive credit for the same course taken in the same or successive years.

B. she does not need to take a course in nontraditional mortgage products to meet her license renewal requirements.

C. she needs to take a 3-hour course in nontraditional mortgage products to meet her requirements.

D. she needs to take classroom-based instruction in nontraditional mortgage products to meet her requirements.

116. *All of following personal information must be included as part of an MLO license application EXCEPT*

A. authorization to obtain criminal findings from any government jurisdiction.

B. copy of licenses issued by other states.

C. credit report.

D. fingerprints for submission to a criminal background check.

117. *In addition to meeting pre-licensing education requirements and passing a written test, applicants must be able to show they have*

A. a degree from an accredited college.

B. at least five years of experience in the mortgage loan industry.

C. financial responsibility, good character, and general fitness.

D. at least three professional references.

118. *Which topic is NOT required as part of the 20 hours of a mortgage loan originator applicant's prelicensing education?*

A. federal law

B. fraud

C. nontraditional mortgage products

D. real estate concepts

119. **According to the SAFE Act, which would be considered a task that would require someone to be a licensed MLO?**

    A. assisting a borrower in obtaining a mortgage loan by offering to negotiate terms with a lender

    B. calling a mortgage loan applicant and asking him to send in three years worth of tax returns

    C. evaluating a mortgage loan application to determine if all the necessary information has been included

    D. submitting the information in a loan file to the mortgage underwriter for a credit decision

120. **Which statement about a loan originator advertising to solicit mortgage business is FALSE?**

    A. The ad must include the loan originator's unique NMLS ID.

    B. The ad must include the license number of employing broker's principal place of business.

    C. The loan originator may advertise exclusively in his or her own name.

    D. The loan originator must obtain the approval of the employing mortgage broker.

121. **A licensed MLO who terminates his affiliation with an employing mortgage broker but wishes to resume working as a mortgage loan originator in the near future may NOT**

    A. originate loans during the time he is not affiliated with an employing entity.

    B. renew his license while not affiliated with an employing broker.

    C. request that the state regulatory authority hold his license in inactive status.

    D. take NMLS approved courses to satisfy his continuing education requirements.

122. **A mortgage loan processor distributes a company business card with her name on it along with the unique identifier of the mortgage lender she works for. The loan processor handwrites a message on the card which states, "I can help you get a loan." This employee is**

    A. assisting her company in soliciting loan business which is permissible.

    B. committing a prohibited act of misrepresentation in advertising which is a violation.

    C. directly soliciting loan business under the unique identifier of a licensee which is legal.

    D. indirectly soliciting loan business which requires her to be licensed as a broker.

123. **Identify which licensee's act is legal.**

    A. Big City Mortgage Co. examined Matthew's net worth, credit score, and employment status to determine his ability to repay a loan.

    B. CapCity bank offered to send appraiser Howard more business if he would appraise a specific property for at least $150,000.

    C. Mortgage broker Dan informed his client that if she stopped making payments on her current mortgage, she would qualify for a lower interest loan.

    D. Sunshine Mortgages, Inc. gave notice to Sally and Ted that they have 90 days to repay their 15-year mortgage, which they have had for 4 years and are in good standing.

124. **Which is NOT a requirement of the Safeguards Rule of the Gramm-Leach-Bliley Act?**

    A. allow consumers to add their phone numbers to a list that prohibits unauthorized calls

    B. ensure the security and confidentiality of customer records

    C. protect against any anticipated threats or hazards to the security of consumer records

    D. protect against the unauthorized access or use of consumer information in ways that could result in substantial harm or inconvenience to customers

125. **If any triggering terms are used in an ad, which fact is EXEMPT from the disclosure requirement?**

    A. amount or percentage of down payment

    B. APR

    C. terms of repayment

    D. total closing costs

Practice Exam #2: MLO National Test with UST

1. *A mortgage broker also owns a title company. Is this business arrangement allowed by RESPA?*

   A. No, this is considered a business conflict of interest
   B. No, this is an illegal business arrangement
   C. Yes, as long as the title company is legitimate and the arrangement is disclosed
   D. Yes, but the two affiliations can never be involved in a single real estate transaction

2. *The minimum down payment contribution needed for a home with an FHA-appraised value of $132,000 (assuming a credit score above 579) is*

   A. $0.
   B. $4,620.
   C. $6,600.
   D. $26,400.

3. *As a mortgage broker puts together an ad to attract some new customers, what law should he be most concerned about?*

   A. FACTA
   B. MARS
   C. RESPA
   D. TILA

4. *Of these loans, which would require reporting under the Home Mortgage Disclosure Act?*

   A. home equity lines of credit
   B. loans purchased for the purpose of servicing those loans
   C. new construction loans
   D. vacant land loans

5. *For a loan that has escrow included, RESPA requires a lender to perform an escrow analysis*

   A. monthly.
   B. quarterly.
   C. semi-annually.
   D. annually.

6. *A borrower's name is on the National Do Not Call Registry and on the lending mortgage company internal "do not call" list. The borrower calls the mortgage company for a loan qualification. The mortgage loan originator*

   A. can call the borrower for up to three months because they have an established business relationship.
   B. can call the borrower for up to 18 months from the transaction date.
   C. cannot call the borrower because she is on the lending company's internal "do not call" list.
   D. cannot call the borrower because she is on the National Do Not Call Registry.

7. *A seller agrees to pay two points on a buyer's loan. The price is $60,000 and the buyer is making a 20% down payment. Two points equal*

   A. $960.
   B. $1,200.
   C. $1,440.
   D. $1,800.

8. *What two regulations require financial disclosures to be provided to the applicant within three business days of a completed mortgage loan application?*

   A. Regulation B and Regulation C
   B. Regulation B and Regulation Z
   C. Regulation C and Regulation X
   D. Regulation X and Regulation Z

9. *Which is NOT a purpose for the Mortgage Servicing Disclosure Statement?*

   A. to disclose the percentages of the loan closings this lender has serviced in the last three years
   B. to explain the resolution of "servicing complaints" required by law
   C. to inform the consumer the likelihood that the mortgage could be sold
   D. to inform the consumer the likelihood that the servicing of the mortgage will be sold

10. *Identify which attribute is NOT considered illegal discrimination in granting credit under the Equal Credit Opportunity Act.*

    A. color
    B. income level
    C. race
    D. source of income

11. *Which Act contains Title X (the Consumer Financial Protection Act) and Title XIV (the Mortgage Reform and Anti-Predatory Lending Act)?*

    A. Bank Secrecy Act/Anti-Money Laundering Act
    B. Dodd-Frank Act
    C. Gramm-Leach-Bliley Act
    D. Secure and Fair Enforcement for Mortgage Licensing Act

12. *Which of these circumstances would NOT be an acceptable reason to provide a revised GFE to a borrower?*

    A. The borrower lost the income from a part-time job and so was no longer eligible for the specific loan terms identified in the GFE
    B. The borrower requested to change the loan term from 15 to 30 years
    C. The mortgage loan originator regretted overlooking certain liabilities in order to qualify the borrower for a better interest rate
    D. The title company discovered a junior lien on the property that was not considered when preparing the GFE

13. *The Safeguards Rule requires financial institutions to*

    A. collect data on loan applications to complete a Loan/Application Register (LAR).
    B. design, implement, and maintain safeguards to protect customer information.
    C. ensure that all mortgage loan originators are registered with the NMLS.
    D. keep separate files on married spouses if requested.

14. *A borrower's stable monthly gross income is $6,800. Every month he pays $485 car payment, $200 revolving credit payment, and $1,500 alimony. What is the maximum monthly mortgage payment for which he would qualify on an FHA mortgage loan?*

    A. $739
    B. $1,423
    C. $2,108
    D. $2,239

15. *Which federal legislation allows a borrower three business days to reconsider an owner-occupied refinance transaction?*

    A. ECOA
    B. FCRA
    C. HMDA
    D. TILA

16. *Which fee would NOT be considered a finance charge and would NOT be part of the APR calculation?*

    A. discount points
    B. escrow deposit for property taxes
    C. mortgage insurance
    D. origination fee

17. *What is the loan-to-value ratio if the loan amount is $100,000, the appraised value is $125,000, and the sales price is $127,000?*

    A. 74%
    B. 79%
    C. 80%
    D. 98%

18. *Generally speaking, a credit agency may NOT report negative credit information in a credit report that is more than how many years old?*

    A. 3
    B. 5
    C. 7
    D. 10

19. *Which Act is primarily focused on protecting consumers from identity theft?*

    A. FACT Act
    B. HMDA
    C. RESPA
    D. TILA

20. *What is the earliest that a mortgage loan may close after a potential borrower completes an application?*

    A. the 3rd business day after completing the application
    B. the 3rd business day after receiving required disclosures or after the disclosures are mailed
    C. the 7th business day after completing the application
    D. the 7th business day after receiving the required disclosures or after the disclosures are mailed

21. **Which is NOT a triggering term according to TILA, requiring additional disclosing in advertising?**

    A. "360 easy payments"
    B. "$3,000 down"
    C. "Pay only $800 a month"
    D. "Terms to fit every budget"

22. **Which requires financial institutions to file reports of cash transactions exceeding $10,000 daily?**

    A. BSA/AML
    B. ECOA
    C. RESPA
    D. TILA

23. **It is a violation of which law to discriminate against a potential borrower on public assistance?**

    A. CRA
    B. ECOA
    C. FCRA
    D. RESPA

24. **Which is NOT a part of the Gramm-Leach-Bliley Act?**

    A. Financial Privacy Rule
    B. Pretexting Provisions
    C. Red Flags Rules
    D. Safeguards Rule

25. **According to the interim final rule on Valuation Independence, a creditor who has information about appraiser misconduct must file a report with the**

    A. Appraisal Foundation.
    B. appropriate state licensing authority.
    C. Consumer Financial Protection Bureau.
    D. Federal Reserve Board.

26. **Under laws related to fair lending and fair housing, which is legal?**

    A. creating and promoting a racially or ethnically exclusive lending image
    B. disregarding income that cannot be verified
    C. refusing to include alimony and child support payments as viable income
    D. subjecting applicants to more extensive credit checks because of race, sex, or national origin

27. **What is the total monthly payment, including escrows, on a 30-year interest only loan of $205,000, taxes of $1,800 per half, hazard insurance of $420 annually, $65 monthly mortgage insurance, and an interest rate of 6%?**

    A. $1,275
    B. $1,315
    C. $1,425
    D. $1,575

28. **RESPA does NOT prohibit**

    A. charging a premium on third-party fees.
    B. kickbacks.
    C. reasonable fees paid for services actually rendered.
    D. referral fees to consumers and service providers.

29. **Which situation is LEAST LIKELY to be an example of predatory lending?**

    A. ABC Mortgage Co. offers a subprime loan to a borrower who is coming out of bankruptcy.
    B. A buyer shows up at closing and finds that the lender has changed the terms of the loan.
    C. A homeowner was 12 days late paying her mortgage, and the lender raised the interest rate 1/4%.
    D. A homeowner paid off his mortgage loan early with lottery winnings and the lender charged a $12,000 prepayment penalty.

30. **Which law requires lenders to disclose consumer credit costs related to adjustable rate mortgages?**

    A. ECOA
    B. RESPA
    C. TILA
    D. Title VIII

31. **Which item is NOT required to appear on the Truth in Lending Statement?**

    A. amount financed
    B. annual percentage rate
    C. finance charge
    D. interest rate

32. **Which is a voluntary lien?**

    A. assessment
    B. judgment
    C. mortgage
    D. property tax

33. *According to the Fair Credit Reporting Act, which situation does NOT entitle someone to a free copy of his credit report?*

    A. An applicant was refused credit due to insufficient income.
    B. A consumer is on public assistance or is unemployed.
    C. A consumer was a victim of identify theft and a fraud alert was inserted in the credit file.
    D. The credit file contains inaccurate information as a result of fraud.

34. *Which situation does NOT involve a straw buyer?*

    A. Ann revises her pay stubs so she can qualify for a loan to buy her dream house.
    B. Bob uses his twin brother's Social Security number and credit information to apply for a loan.
    C. Dave agrees to secure a loan under his name, even though it's his sister with bad credit who intends to live in the house and make the payments.
    D. Tina tells Rob, who is facing foreclosure, that if he deeds the property to her, she will refinance on good terms and let him stay in the house.

35. *A mortgage lending company refuses to make loans for homes in a minority neighborhood. This is an illegal action called*

    A. blockbusting.
    B. coercion.
    C. redlining.
    D. steering.

36. *What federal law prohibits making a loan to a customer without verifying the customer's ability to repay the loan?*

    A. CRA
    B. HMDA
    C. HOEPA
    D. RESPA

37. *MLO Dave knew that his customer worked at a factory that was two weeks away from closing, but in his eagerness to close the deal, he decided to ignore that fact. This might be considered an example of*

    A. actual fraud.
    B. constructive fraud.
    C. good business.
    D. negligent misrepresentation.

38. *What fee may be collected prior to delivering required disclosures?*

    A. appraisal
    B. credit report
    C. origination
    D. rate-lock

39. *While it is illegal to ask or consider the race or national origin of an applicant, which federal legislation requires that this information be requested from every applicant to monitor whether discriminatory practices are being used?*

    A. Equal Credit Opportunity Act
    B. Fair Credit Reporting Act
    C. Home Mortgage Disclosure Act
    D. Truth in Lending Act

40. *Marvin and Juanita have a reverse mortgage. Over the term of this mortgage, their*

    A. debt grows and their equity shrinks.
    B. debt shrinks and their equity grows.
    C. debt grows and their equity remains stable.
    D. debt remains stable and the equity shrinks.

41. *Your refinancing borrower qualifies for a 95% LTV and has a payoff of $70,000. How much cash is available if the appraisal is $95,000 and the closing costs are $3,000?*

    A. $17,250
    B. $20,250
    C. $22,000
    D. $90,250

42. *Which of these situations would NOT violate ECOA?*

    A. While looking at your customer's paycheck stubs, you see that child support is being paid and ask, "Do you pay child support, alimony, or separate maintenance?"
    B. Your customer's income information includes aid to dependent children from the state. You ask, "Are you sure you want to include this as part of your income on this application? It won't look good."
    C. Your customer's last name is Patel and you observe, "That's Indian, right?"
    D. Your very pregnant customer is sitting at your desk while two more little ones who came in with her are running around your office. You ask her, "Do you think this is your last child?"

43. **On the loan application (Form 1003), which section ensures compliance with HMDA?**

    A. III: Borrower Information
    B. VII: Details of Transactions
    C. VIII: Declarations
    D. X: Information for Government Monitoring Purposes

44. **ABC Bank receives a change of address request from a consumer. What requires the bank to follow up with her to verify the validity of the request?**

    A. Federal Reserve
    B. Red Flag Rules
    C. SAFE Act
    D. Truth in Lending Act

45. **If a home is in a federally designated flood hazard area, the lender will require specific flood insurance**

    A. only if the homeowner does not carry a flood rider on his homeowner's insurance.
    B. until the LTV is 80%.
    C. until the LTV is 78%.
    D. for the life of loan.

46. **The type of mortgage that requires regular payment of principal and interest calculated to pay off the entire balance by the end of the loan term is called**

    A. adjustable rate.
    B. balloon payment.
    C. fully amortizing.
    D. partially amortizing.

47. **Protected classes under the Fair Housing Act include race, color, national origin, sex, disability, religion, and**

    A. familial status.
    B. marital status.
    C. military status.
    D. sexual orientation.

48. **The portion of an adjustable rate mortgage used to compute the interest rate that can change and is based on the T-Bill, LIBOR, or any other factor outlined in the note is known as the**

    A. ARM.
    B. index.
    C. margin.
    D. rate.

49. **Which borrower would be the best candidate for a reverse equity mortgage?**

    A. a borrower with a poor credit history but who has a large down payment
    B. a borrower who is age 62 or older who owns his or her home free and clear
    C. a borrower whose income is at or below 80% of the adjusted median income level
    D. a borrower whose spouse was a veteran who died in the line of active duty

50. **Which type of loan is LEAST LIKELY to result in payment shock?**

    A. adjustable rate mortgage
    B. hybrid ARM
    C. I/O
    D. reverse mortgage

51. **A borrower has an ARM with an initial rate of 6% and a rate cap 2/6. What's the highest his interest rate could be over the life of the loan?**

    A. 8%
    B. 12%
    C. 18%
    D. It depends on the index.

52. **What is another name for a nonconforming loan?**

    A. adverse loan
    B. indexed loan
    C. jumbo loan
    D. conventional loan

53. **Advance fee bans are prohibited by the**

    A. Financial Privacy Rule.
    B. Loan Originator Compensation Rule.
    C. MARS Rule.
    D. Safeguards Rule.

54. **Some lenders and investors are willing to make subprime loans because**

    A. borrowers typically have greater income stability than with other real estate loans.
    B. borrowers typically have greater net worth than with other real estate loans.
    C. lenders can charge much higher rates than they can with other real estate loans.
    D. lenders experience less risk with subprime loans than with other real estate loans.

55. **Discount points refer specifically to points paid**

    A. for documentation and closing fees.
    B. for servicing charges and administration costs.
    C. to cover loan origination fees.
    D. to lower borrower's interest rate.

56. **All of the following are parts of the Dodd-Frank Act legislation EXCEPT for**

    A. amendments to the Truth in Lending Act related to loan originator compensation.
    B. establishment of the Consumer Financial Bureau.
    C. goals for establishing qualified mortgage (QM) criteria.
    D. requirements for financial institutions to assist in detecting and preventing money laundering.

57. **In order to comply with HMDA, which is NOT a question a mortgage loan originator may ask a borrower?**

    A. "What is your marital status?"
    B. "What is your national origin?"
    C. "What is your race?"
    D. "What is your religion?"

58. **A borrower is buying a house for $100,000. He provides a down payment of $5,000. If he pays two discount points, what is the total cost of the points?**

    A. $1,500
    B. $1,900
    C. $2,000
    D. $2,100

59. **Under Regulation Z, once the APR differs from the lender's original estimate by _____% a new Truth in Lending statement must be issued.**

    A. 1
    B. 1/2
    C. 1/4
    D. 1/8

60. **RESPA applies to what types of properties?**

    A. commercial
    B. one- to four-family residential properties
    C. residential properties with five or fewer units
    D. residential property and unimproved land

61. **What type of mortgage allows personal property (like appliances) to be included in the property sale and financed together with one loan?**

    A. bridge mortgage
    B. equity participation mortgage
    C. package mortgage
    D. wraparound mortgage

62. **Calculating the housing expense ratio by taking stable monthly income and multiplying by 0.31 is the ratio used to qualify for a**

    A. conventional loan.
    B. FHA-insured loan.
    C. subprime loan.
    D. VA loan.

63. **The annual percentage rate (APR) is also referred to as**

    A. effective rate of interest.
    B. equity.
    C. escrow account.
    D. nominal rate of interest.

64. **A mortgage broker rents office space from a title company at a discount in exchange for referring customers for settlement services. Which federal law does this arrangement violate?**

    A. RESPA
    B. SAFE Act
    C. TILA
    D. It does not violate any federal law.

65. **One of the most critical points of the Federal Reserve Loan Originator Compensation Rule is the prohibition of the practice of**

    A. collecting any advance fees for loan modifications or short sales the consumer has been provided with an acceptable written offer.
    B. giving or accepting a fee, kickback, or anything of value in exchange for referrals of settlement service business.
    C. inquiring about a consumer's marital status or intentions related to having or raising children.
    D. steering" consumers to a lender to receive greater compensation.

66. **While taking a loan application, a mortgage loan originator will NOT gather**

    A. bankruptcy papers from 10 years ago.
    B. income information.
    C. liabilities information.
    D. rent/mortgage history.

67. *A borrower's stable monthly gross income is $2,500. He has three monthly debts: $250 car payment, $100 personal loan payment, and $50 credit card payment. What is the maximum monthly mortgage payment he would qualify for using the total debt to income ratio for a conventional loan?*

   A. $900
   B. $800
   C. $600
   D. $500

68. *Which law requires that state-licensed mortgage loan originators pass a national exam which includes a uniform state content section (UST)?*

   A. CRA
   B. FACT Act
   C. HOEPA
   D. SAFE Act

69. *How many years of employment are required to be disclosed on the mortgage loan application?*

   A. one
   B. two
   C. three
   D. four

70. *A borrower has been at her job for 10 years and typically works overtime 5 hours per week at time and a half. Her hourly rate is $15.75. What is the gross monthly income you can use to qualify her?*

   A. $2,614.5
   B. $2,830.22
   C. $3,170.05
   D. $3,241.88

71. *Total debt to income ratio is the relationship between the borrower's*

   A. equity in the home and the amount of the loan.
   B. monthly housing costs and other debt obligations.
   C. stable monthly income and the area mean income (AMI).
   D. total monthly debt obligation and gross monthly income.

72. *When using the sales comparison approach to arrive at an opinion of value, an appraiser looks*

   A. into the future to anticipate the home's appreciation.
   B. at current prices of all homes on the market in a given neighborhood.
   C. into the recent past to analyze similar sales.
   D. into the past to see what an owner originally paid for a property.

73. *Which is NOT a trigger used to define a high cost loan under the Home Ownership and Equity Protection Act (HOEPA)?*

   A. excessive annual percentage rate
   B. excessive points and fees
   C. excessive prepayment penalty
   D. excessive total finance charge

74. *A mortgage loan that allows the borrower to obtain multiple advances of funds up to an approved amount is known as a(n)*

   A. bi-weekly mortgage.
   B. bridge loan.
   C. HELOC.
   D. installment second mortgage.

75. *A veteran needs two documents to obtain a VA loan. One is a DD-214 and the other is a*

   A. birth certificate.
   B. Certificate of Eligibility.
   C. Certificate of Occupancy.
   D. military discharge paper.

76. *Which of the following types of income will NOT require additional information, such as likelihood that it will continue, to determine if the income can be used to qualify the borrower?*

   A. alimony
   B. disability
   C. salary
   D. unemployment

77. *Which was the first major legislation to directly affect equal rights to ownership of real property?*

   A. Civil Rights Act
   B. Emancipation Proclamation
   C. Federal Fair Housing Act
   D. Homeowners Protection Act

78. *An appraiser has been contracted to determine the value of a large apartment building for a potential investor. Which appraisal method is probably the most useful for this situation?*

    A. competitive market analysis
    B. cost approach
    C. income approach
    D. sales comparison approach

79. *Conventional mortgages require mortgage insurance once the LTV exceeds*

    A. 75%.
    B. 80%.
    C. 85%.
    D. 90%.

80. *An acceleration clause in a mortgage instrument*

    A. allows the interest rate to be increased.
    B. increases payments at periodic intervals.
    C. permits the lender to declare the loan in default and demand the balance due.
    D. states one late payment is an act of default.

81. *Which document is NOT required by RESPA to be given to consumers within three business days of a completed loan application?*

    A. GFE
    B. HUD-1
    C. Mortgage Servicing Disclosure Statement
    D. Settlement Costs and You Booklet

82. *The main advantage of a 15-year loan versus a 30-year loan is*

    A. it never requires mortgage insurance since the term is shorter.
    B. the monthly payments are usually lower.
    C. there are more tax deductions for interest paid.
    D. the total paid to the lender is less.

83. *The Equal Credit Opportunity Act is a law that requires the lender to provide the borrower a reason for rejection of credit in writing within how many days of loan application?*

    A. 3
    B. 10
    C. 30
    D. 45

84. *A document that conveys ownership of real property from the grantor to the grantee is known as a*

    A. deed.
    B. mortgage.
    C. note.
    D. title commitment.

85. *The SAFE Act requires at least how many hours of continuing education annually for state-licensed mortgage loan originators?*

    A. 4
    B. 8
    C. 12
    D. 20

86. *Which document is NOT required at closing?*

    A. GFE
    B. HUD-1 or HUD-1A
    C. initial escrow statement
    D. promissory note

87. *According to the Fair Credit Reporting Act, when is a consumer entitled to a free copy of his credit score (assuming there has been no fraud)?*

    A. once a year
    B. when he has been turned down for credit
    C. when he is on public assistance
    D. A consumer has no right to a free copy of his credit score.

88. *Of these, which law is intended to combat the crime of identity theft?*

    A. FACT Act
    B. Homeownership and Equity Protection Act
    C. Gramm-Leach-Bliley Act
    D. SAFE Act

89. *If an MLO or real estate agent suggests to a client that he move to a particular area to reside in a community that he will "fit into," they would be guilty of*

    A. blockbusting.
    B. flipping.
    C. redlining.
    D. steering.

90. *Form 4506-T is used to*

A. apply for a mortgage loan.
B. communicate the appraiser's opinion of value on a property.
C. request transcripts of federal tax returns.
D. verify a veteran's discharge from the armed services.

91. *A loan defined as a high cost loan under the Home Ownership and Equity Protection Act is also known as a*

A. Section 30 loan.
B. Section 31 loan.
C. Section 32 loan.
D. Section 33 loan.

92. *A borrower is applying to refinance his mortgage. His first mortgage is $25,000 at a 9% rate. He plans to get cash out, up to $40,000. He qualifies for an 80% LTV and his house appraises for $100,000. Shortly before closing, the title exam shows $23,000 in bond liens. Closing costs total $6,000. How much cash will he receive at closing?*

A. $9,000
B. $26,000
C. $46,000
D. $49,000

93. *What federal legislation allows the borrower to challenge the value stated on an appraisal report?*

A. ECOA
B. FCRA
C. RESPA
D. TILA

94. *Regulation Z applies to all residential loans*

A. made to corporations or businesses.
B. that do not have finance charges.
C. with four or less installments.
D. with more than four installments.

95. *An appraisal*

A. establishes the selling price of a property.
B. guarantees the value of a piece of real estate.
C. is an opinion of value.
D. is a prediction of future worth.

96. *At closing, who issues a clear to close?*

A. lender
B. mortgage broker
C. real estate broker
D. title agency

97. *The legislation that restricts the circumstances under which a financial institution may disclose a consumer's personal financial information to non-affiliated third parties is the*

A. Fair and Accurate Credit Transaction Act.
B. Fair Credit Reporting Act.
C. Gramm-Leach-Bliley Act.
D. Home Mortgage Disclosure Act.

98. *According to the Interagency Guidance on Nontraditional Mortgage Product Risks, loans to borrowers who do not show capacity to repay the loan from sources other than the collateral are*

A. acceptable as long as the interest rate is fixed.
B. acceptable if the borrower pays PMI.
C. acceptable with superior credit scores.
D. unsafe and should be avoided.

99. *Which statement would trigger additional loan term disclosure for advertising purposes according to TILA?*

A. "FHA financing available"
B. "Low monthly payment"
C. "Pay only $700 per month"
D. "We make VA loans"

100. *A nontraditional loan is defined by the SAFE Act as*

A. any loan that could not be sold in the secondary market.
B. any loan that is insured by a government agency.
C. anything other than a 30-year fixed rate loan.
D. anything that exceeds the maximum loan limit set by Fannie Mae.

101. *Against any licensee who is in violation of laws and regulations under state law, the state regulatory authority is authorized*

A. close a business office without notification.
B. deny an application without providing a reason.
C. impose fines and/or initiate suspension or revocation of a license.
D. refuse a licensee's request for a hearing on charges.

102. *The unique identifier licensees are required to show on all residential mortgage forms, solicitations, or advertisements is issued by the*

   A. Department of Housing and Urban Development.
   B. Federal Bureau of Investigation.
   C. Nationwide Mortgage Licensing System and Registry.
   D. state regulatory authority.

103. *Which should be included in a state's system of supervision and enforcement of the SAFE Act?*

   A. authority to change annual renewal education requirements
   B. authority to make no documentation loans
   C. authority to issue unique identifiers
   D. authority to subpoena witnesses and documents

104. *The state regulatory authority may refuse to renew a license for an MLO, broker, or lender if there is a finding that the licensee has*

   A. acquired additional real estate holdings not related to the business.
   B. demonstrated unfairness in the transaction of business.
   C. invested personal funds in another company in another state.
   D. requested a partner be placed on inactive or escrow status for medical reasons.

105. *When conducting an examination, designated officers for the state regulatory authority have the authority to*

   A. arrest an employee of a lender.
   B. compel production of papers and objects.
   C. suspend a license.
   D. revoke a license.

106. *Under the SAFE Act, each state has the authority to*

   A. approve the prelicensing and continuing education offerings for persons licensed under this Act.
   B. issue a state specific license ID number that a licensee may use instead of their NMLS unique identifier.
   C. replace the national testing requirements for MLOs with only state-specific requirements.
   D. write state-specific rules or regulations or adopt procedures related to licensing of persons covered under this Act.

107. *Registered mortgage loan originator refers to*

   A. a mortgage loan originator who is licensed under the state regulatory authority but has an office that is in another state.
   B. a mortgage loan originator who is registered with and maintains a unique identifier through the Nationwide Mortgage Licensing System and Registry.
   C. any licensed mortgage loan originator whose license has been suspended or revoked by the state regulatory authority.
   D. any licensed mortgage loan originator that is employed by a lender licensed under the state regulatory authority.

108. *A loan modification refers to*

   A. authorizing a mortgage lender to service a loan for more than four months.
   B. changing the terms of an existing loan.
   C. performing administrative or clerical functions related to a mortgage loan.
   D. refinancing an existing loan.

109. *Which is FHA's reverse mortgage program?*

   A. Blanket Mortgage
   B. Bridge Mortgage
   C. Gradual Payment Mortgage
   D. Home Equity Conversion Mortgage

110. *Of these, which is NOT a third party fee?*

   A. appraiser fee
   B. courier fee
   C. credit report fee
   D. rate lock fee

111. *Mortgage brokers*

   A. act as intermediaries between borrowers and lenders.
   B. originate and service mortgage loans.
   C. provide funding for mortgage loans.
   D. underwrite mortgage loans.

112. *Of these, who must have a mortgage loan originator license?*

   A. Bella, who is paid a fee for taking mortgage loan applications for a mortgage broker
   B. Pam, who is employed by a federally chartered bank to take mortgage loan applications
   C. Tom, who is paid a fee for originating commercial mortgage loans
   D. XYZ Mortgage Company, who solicits mortgage loans for a fee

113. *Which topic is required to be included as part of the 8 hours of a MLO's annual continuing education for license renewal?*

    A. customer service
    B. economics
    C. ethics
    D. loan servicing

114. *Which mortgage loan originator applicant would definitely be considered ineligible by the state regulatory authority to be granted a mortgage loan originator license in his state?*

    A. Daryl, who had a mortgage loan originator license revoked due to a violation when he was working in another state
    B. Fern, who scored only 75% on her written MLO test
    C. Joseph, who forgot to include one of his past employers on his personal history form
    D. Zelda, who received a community service sentence for an assault conviction 10 years ago

115. *When can a mortgage broker employ an unlicensed and unregistered mortgage loan originator?*

    A. when the mortgage loan originator has met the requirements for a loan originator but has yet to be registered by the NMLS
    B. when the loan originator is already licensed and registered in another state
    C. when the mortgage loan originator originates less than 30 loans for the broker annually
    D. under no circumstances

116. *The application of a mortgage loan originator would likely be denied if the applicant had*

    A. been convicted of fraud 10 years ago.
    B. been pardoned for a conviction of fraud 10 years ago.
    C. a long outstanding hospital bill for a surgery.
    D. surrendered his license in another state to move to this state.

117. *A nontraditional loan is defined by the SAFE Act as*

    A. any loan that could not be sold in the secondary market.
    B. any loan that is insured by a government agency.
    C. anything other than a 30-year fixed rate loan.
    D. anything that exceeds the maximum loan limit set by Fannie Mae.

118. *Performing which task requires licensing?*

    A. analyzing a loan application that is received from a consumer
    B. communicating details of loan closing arrangements
    C. making an underwriting decision
    D. offering or negotiating loan terms

119. *A licensed mortgage lender MAY NOT publish an advertisement that uses*

    A. an insignia designating membership in a particular professional or local association.
    B. the lender's exact name as it appears on the license.
    C. the lender's unique NMLS identifier.
    D. a post office box number in place of the business address that appears on the license.

120. *Mortgage broker Greg accidentally failed to include an applicant's car payment as a debt on the mortgage loan application. The lender approved the loan, despite the fact that the borrower was unlikely to be able to afford it. Greg's conduct could best be described as*

    A. fraudulent.
    B. illegal.
    C. negligent.
    D. unfair.

121. *Which mortgage broker's act is a violation?*

    A. Dorian collects a rate lock-in fee from a client payable to the broker
    B. Lily collects a rate lock-in fee from a client on the mortgage lender's behalf, payable to the mortgage lender
    C. Shaun presents a lender's offer that a loan will be made at a specified rate if the loan is closed by the given expiration date and if the applicant can meet the qualification standards
    D. Travis collects a rate lock-in fee required by a governmental agency to be collected directly by the mortgage broker

122. *Steering consumers to loan products that would result in greater compensation for a mortgage loan originator is prohibited by what legislation?*

    A. Dodd-Frank Act
    B. Fair Housing Act
    C. Home Ownership and Equity Protection Act
    D. SAFE Act

123. **Mortgage loan originators are prohibited from**

    A. asking an appraiser to consider other comparable properties.

    B. obtaining multiple appraisals on a property.

    C. telling an appraiser a minimum value needed to approve the loan.

    D. withholding fees from appraisers for substandard performance.

124. **A lender has how many days to notify the borrower of an underwriting decision?**

    A. 3

    B. 10

    C. 30

    D. 60

125. **If an ad mentions the interest rate on a specific loan product, that interest rate must be**

    A. available for at least 10 business days.

    B. given to every applicant.

    C. locked in without a lock-in fee.

    D. made available to a reasonable number of qualified applicants.

UST Standalone Practice Exam #1

1. **Which number must be used to identify a mortgage loan originator on all forms, business cards, and advertising?**

    A. license number issued by the state regulatory authority

    B. Federal Tax ID number

    C. NMLS unique identifier

    D. Social Security number

2. **The state regulatory authority may suspend or revoke a license for failure to**

    A. declare bankruptcy if personal financial situation warrants this action.

    B. file an income tax return by April 15.

    C. fully cooperate with any examination or investigation ordered by the regulatory authority.

    D. request a hearing to contest an order to cease and desist.

3. **How often may the state regulatory authority investigate a mortgage licensee's books, accounts, records, and files?**

    A. monthly

    B. quarterly

    C. annually

    D. at any time

4. **The intent of the SAFE Act is for the state regulatory authority to have a _____ administrative authority.**

    A. broad

    B. conditional

    C. limited

    D. restricted

5. **Each state's regulatory authority must establish procedures for**

    A. approving education courses for loan originators.

    B. assigning unique identifiers to loan originators.

    C. endorsing course providers for loan originators.

    D. examining records of loan originators.

6. **What is NOT a penalty that the state regulatory authority may impose on a licensee who violates state law?**

    A. fines

    B. imprisonment

    C. license revocation

    D. restitution

7. *A loan processor refers to any person who*

A. directly or indirectly originates a mortgage loan.

B. extends credit that is subject to a finance charge.

C. is obligated to repay a mortgage loan.

D. performs administrative or clerical duties related to mortgage loans.

8. *The term person may refer to a*

A. company.

B. natural person.

C. partnership.

D. All of these choices are included in the definition.

9. *Who is NOT "taking" a loan application?*

A. Pat presents particular loan terms to a borrower for consideration but other individuals will be responsible for completing the loan process

B. Quinn assists a borrower filling out an application by explaining the residential mortgage loan terms in order to reach a mutual understanding of these loan terms

C. Rita describes for a borrower the loan application process without any discussion of particular loan products

D. Sid collects all the necessary information from a borrower to complete a loan application form and sends that information to a lender for final verification

10. *A loan originator license would NOT necessarily be denied if the applicant*

A. has had a mortgage loan origination registration revoked by another state.

B. pled guilty to money laundering in Canada 10 years ago.

C. pled no contest in a fraud case 3 years ago.

D. was convicted on a felony charge of assault 10 years ago.

11. *Doris performs only clerical duties for a licensed mortgage broker putting together loan packages. She is most likely a loan _____ and _____ from needing to be licensed.*

A. originator / is not exempt

B. originator / is exempt

C. processor / is not exempt

D. processor / is exempt

12. *The state regulatory authority can deny a mortgage loan originator applicant a license if the applicant has*

A. been convicted of any felony in the last ten years.

B. ever been convicted of an act of domestic violence or endangering a minor, unless pardoned.

C. ever been convicted of an act of fraud, dishonesty, breach of trust, or money laundering, unless pardoned.

D. ever been convicted of driving under the influence.

13. *The application fee for a mortgage loan originator license is refundable if the license is*

A. denied.

B. surrendered.

C. suspended.

D. The application fee is not refundable under any circumstance.

14. *A person who only works part time as a mortgage loan originator*

A. is exempt from being licensed and need not be registered with the NMLS.

B. is exempt from being licensed but must be registered with the NMLS.

C. is required to be licensed and must be registered with the NMLS.

D. is required to be registered with the NMLS only.

15. *A licensed mortgage loan originator must comply with requirements for license renewal*

A. annually by June 30.

B. annually by December 31.

C. annually by the anniversary date the license was first issued.

D. bi-annually by December 31.

16. *Which characteristic would NOT automatically deny a loan originator of receiving a license?*

A. criminal fraud

B. financial irresponsibility

C. licensed out-of-state

D. unacceptable character

17. *The SAFE Act mandates specific topics that must be covered as part of a state-licensed mortgage loan originator's continuing education every year. Which topic is NOT required?*

    A. conventional mortgage products
    B. ethics
    C. federal law
    D. nontraditional mortgage products

18. *A mortgage broker with 20 years of experience is neither registered nor licensed as a mortgage loan originator. If he continues his loan origination activities, he would be in violation of what law?*

    A. Gramm-Leach-Bliley Act
    B. Real Estate Settlement and Procedures Act
    C. SAFE Act
    D. Truth in Lending Act

19. *A mortgage industry ad is considered misleading if it includes*

    A. the name, address, phone number, and unique identifier of the loan originator.
    B. the name of the loan originator's employer.
    C. the words "immediate approval."
    D. the unique identifier of the loan originator.

20. *Within ___ days after receipt of a loan application, a mortgage broker must fully disclose to the borrower total compensation that the broker would receive from any loan options that the lender or mortgage broker presents to the borrower.*

    A. 3
    B. 10
    C. 15
    D. 21

21. *Which conduct by a mortgage loan originator would NOT be prohibited?*

    A. accepting a deposit to induce the lender to produce a loan
    B. conducting business with a known unlicensed broker
    C. disbursing the mortgage loan proceeds into a customer's account via direct deposit
    D. imposing an undisclosed charge on a borrower for establishing an escrow account

22. *If a licensee has a particular conflicting interest in a mortgage loan transaction, the licensee must*

    A. disclose in writing that an affiliated business relationship exists among providers.
    B. pay an additional $100 to the state's mortgage guaranty trust fund.
    C. retain an attorney to represent the borrower's interest.
    D. withdraw from the transaction prior to making or accepting a commitment.

23. *An advertisement promoting the tax deductibility of home equity credit would NOT be misleading if it includes a statement that a consumer*

    A. could be eligible for reduced tax rates by taking out a home equity loan.
    B. may earn tax credits by taking out a home equity loan.
    C. may be entitled to "free money" by taking out a home equity loan.
    D. should consult a tax advisor regarding the deductibility of interest costs.

24. *MLO Cindy's customer purposely does not tell her that he just co-signed his nephew's auto loan. The credit report shows neither that loan nor a credit inquiry, and so that debt is not considered when the lender pre-approves him for a larger mortgage than he really should have. Do you think Cindy did anything wrong?*

    A. No, she can't be held responsible if a client withholds information that does not show on his credit report.
    B. Yes, she colluded with the customer to withhold material information.
    C. Yes, she committed actual fraud by approving a purposely false application.
    D. Yes, she committed constructive fraud by not confirming the customer's debts.

25. *All may be included in a borrower's income analysis EXCEPT*

    A. pensions, interest, and dividends.
    B. regular earnings and overtime.
    C. revealed alimony and child support.
    D. sporadic overtime and bonuses.

UST Standalone Practice Exam #2

1. *After investigating a charge of fraud against loan originator Mark, the state regulatory authority permanently withdraws his license. What is this known as?*

   A. cancellation
   B. revocation
   C. suspension
   D. termination

2. *Which occurrence WOULD NOT require the licensee to file a written report with the state regulatory authority?*

   A. Elliot, a licensed mortgage loan originator for a licensed lender, is indicted on a felony charge
   B. Marsha, a licensed mortgage loan originator, is cited for driving while intoxicated
   C. Quinn, a licensed broker, files a petition for bankruptcy
   D. Richard, a senior officer for a licensed lending company, is convicted on a felony charge

3. *Any actual travel and reasonable living expenses incurred by an officer of the regulatory authority conducting an examination or investigation of a licensed lender or broker are the responsibility of the*

   A. the individual conducting the examination or investigation of the licensee.
   B. the lender or broker being examined or investigated.
   C. the lender or broker being examined only if violations are discovered.
   D. the regulatory authority who is requesting the examination or investigation of a licensee.

4. *After the state regulatory authority revokes Lisa's mortgage loan originator license, does she have any options for appeal?*

   A. No, the state regulatory authority's decision is final.
   B. Yes, she can appeal to her employer.
   C. Yes, she can appeal to the State Supreme Court.
   D. Yes, she can appeal to the State Attorney General.

5. *MLO applicants may request a(n) _____ if their application has not been approved or is denied by the state regulatory authority within the allotted timeframe for the state*

   A. exception
   B. extension
   C. hearing
   D. waiver

6. *What type of loan requires a lender or mortgage broker licensed in a state to deliver a notice recommending financial counseling?*

   A. adjustable rate mortgage
   B. graduated payment mortgage
   C. home equity conversion mortgage
   D. home equity line of credit

7. *An individual who takes a mortgage loan application or negotiates the terms of mortgage loan for compensation is NOT a mortgage*

   A. broker.
   B. lender.
   C. loan originator.
   D. processor.

8. *A written or electronically transmitted confirmation issued to a mortgage applicant prior to a commitment of a particular rate, number of points, or variable rate terms which will be the rate, number of points, or variable rate terms at which the lender will make the loan, provided that the first mortgage loan is closed by a specified date and that the applicant qualifies for the loan is referred to as a*

   A. adjustable rate.
   B. good faith estimate.
   C. mortgage lock-in rate.
   D. prime rate.

9. **All of the following would likely be considered examples of conflicting interest EXCEPT**

   A. the licensee's brother-in law is a principal loan originator and a board member of the company providing additional products and services in the loan transaction.

   B. the licensee's father-in-law holds 10% of the shares of a title company.

   C. the licensee's son is designated as the principal loan originator.

   D. the licensee's spouse has a partnership in an appraisal company.

10. **Of these, which is considered a residential mortgage loan?**

    A. a loan for a dwelling located on a 30-acre working farm

    B. a loan for a multi-unit investment property

    C. a loan for one to four family property which is to be lived in

    D. a loan for a retail property to be used for business

11. **The term individual may refer to a**

    A. company.

    B. natural person.

    C. organization.

    D. All of these choices are included in the definition.

12. **Which activity is defined as an administrative/clerical task?**

    A. present for consideration by a borrower or prospective borrower particular residential mortgage loan terms

    B. receive, collect, and/or distribute information common for the processing or underwriting of a loan

    C. recommend, refer, or steer a borrower or prospective borrower to a particular lender or set of residential mortgage loan terms

    D. take a residential mortgage loan application

13. **The application of a mortgage loan originator would likely be denied if the applicant had**

    A. a pre-existing medical condition.

    B. completed only 20 hours of pre-licensing education.

    C. resigned his previous position with a previous employer.

    D. scored only 70% on the licensing exam.

14. **Lance has been hired by Reasonable Mortgage Company to analyze information collected for processing of a residential mortgage loan. Lance's job duties suggest that he is acting as**

    A. a mortgage broker and requires licensing.

    B. a mortgage loan originator and requires licensing.

    C. a mortgage processor or underwriter and does not require licensing.

    D. a mortgage servicer and does not require licensing.

15. **Applicants are required to provide a credit report as part of an initial MLO application primarily so the state regulatory authority can evaluate**

    A. the amount of the application fee the applicant must pay.

    B. the amount of the surety bond the applicant must file.

    C. the overall financial responsibility of the applicant.

    D. the overall net worth of the applicant.

16. **Which task requires licensing?**

    A. collecting only basic identifying information about the borrower on behalf of that lender

    B. performing clerical or support duties on behalf of a loan originator

    C. taking a mortgage loan application on behalf of a loan originator

    D. transmitting a completed form to a lender on behalf of a borrower

17. **After investigating an advertising violation against the High Dollar Mortgage Company, the State Regulatory Authority notifies High Dollar in writing of the disapproval of a particular print ad they have been using. To be in compliance, High Dollar Mortgage Company must**

    A. add a disclaimer to the advertising copy that is in at least 12 point type.

    B. immediately cease publication of the disapproved print advertisement.

    C. revise the objectionable text that appears in the print advertisement.

    D. rescind any loan offers made as a result of using this print advertisement.

18. *Which loan advertisement content DOES NOT include a triggering term?*

    A. 10% down
    B. 30-year mortgages available
    C. monthly payments only $230
    D. terms to fit your budget

19. *Which type of loan is NEVER considered to be a high cost loan?*

    A. open end loan
    B. refinance
    C. reverse mortgage
    D. second lien loan

20. *The Privacy Rule of the Gramm-Leach-Bliley Act requires that financial institutions provide the consumer with a Consumer Privacy Policy*

    A. before disclosing information to non-affiliated third parties.
    B. each time the servicing is transferred.
    C. three business days prior to closing.
    D. within three business days of applying for a loan.

21. *What is the earliest that a mortgage loan may close after a potential borrower completes an application?*

    A. the 3rd business day after completing the application
    B. the 3rd business day after receiving required disclosures or after the disclosures are mailed
    C. the 7th business day after completing the application
    D. the 7th business day after receiving the required disclosures or after the disclosures are mailed

22. *When taking an application for a mortgage loan, what are creditors NOT permitted to ask?*

    A. "Are you required to pay child support?"
    B. "Do you receive child support?"
    C. "What is your home address?"
    D. "Who is your employer?"

23. *What terminology is the only correct way to ask a client about his or her marital status?*

    A. "Are you married or divorced?"
    B. "Are you married, unmarried, or separated?"
    C. "Are you single, married, or widowed?"
    D. "You cannot ask this question since marital status is a protected class."

24. *Which of the following is an acceptable condition on which to base a mortgage loan originator's compensation?*

    A. fixed percentage of the loan amount
    B. percentage of all fees collected on the loan
    C. premium based on the interest rate selected
    D. premium for lower LTV loans

25. *Which situation is LEAST likely to be an example of predatory lending?*

    A. ABC Mortgage Co. offers a subprime loan to Mark, who is coming out of bankruptcy.
    B. Dave shows up at closing and finds that the lender has changed the terms of the loan.
    C. Ellie was 12 days late paying her mortgage, and the lender raised the interest rate 1/4%.
    D. Frank paid off his mortgage loan early with lottery winnings and the lender charged a $12,000 prepayment penalty.

Glossary

2-1 Buydown A graduated payment buydown where the payments are subsidized for only two years.

3-2-1 Buydown A graduated payment buydown where the payments are subsidized for three years.

3/7/3 Rule A provision of the Truth in Lending Act related to required disclosures and waiting periods. Initial disclosure to be delivered within three business days of receipt of a completed application; earliest to close a loan is the seventh business day after disclosures are provided; a three business-day waiting period before a loan can close is imposed after borrower receives re-disclosures.

Abstract of Title A summarized chronological history of title to a property, listing all recorded documents that affect the title, generally created by a title abstractor after examining records of deeds, taxes, special assessments, liens, judgments, mortgages, and other encumbrances that have ever affected the property, even if the encumbrance has been removed or satisfied. An abstract of title does not ensure the validity of the title, and there is no guarantee associated with this type of title evidence, so the homeowner or lender does not have any recourse if title defects are discovered later.

Acceleration Clause Gives the lender the right to declare the entire loan balance due immediately because of borrower default or for violation of other contract provisions. Most promissory notes, mortgages, trust deeds, and land contracts contain an acceleration clause allowing the lender to accelerate the debt upon default as defined in the contract.

Adverse Possession Acquiring title to someone else's real property by possession of it. Possession and use of property can mature into title. Acquiring title to land by adverse possession requires open and notorious, hostile and adverse, exclusive and continuous use of another's land for a number of years (as specified by state law).

Affiliated Business Arrangement A situation where a person in a position to refer settlement services—or an associate of that person—has either an affiliate relationship with or a direct or beneficial ownership interest of more than **1%** in a provider of settlement services and who then refers business to that provider or in some way influences the selection of that provider.

Alienation Clause Gives the lender the right to exercise certain rights upon transfer of the property, such as declare the entire loan balance immediately due and payable. The alienation clause may give the lender the right to declare the entire loan balance immediately due and payable (hence, referred to as a due on sale clause), the right to raise the interest rate on the loan, the right to charge an assumption fee, or the right to exercise other rights stated in the contract. A loan is generally not assumable if it contains an alienation clause.

Amortization Schedule A tool that shows exactly how much of each payment of a fully amortizing loan will be applied toward principal and how much toward interest over the life of the loan. Some amortization schedules show only a year-to-year schedule, while others show a month-to-month breakdown. All amortization schedules will show the total amount that the loan is costing the borrower over its entire term.

Amortize To calculate payments to pay off a debt by periodic installments, with payments going to pay principal and interest.

Annual Percentage Rate (APR) The relationship between the cost of borrowing and the total amount financed, represented as a percentage.

Arm's Length Transaction One that occurred under typical conditions in the marketplace, with each party acting in his own best interests.

As-Is A typical appraisal where the property value was determined based on a complete and thorough examination of the subject property as it currently sits and in its present condition, as opposed to being subject to other hypothetical conditions, extraordinary assumptions, or repairs.

Assumption One party (buyer) takes over primary liability for the loan of another party (seller), usually implying no change in loan terms. When a buyer assumes the seller's mortgage, the seller remains secondarily liable unless the lender provides a release. Loan assumption is not always an option with loans written today as lenders try to protect their interests by being able to approve a new buyer. A new loan allows a lender to change interest rates, charge fees, or change loan terms for a new party.

Automated Valuation Model (AVM) Part of an automated underwriting system that is able to provide a probable value range for properties by performing a statistical analysis of available data. While not true appraisals, AVMs can reduce the time and costs necessary to close a loan.

Automated Underwriting Process where loan applicant information is entered into a computer and an evaluation comes back within minutes advising the lender to accept the loan, or refers the loan application for further review.

Balloon Payment A final payment at the end of a loan term to pay off the entire remaining balance of principal and interest not covered by payments during the loan term.

Basis Point A unit that is equal to 1/100th of 1% and is used to denote the change in a financial instrument, commonly used for calculating changes in interest rates. The relationship can be summarized as 1% change = 100 basis points.

Blockbusting The illegal practice of inducing owners to sell their homes (often at a deflated price) by suggesting that the ethnic or racial composition of the neighborhood is changing, with implication that property values will decline as a result. Also called **panic selling** and **panic peddling**.

Buydown Additional funds in the form of points paid to a lender at the beginning of a loan to lower the interest rate and monthly payments.

Buydown, Permanent When points are paid to a lender to reduce the interest rate and loan payments for the entire life of the loan.

Buydown, Temporary When points are paid to a lender to reduce the interest rate and payments early in a loan, with interest rate and payments rising later.

Cap, Interest Rate A limit on the amount of interest rate increase that can occur with an adjustable rate mortgage.

Cap, Mortgage Payment A limit on the amount of mortgage payment increase that can occur with an adjustable rate mortgage.

Cap, Negative Amortization A limit on the amount of negative amortization that can occur with an adjustable rate mortgage.

Certificate of Eligibility A certificate issued by the Department of Veteran's Affairs to establish status and amount of a veteran's eligibility to qualify for loan guarantee.

Certificate of Reasonable Value (CRV) A document issued by the VA which states the value of the subject property based on an approved appraisal. The VA loan amount cannot exceed the CRV.

Chain of Title Chain of deeds passing title for land from owner to owner.

Closing The final stage in a real estate transaction where ownership of real property is transferred from seller to buyer according to the terms and conditions set forth in a sales contract or escrow agreement.

Co-Mortgagor A person who signs a mortgage with the primary mortgagor and thus accepts a joint obligation to repay the loan. Also called **Co-Borrower** or **Co-Signer**.

Co-Ownership Also known as concurrent ownership, this is any form of ownership where two or more people share title to real property, with each person having an undivided interest in the property. **Undivided interest** gives each co-owner the right to possession of the whole property, not just part of it. Under the law, any number of people may join in the co-ownership of real property: **Tenancy in common** (form of co-ownership with two or more people having an undivided interest in the entire land, but no right of survivorship), **joint tenancy** (when each co-owner has an equal undivided interest in the land and right of survivorship), and **tenancy by the entirety** (form of co-ownership that involves only owners who are husband and wife with each having an equal and undivided share of the property).

Commercial Banks Financial institutions that provide a variety of financial services, including loans. Although banks remain the largest source of investment funds in the country today, their activities are focused on relatively short-term commercial and consumer loans.

Community Reinvestment Act (CRA) Enacted by Congress in 1977 to encourage financial institutions to help meet the credit needs of the communities in which they operate, including low- and moderate-income neighborhoods, consistent with safe and sound lending practices. The CRA requires that each insured depository institution's record in helping meet the credit needs of its entire community be evaluated periodically. That record is taken into account in considering an institution's application for deposit facilities, including mergers and acquisitions.

Condition 1. A provision in a contract, deed, law, regulation, guideline, etc., that makes the parties' rights and obligations depend on the occurrence, or non-occurrence, of a particular event. Also called a **Contingency Clause**. 2. A provision of a contract, law, regulation, guideline, etc., that allows, or does not allow, something else to occur based on whether or not certain other events occur or do not occur. 3. Other factors that reflect the general state of something as good or bad; (e.g., economic conditions of an area, property condition, etc.)

Condominiums Properties developed for co-ownership where each co-owner has a separate fee simple interest in an individual unit and an undivided interest in the common areas of the property. Common areas are areas of the development that all residents use and own as tenants in common, such as the parking lot, hallways, and recreational facilities. Condominium residents must follow the declarations and by laws set forth by the condominium founder, and maintained and enforced by the owners' association. Most condominiums are designed for residential use. Each owner may give a lender a mortgage on his or her unit and undivided interest in common areas. Each owner's creditors can claim a lien against that unit and undivided interest. If a lien holder forecloses, only that unit and its undivided interest are affected without jeopardizing the entire condominium. Property taxes are also levied against each unit separately, and thus do not affect the whole property. Owners' association levies to pay for common area expenses are divided among unit owners, and can also result in a lien if unpaid.

Contribution The concept that a particular item or feature of a home is only worth what it actually contributes in value to that piece of property. Thus, if a five-bedroom home is not desirable, putting an addition onto a house to add a fifth bedroom doesn't increase the value of the home that much.

Conveyance The transfer of title to real property from one person to another by means of a written document, such as a deed.

Cooperatives (or Co-ops) Buildings owned by corporations, with the residents as shareholders who each receive a proprietary lease on an individual unit and the right to use common areas. The title to the cooperative building is held by a corporation formed for that purpose. A person who wants to live in the building buys shares in the corporation, instead of renting or buying a unit, and is given a proprietary lease for a unit in the building. **Proprietary leases** have longer terms than ordinary leases and give the shareholder more rights than an ordinary tenant. A cooperative shareholder pays a prorated share of the building's expenses, including property taxes for the whole building.

Credit Report A listing of a borrower's credit history, including amount of debt, record of repayment, job info, address info, etc.

Credit Scoring A means by which the lender makes certain determinations regarding the creditworthiness of potential borrowers. This involves a lender assigning specified numerical values to different aspects of a borrower.

Declaration of Covenants, Conditions, and Restrictions (CC&Rs) Often placed in the deed by the original sub-divider of land, although it can also be added later. The purpose of CC&Rs is to keep the subdivision attractive and protect the market value of properties. Deed restriction examples include setting a minimum house size that must be built on the land or prohibitions against certain types of fences. These types of deed restrictions can have a positive impact on value because they promote conformity in the neighborhood. Severe restrictions can hurt property value, but this is usually not the case with subdivision CC&Rs.

Deed An instrument that conveys a grantor's (seller's) interest, if any, in real property. The deed is the document used by the owner of real property to transfer all or part of his interests in the property to another. The deed serves as evidence of title. **Warranty deeds** carry warranties of clear title and grantor's right to convey title.

Deed of Trust An instrument held by a third party as security for the payment of a note. Also called a **Trust Deed**. Like a mortgage, it creates a voluntary lien on real property to secure repayment of a debt. Parties to a deed of trust are grantor or trustor (borrower), beneficiary (lender), and trustee (neutral third party). Unlike a mortgage, a trust deed has a power of sale, allowing trustee to foreclose non-judicially. Compare to **Mortgage**.

Deed Restrictions Limitations on real property use, imposed by a former owner through language included in the deed. These may also be called **restrictive covenants**, especially if they are recorded in a later document. Deed restrictions and restrictive covenants that are recorded **run with the land** and are thus *enforceable against future property owners*. Note, however, that deed restrictions and restrictive covenants must touch and concern the land to be legal and binding on future transfers.

Default Failure to fulfill an obligation, duty, or promise, as when borrower fails to make payments, tenant fails to pay rent, or party fails to perform a contract. Mortgage, note, or other document defines what constitutes default.

Defeasance Clause Used to defeat or cancel a certain right on the occurrence of a specific event. This clause can appear in contracts or mortgages. A defeasance clause can also give a borrower the right to redeem real estate after default on a note, by paying the full amount owed plus fees and court costs incurred in pursuing the defaulting party. The defeasance clause will outline the circumstances, procedures, and rules for the redemption to be successful. For example, a debtor fails to make a balloon payment when due. The debtor can make the payment in full within the time frame specified in the defeasance clause and regain title to the property, thus overriding another clause in the contract that transferred the property title to the creditor upon default.

Deficiency Judgment A court order stating that the debtor owes money to the creditor when the collateral property does not bring enough at foreclosure sale to cover the entire loan amount, accrued interest, and other costs.

Depreciation Expensing of the cost of business or investment property over a set number of years, determined by the IRS to be the asset's useful life. For example, the cost of a **residential** building is divided by a depreciation life of **27.5** years, whereas the cost of a **commercial** building is divided by a depreciation life of **39** years. For a property to be depreciable, it must be used in a trade or business.

Desktop Underwriter® (DU®) Fannie Mae's electronic Automated Underwriting System (AUS) that puts lenders in direct contact with Fannie Mae, providing a streamlined process of document submission, underwriting, and loan approval.

Direct Endorsers Lenders authorized to underwrite their own FHA loan applications and who are responsible for the entire loan process through closing.

Discount Points An amount paid to a lender when a loan is made to make up the difference between the current market interest rate and the rate a lender gives a borrower on a note. Discount points increase a lender's yield, allowing the lender to give a borrower a lower interest rate. Also referred to as **discounts** or **points**.

Due on Sale Clause Mortgage clause that prohibits assignment by making the entire mortgage balance due when property is sold.

Easement A right to use another person's real property for a particular purpose. Easements can be public (e.g., for road expansion) or private (e.g., for access to a landlocked parcel). It's important to understand that easements restrict how a parcel of land may be used because, usually, a structure cannot be put on an easement. The easement creates limited rights for the easement holder. An easement that grants access is referred to as a **right of way** (ROW).

Eminent Domain The government's constitutional power (right) to take (or appropriate or condemn) private property for public use, as long as the owner is paid just compensation. Eminent domain affects real estate because of government involvement in fair market pricing, and by making adjacent land more or less valuable, depending on a proposed use (e.g., freeway interchange vs. a landfill). Remember, eminent domain is the right; **condemnation** is the action.

Encroachment A physical object intruding onto neighboring property, often due to a mistake regarding the boundary.

Encumbrance A non-possessory interest in property; a lien, easement, or restrictive covenant burdening the property owner's title.

Equitable Title An interest in real property created with the execution of a valid sales contract.

Equity The difference between the value of the property and the outstanding indebtedness secured by the property.

Equity Exchange When value in a property is traded for value in another property. Properties must be of **like kind**, held for use in trade or business, or as investment to qualify for tax deferment. An equity exchange can also be a **delayed exchange**, with a promise to provide a replacement property. To qualify for tax deferment, the replacement property must be located within 45 days and closed within 180 days of the first exchange. Also called **Tax-Deferred Exchange, Tax-Free Exchange, Like Kind Exchange,** or **Section 1031** (from the section number of IRS law).

Escrow The system in which things of value, like money or documents, are held on behalf of the parties to a transaction by a disinterested third party, or escrow agent, until specified conditions have all been met.

Estoppel A legal doctrine that prevents a person from asserting rights or facts that are inconsistent with earlier actions or statements when he or she failed to object or attempt to stop another person's actions.

External Obsolescence Occurs when something *outside the control of the property* makes it less desirable, such as loss of an area's economic base or the construction of a new highway that creates noise or re-routes traffic. External obsolescence is always considered incurable since the property owner cannot remedy it. Also known as **economic obsolescence.**

Familial Status A protected class under the Federal Fair Housing Act and many state Civil Rights Laws, making it illegal to discriminate against a person because he or she is the parent or guardian of a child younger than 18 years of age.

Federal Home Loan Mortgage Corporation (Freddie Mac or FHLMC) Created in 1970 as a nonprofit, federally chartered institution controlled by the Federal Home Loan Bank System. Like Fannie Mae, Freddie Mac is currently under the conservatorship of the Federal Housing Finance Agency. Unlike Fannie Mae, Freddie Mac does not guarantee payment of its mortgages. The primary function of Freddie Mac was to help S & Ls acquire additional funds for lending in the mortgage market by purchasing the mortgages they already held. Freddie Mac may deal in FHA, VA, and conventional mortgages. While Fannie Mae emphasizes the purchase of mortgage loans, Freddie Mac also actively sells the mortgage loans from its portfolio, thus acting as a conduit for mortgage investments. The funds generated by the sale of the mortgages are then used to purchase more mortgages.**Federal Housing Administration (FHA)** Government agency that insures mortgage loans.

Federal Housing Finance Agency (FHFA) Government agency that merged the powers and regulatory authority of the Federal Housing Finance Board (FHFB) and the Office of Federal Housing Enterprise Oversight (OFHEO), as well as the GSE mission office at the Department of Housing and Urban Development (HUD); the conservator of Fannie Mae and Freddie Mac.

Federal National Mortgage Association (Fannie Mae or FNMA) The leading investor in the secondary mortgage market, Fannie Mae is able to purchase conventional mortgages as well as FHA and VA mortgages. Fannie Mae was created in 1938 as the first government-sponsored secondary market institution and is currently under the conservatorship of the Federal Housing Finance Agency (FHFA).

Federal Reserve Banks Banks that provide services to financial institutions (e.g., check clearing), which have one main office in each Federal Reserve district. All nationally chartered commercial banks must join the Federal Reserve and buy stock in its district reserve bank.

Federal Reserve Board The body responsible for U.S. monetary policy, maintaining economic stability, and regulating commercial banks. Also referred to as **Board of Governors**, but most commonly called **the Fed**.

Federal Reserve System Established by the Federal Reserve Act of 1913 with 12 Federal Reserve Banks as a lender of last resort.

Fee Simple Estate The fullest freehold estate interest that exists in real property. It is also called fee title or fee simple absolute. Fee simple ownership includes such other appurtenances as access rights, surface rights, subsurface rights, mineral rights, some water rights, and limited air rights.

Finance Instrument A written document used in the borrowing or lending of money. The most common type is a **promissory note**.

Financial Statement A document that shows assets and liabilities for an individual, covering a specific period of time or a specific point in time.

First Lien Position The spot held by the lien with highest priority when there's more than one mortgage or other debt or obligation secured by the property.

Fixed Rate Loan Loan with a constant interest rate remaining for the duration of the loan.

Flipping Defined by Fannie Mae as the process of purchasing existing properties with the intention of immediately reselling them for a profit.

Flipping, Illegal Property purchased at a low price, appraised at a high value without valid reason, and resold at the higher price.

Foreclosure When a borrower is in **default** on a loan, the lender accelerates the due date of the debt to the present and gives the debtor notice of default, demanding the full loan balance be paid at once. If the debtor fails to do so, the lender files a lawsuit, called a foreclosure action, in a court of jurisdiction where the land is located. There are some differences in how foreclosure proceedings progress, depending on the state and county in which the action takes place. One other option debtors have to avoid foreclosure is to make a voluntary conveyance, also called **deed in lieu of foreclosure**. With this action, debtors still lose the property, but by returning it voluntarily before final court action, they avoid having a foreclosure on their credit record. After confirmation of sale, however, it is too late.

Fraud An intentional or negligent misrepresentation or concealment of a material fact; making statements that a person knows, or should realize, are false or misleading.

Freehold Estate A possessory interest of uncertain duration; it may end, but no one knows when. Some events that will end a freehold estate include the transfer of the property to someone else, the death of the owner, foreclosure, and confiscation for back taxes.

Fully Amortizing Loans Loans where the total payments over the life of the loan pay off the entire balance of principal and interest due at the end of the loan term.

Functional Obsolescence Describes a building that is less desirable because of something *inherent in the structure itself,* such as a house with an outdated style, inadequate fixtures, impractical floor plan, etc. This too may be curable or incurable.

Funding Fee A non-refundable fee charged on VA-guaranteed loans in place of mortgage insurance.

Good Faith Estimate (GFE) An estimate by the mortgage loan originator of the closing costs that the borrower must pay for a real estate loan. The MLO must give a GFE to the borrower at the time of the loan application (or within three business days of a completed application); disclosure of certain third party fees has to be exact or higher or the mortgage company will have to pay the shortages, the MLO cannot pay nor be penalized in their compensation. Often referred to as **Good Faith Statement**.

Government National Mortgage Association (Ginnie Mae or GNMA) Created in 1968 as a government-owned corporation, operating under the Department of Housing and Urban Development (HUD). A primary function of Ginnie Mae is promoting investment by guaranteeing the payment of principal and interest on FHA and VA mortgages through its mortgage backed securities program. This program, supported by the federal government's borrowing power, guarantees interest and principal mortgage payments to mortgage holders.

Government-Sponsored Enterprise (GSE) A group of financial services corporations created by the United States Congress to enhance the flow of credit to targeted sectors of the economy and to make those segments more efficient and transparent. Federal National Mortgage Association (Fannie Mae) and FNMA and Federal Home Loan Mortgage Corporation (Freddie Mac) are examples of GSEs.

Gross Income Income before taxes and other expenses have been deducted.

Gross Living Area (GLA) Residential space that's finished, heated, and above grade. Garages, finished basements, and storage areas don't count in GLA.

Highest and Best Use The use that is the most physically possible, legally permissible, economically feasible, and maximally profitable or productive. This is the most important property-specific factor that an appraiser considers before making a determination of value.

Home Equity Line of Credit (HELOC) Available money that can be borrowed by a homeowner, secured by a second mortgage on the principal residence. Home equity lines of credit can be accessed at any time up to a predetermined borrowing limit and are often used for non-housing expenditures. Compare to **Home Equity Loan**.

Home Equity Loan A loan taken by a homeowner, secured by a second mortgage on the principal residence. Home equity loans are usually a one-time loan for a specific amount of money and obtained for a specific, and often non-housing, expenditure. Compare to **Home Equity Line of Credit**.

Home Mortgage Disclosure Act A law requiring all institutional mortgage lenders with assets of more than $10 million to make annual reports of all mortgage loans made in a given geographic area where they have at least one office. This law is designed to help the government detect patterns of **redlining**.

Home Ownership Equity Protection Act (HOEPA) Section **32** of Regulation Z Truth in Lending Act establishing disclosure requirements and prohibiting equity stripping and other abusive practices associated with high cost loans.

Homeowners Protection Act (HPA) Federal law passed in 1998 that requires lenders or servicers to provide certain disclosures and notifications concerning **private mortgage insurance** (PMI) on single-family residential mortgage transactions. Most provisions of the Act do not apply to home loans made before July 29, 1999, or to mortgages where the lender pays the mortgage insurance (special disclosure rules apply to loans in these categories). The HPA requires that lenders provide an initial written disclosure regarding PMI cancellation—and annual reminders of this right, including: The borrower's right to request cancellation of PMI when a mortgage has been paid down to **80%** of its original value and the automatic cancellation of PMI by the lender when a mortgage has been paid down to **78%** of its original value. The Act requires written disclosure for both adjustable rate and fixed rate home mortgages on primary residences.

Housing and Economic Recovery Act of 2008 (HERA) Major federal law designed to assist with the revitalization of the U.S. housing market; includes provisions related to foreclosure prevention and consumer protections, as well as establishing minimum standards for licensing and registration of mortgage loan originators. See the **Secure and Fair Enforcement for Mortgage Licensing Act.**

Housing Expense Ratio The relationship of a borrower's total monthly housing expense to income, expressed as a percentage.

HUD The Department of Housing and Urban Development; government agency that deals with housing issues.

HUD Uniform Settlement Statement (HUD-1) A settlement statement, required under RESPA, that details all costs associated with closing a loan, showing how much was paid, to what companies or parties, and for what purpose.

Hypothecation The voluntary process which allows a debtor to pledge property as security for a debt without giving up possession of it. This serves as security for the creditor and motivation for the debtor to make sure that the terms of the note are fulfilled and the note is repaid as agreed. Failure to do so could result in loss of possession.

Index A statistical report that is generally a reliable indicator of the approximate change in the cost of money, and is often used to adjust the interest rate in ARMs.

Instrument Any document that transfers title (such as a deed), creates a lien (such as a mortgage), or gives a right to payment (such as a note or contract).

Interest 1. A right or share in something, such as a piece of real estate. 2. A charge a borrower pays to a lender for the use of the lender's money. Compare to **Principal**.

Interest Rate The rate which is charged or paid for the use of money, generally expressed as a percentage of the principal.

Interest Only Loan A loan where scheduled payments only pay accrued interest and not any portion of the principal. A balloon payment equal to the entire principal amount of the loan is due at the end of the loan term.

Jumbo Loans Loans that exceed the maximum loan amount that Fannie Mae/Freddie Mac will buy, making them nonconforming.

Junk Fees Charges assessed to a borrower by a loan originator that serve little if any function and are often hidden in mortgage documents.

Kickbacks Fees or other compensation given for services not performed, but as a means of undisclosed commission for business referrals. Kickbacks are prohibited by RESPA.

Land Contract A real estate installment agreement where the buyer, the **vendee**, makes payments to the seller, the **vendor**, in exchange for the right to occupy and use the property, but no deed or title is transferred until all, or a specified portion, of the payments have been made. The seller retains legal title to the subject property—the buyer only becomes an owner in fact, having possession and equitable title, but no actual title and no deed.

Lease A contract where one party pays the other rent in exchange for possession of real estate; a conveyance of a leasehold estate from the fee owner to a tenant.

Lease/Option When a seller leases property to someone for a specific term, with an option to buy the property at a predetermined price during the lease term. The lease/option plan is comprised of two elements—a lease and an option. A **lease** is a contract where one party pays the other rent in exchange for possession of real estate. An **option** is a contract giving one party the right to do something within a designated time period, without obligation to do so. The seller/lessor leases the property to the buyer/tenant for a specific term (six months, one year, etc.) with the provision that part of the rental payments may be applied to the purchase price if the tenant decides to buy before the lease expires.

Lease/Purchase When a seller leases property to someone for a specific term, with the tenant agreeing to buy the property at a set price during or following the lease term. The lease/purchase plan is comprised of two elements: A lease and a purchase contract. The lease/purchase is the equivalent of a sale, but there are additional considerations to take into account because the sale is delayed until a later date. The seller/lessor leases the property to the buyer/tenant for a specific term (six months, one year, etc.,) with the provision that part of the rental payments may be applied to the purchase price. In addition to a lease agreement, a purchase agreement is also prepared, which details the exact terms and conditions of the purchase, as well as the date it is to take place. Both contracts must conform to all laws governing real estate contracts.

Leasehold Estate An interest in real estate that gives the holder a temporary right to possession, without conveying title. The holder of a leasehold estate is known as a **tenant** or **lessee**. The property owner is known as the **landlord** or **lessor**.

Lien Not only a financial interest in property; it is also a financial encumbrance. Liens are typically security for a debt that gives the creditor, or lien holder, the right to foreclose on the debtor's property if the debt is not paid. In **foreclosure**, the property is sold and the lien holder collects the amount of the debt from the proceeds of the foreclosure sale.

Lien, Materialman's Similar to a mechanic's lien, but based on a debt owed to someone who supplied materials, equipment, or fuel for a project rather than labor.

Lien, Mechanic's A specific lien claimed by someone who performed work on the property (construction, repairs, or improvements) and has not been paid. This term is often used in a general sense, referring to materialman's liens as well as actual mechanics' liens.

Lien Position Any mortgage in a higher lien position is said to be a **senior mortgage**, so a first mortgage is always a senior mortgage. A **junior mortgage** is any mortgage with a lower lien position than another. Thus, a second mortgage is a junior mortgage to a first mortgage, but a second mortgage is a senior mortgage to a third mortgage. In the event of **foreclosure**, liens for real estate taxes always have the highest priority and get paid first, then the first recorded lien gets paid, and then if there's money left, the second lien gets paid, and so on. Once the funds are exhausted, liens in a later position get nothing.

Lien Theory/Title Theory In **lien theory** states, the mortgage creates a lien against the property which must be repaid by the debtor. The property serves as collateral that is hypothecated to the lender as security for the debt. The lender must go through a foreclosure proceeding to reclaim title in the event of default. In **title theory** states, the mortgage instrument actually gives title to the property to the lender while the debt is outstanding, with the owner getting only possession and use of the land. Once the mortgage amount has been repaid, title reverts back to the owner.

Life Estate A freehold estate that lasts only as long as a specified person, the "measuring life," lives. The holder of a life estate is called a **life tenant**. A life estate may also be based on another person's life. This is called a life estate **pur autre vie** (for another's life).

Like-Kind Exchange (Equity Exchange) When the value in one property is traded for value in another property. This is also called a tax-deferred exchange, tax-free exchange, like-kind exchange, or Section 1031 (from the section number of IRS law). When property is exchanged as part of an equity exchange, the parties defer paying taxes until a capital gain (profit) is actually realized from the transaction. General rules for a tax-deferred equity exchange of real estate are: (1) The properties must be exchanged, or qualify as delayed exchange, which is a promise to provide a replacement—located within 45 days, closed within 180 days. (2) The properties must be like-kind property, i.e., real estate for real estate. (3) The properties must be held for use in a trade or business, or held by the party as an investment.

Loan Origination Fee Fee charged by lender to cover the administrative costs of making a loan, usually based on a percentage of the loan amount (1% = 1 point).

Loan-to-Value Ratio (LTV) The amount of money borrowed compared to the value or price of the property.

Margin The difference between the index value and the interest rate charged to the borrower with an ARM loan.

Market Price The price for which a piece of real estate actually sold.

Market Value The theoretical price a property is most likely to bring in a typical transaction.

Marketable Title A title that is free and clear from undisclosed encumbrances or other defects that would expose a purchaser to litigation or impede a purchaser's ability to enjoy the property or to later sell the property easily.

Mortgage Instruments that create a voluntary lien against real property as security for the payment of a note. A mortgage is a type of security instrument, where the borrower (the **mortgagor**) pledges property to the lender (the **mortgagee**) as collateral for the debt. A promissory note is almost always accompanied by a security instrument to give the creditor some leverage against the debtor, and the debtor an extra incentive to pay.

Mortgage, Adjustable Rate (ARM) A mortgage that permits the lender to periodically adjust the interest rate to reflect fluctuations in the cost of money.

Mortgage, Bi-Weekly A fixed-rate mortgage, similar to a standard mortgage, but with payments made every two weeks instead of every month, thus making an extra payment each year.

Mortgage, Blanket 1. Mortgage that covers more than one parcel of real estate. 2. Mortgage that covers an entire building or development, rather than an individual unit or lot.

Mortgage, Bridge A mortgage that occurs between the termination of one mortgage and the commencement of another. When the next mortgage is taken out, the bridge is repaid.

Mortgage, Cash-Out A mortgage that a borrower gives to lenders so that the borrower can get cash for the equity that has built up in property (e.g., a home equity loan taken out for a non-house purpose, or an investor trying to recoup money invested in fixing up a property).

Mortgage, Construction A temporary loan used to finance the construction of a building on land. Replaced with a takeout loan.

Mortgage, Conventional A loan that is not insured or guaranteed by a government entity.

Mortgage, Equity Participation A mortgage that lets the lender share part of the earnings, income, or profits from a real estate project.

Mortgage, Graduated Payment (GPM) Payment structure that allows the borrower to make smaller payments in the early years of the mortgage, with payments increasing on a scheduled basis at a predetermined point until they are sufficient to fully amortize the loan over the remainder of its term.

Mortgage, Growth Equity (GEM) A fixed-rate mortgage set up like a 30-year conventional loan, but payments increase regularly like an ARM. Also called a **Rapidly Amortizing Mortgage**.

Mortgage, Hard Money A mortgage where the borrower receives cash (e.g., cash out mortgage).

Mortgage, Junior Any mortgage that has a lower lien position than another mortgage.

Mortgage, Open-End A mortgage where the borrower can request more funds from the lender, up to a certain pre-defined limit, even re-borrowing part of the debt that's been repaid (at lender's discretion) without having to renegotiate the loan. (*Note*: Most mortgage documents say *open-end* mortgage, but it's rare for lenders to loan more money without re-assessing the borrower and renegotiating the loan. Borrowers usually need to get a line of credit because it has an adjustable interest rate.)

Mortgage, Package A mortgage where personal property (e.g., appliances) is included in a real estate sale and financed with one contract.

Mortgage, Purchase Money A mortgage where the seller finances all or part of the sale price of a piece of property for a buyer.

Mortgage, Purchase Money Second A purchase money mortgage in a second lien position.

Mortgage, Reduction Option A fixed-rate mortgage that gives the borrower a limited opportunity to reduce the interest rate one time during the course of the loan, provided certain conditions are met.

Mortgage, Refinance A mortgage that a borrower gives to a lender to redo or expand the loan on the property, usually to get a better interest rate or pay off other debts.

Mortgage, Reverse A loan used by qualified homeowners age 62 or older to convert equity in the home into a lump sum, a monthly cash stream, and/or a line of credit; generally repaid when the last surviving borrower dies, sells the home, or ceases to live in the home for 12 consecutive months.

Mortgage, Shared Appreciation (SAM) A mortgage where the lender charges below-market interest rates in exchange for a share of the borrower's equity.

Mortgage, Soft Money A mortgage where the borrower receives credit instead of actual cash (e.g., a purchase money mortgage).

Mortgage, Subject to Existing *See* **Subject to.**

Mortgage, Variable Balance (VBM) A mortgage with an adjustable interest rate, but with payments that never change. Instead, as the rate goes up or down, the balance due on the mortgage changes.

Mortgage, Wraparound When an existing loan on a property is retained, while the lender (or seller) gives the buyer another, larger loan. Often the seller keeps the existing mortgage, still pays on it, and gives the buyer another mortgage.

Mortgage Backed Security (MBS) Any security that represents an undivided interest in a group of mortgages. Principal and interest payments from the individual mortgage loans are grouped and paid out to the MBS holders. **Bond-type securities** are long-term, pay interest semi-annually, and provide for repayment at a specified date. **Pass-through securities**, which are more common, pay interest and principal payments on a monthly basis.

Mortgage Banker One who originates mortgage loans, usually funding loans with the company's own funds. Mortgage bankers may sell the loans or do the servicing. Mortgage bankers often act as originators and servicers of loans on behalf of large investors such as insurance companies, pension plans, or Fannie Mae. Since these large investors operate on a national scale, they have neither the time nor resources to understand the particular risks of local markets, or to deal with the day-to-day management of their loans. Even if loans are sold on the secondary market, mortgage bankers may continue to act as agents and service loans for a fee.

Mortgage Broker One who, for a fee, brings borrowers and lenders together, but typically does not service the loans made. Mortgage brokers do not underwrite or fund their loans, but act as a conduit in residential mortgages. Among the services that a mortgage broker typically provides are: Collecting financial and other required information from borrowers, analyzing income and debt to determine maximum mortgage amounts the borrower can afford, advising borrowers on available loan programs, explaining the loan process, filling out a loan application, providing required disclosures, processing the loan file and submitting it to lenders, assisting borrowers to understand and respond to lender decisions, and participating in the loan closing process.

Mortgage Companies Institutions that function as the originators and servicers of loans on behalf of large investors such as insurance companies, pension plans, or the Federal National Mortgage Association (Fannie Mae). Since these large investors often operate on a national scale, they have neither the time nor the resources to understand the particular risks of local markets or to deal with the day-to-day management of their loans. Mortgage companies fill the gap functioning more as intermediaries than as sources of lending capital.

Mortgage Disclosure Improvement Act (MDIA) An amendment to the Truth in Lending Act enacted in 2009 that adds additional disclosure requirements, APR tolerances, and waiting periods on closing mortgage loans, as well as limiting fees that can be charged prior to disclosure.

Mortgage Insurance Premium (MIP) The fee charged for FHA mortgage insurance coverage. The initial premium (**upfront mortgage insurance premium** or **UFMIP**) can be financed and there may be a renewal premium.

Mortgage Loan Originator As defined by the SAFE Act, an individual who either takes a residential mortgage loan application or offers or negotiates terms of a residential mortgage loan for compensation or gain.

National Mortgage Licensing System (NMLS) The agency that maintains the data for loan officers including felony records through fingerprints, education records, credit history, and the test results for federal and state tests. All loan officers are required to be registered on the NMLS system, but all MLOs that work for mortgage bankers or mortgage brokers must complete the testing, education, and credit-report requirements.

Negative Amortization A situation that occurs when the minimum required periodic payment for principal and interest does not cover the accrued interest due for that period, resulting in the unpaid interest being added to the principal balance.

Negotiable Instruments Promissory notes or other finance instruments that are freely transferable from one party to another. Most promissory notes used in real estate are negotiable instruments. When a note is freely transferable, the lender or other creditor can obtain immediate cash by selling the note, such as when real estate notes are sold to the secondary market. The sale is usually at a discount, meaning the note is sold for a cash amount less than the note's face value.

Nonconforming Loans Loans that do not meet Fannie Mae/Freddie Mac standards, and thus cannot be sold to them but can be sold to other secondary markets. Compare to **Conforming Loans**.

Nontraditional Mortgage Product As defined by the SAFE Act, anything other than a 30-year fixed rate loan.

Office of Thrift Supervision (OTS) The government entity that regulates Savings and Loans in the same manner the Federal Reserve regulates commercial banks.

Origination Fee Lenders charge loan **origination fees** in order to cover the lender's administrative costs in processing a loan. These can also be called loan fees, service fees, or even administrative fees. Additional points may be charged as fees for other reasons, such as closing fees, documentation fees, etc. While these are sometimes called points—remember, each point is 1% of the loan amount—loan fees are not discount points.

Ownership in Severalty The simplest form of ownership; is a sole form of ownership, meaning that only one person or legal entity holds the title to that property. With ownership in severalty, the owner's interest has been severed from the interests of all others.

Par Rate The rate that lenders offer only to mortgage brokers, also known as the "wholesale" rate, when neither discounts points or yield spread is paid.

Partial Release, Satisfaction, or Conveyance Clause Obligates the creditor to release part of the property from lien and convey title to that part back to the debtor once certain provisions of the note or mortgage have been satisfied. Usually, this occurs after a certain percentage of the mortgage balance has been paid. This is an important clause that appears in many blanket mortgages and some construction mortgages so the developer or builder can sell off completed homes with clear title before having to pay back the entire amount borrowed for the entire development project. Also, if the land is bought with a mortgage, construction financing is much easier to obtain later when the builder owns part of the land free of liens.

Partially Amortizing Loans Loans for which payments are applied to principal and interest, but the payments do not retire the debt when the agreed upon loan term expires, thus requiring a balloon payment at the end of the loan term.

Periodic Re-Amortization When the payments on a loan are recalculated at a specific time based on the loan balance at that time so the new payments will fully amortize the loan over the remaining loan term.

PITI A typical mortgage payment that includes **P**rinciple, **I**nterest, **T**axes, and **I**nsurance (homeowners).

Planned Unit Development (PUD) A special type of subdivision that may combine nonresidential uses with residential uses, or otherwise depart from ordinary zoning and subdivision regulations; some PUDs have lot owners co-own recreational facilities or open spaces as tenants in common.

Point One percent of the loan amount. **Discount points** are additional funds paid to a lender at the beginning of a loan to lower the interest rate and monthly payments. The effect of discount points is to make up the difference between the current market interest rate and the rate a lender gives a borrower on a note.

Police Power The constitutional power of state (and local) governments to enact and enforce laws that protect the public's health, safety, morals, and general welfare. From the lender's standpoint, the most important restrictions that government can place on land come from its police power, which can take the form of land use controls (primarily zoning laws and building codes) and environmental protection laws.

Portfolio Lenders Financial institutions that make real estate loans they keep and service in-house, instead of selling on the secondary market. Portfolio lenders can be major financial institutions, such as banks, or other types of non-traditional lenders or investors.

Power of Sale Clause A clause that allows the trustee to sell trust deed property, without court supervision, when terms of the trust deed are not kept.

Pre-Approval Process by which a lender determines if potential borrowers can be financed through the lender, and for what amount of money.

Predatory Lending Loans that take advantage of ill-informed consumers through excessively high fees, misrepresented loan terms, frequent refinancing that does not benefit the borrower, and other prohibited acts.

Pre-Qualification Process by which a mortgage loan originator estimates the amount of loan for which a borrower might be approved; this is non-binding.

Prepayment Penalty A fee that a lender charges the borrower for paying off a loan early. While the time periods and amount of the prepayment penalty may vary considerably, the basic effect of these penalties is to charge the debtor extra money to make up for interest income a lender loses when the debtor pays off the loan early. Standard Fannie Mae and Freddie Mac notes and mortgages do not have prepayment penalties, and prepayment penalties are prohibited in FHA and VA loans.

Primary Mortgage Markets Lenders who make mortgage loans directly to borrowers. The primary market is comprised of the various lending institutions in local communities—commercial banks, S & Ls, and mortgage companies. The source of funds for the primary market is largely made up of the savings deposits of individuals and businesses in the local area. Lenders use those savings to make real estate loans.

Prime Rate The lowest interest rate that banks charge their best commercial customers.

Principal 1. With regard to a loan, the amount originally borrowed or the current balance. Compare to **Interest**. 2. A person who grants another person (an agent) authority to represent him or her in dealing with third parties.

Private Mortgage Insurance (PMI) Insurance offered by private companies to insure a lender against default on a loan by a borrower.

Promissory Note Instruments that evidence a promise to pay a specific amount of money to a specific person within a specific time frame. Before a lender will finance the purchase of a house, the borrower must promise to repay the funds. The one promising to pay the money is called the **maker** of the note, usually the homebuyer. The one to whom payment is promised is called the **payee**, usually the lender, which could also be the seller. Promissory notes are basic evidence of debt, showing who owes how much to whom.

Property Something that is owned—real or personal—and includes the rights of ownership. The rights of ownership allow the owner to use, possess, transfer, or encumber the property owned. **Real property** is defined as the physical land and everything attached to it, plus the rights of ownership (bundle of rights) in real estate. Real property is also called **realty**. **Personal property** is defined as tangible items not permanently attached to, or part of, the real estate as well as intangible items. Personal property is also called **personalty** or **chattel**.

Quitclaim Deeds Deeds that convey any interest in a piece of real property that the grantor has at the time the deed is executed. It makes no warranties whatsoever regarding the title, if any, held by the grantor. It simply conveys whatever right, title, or interest the grantor holds in the property without representation that there is any interest at all. Often, quitclaims are used to clear up title problems, known as clouds on the title.

Real Estate Investment Trust (REIT) A real estate investment business with at least 100 investors, organized as a trust.

Real Estate Owned (REO) Property acquired by a lending institution through foreclosure and held in inventory.

Real Estate Settlement Procedures Act (RESPA) Federal law dealing with real estate closings that provides specific procedures and guidelines for the disclosure of settlement costs.

Recertification of Value (Recert) Completed to confirm whether or not the conditions of a prior appraisal have been met. A Recertification of Value does not change the effective date of the value opinion.

Red Flag Rules Section 114 of the Fair and Accurate Credit Transaction Act requiring financial institutions to implement identity theft prevention programs.

Redemption Debtors may be able to redeem (save) their property from the time a notice of a pending foreclosure, called a **lis pendens**, is filed until the confirmation of the foreclosure sale. This is done by paying the court what is due, which may include court costs and attorneys' fees. In some states, this right to save or redeem the property prior to the confirmation of sale is called the **equitable right of redemption.** Some other states use the **statutory right of redemption,** which allows debtors to redeem themselves after the final sale. Once the redemption is made, the court will set aside the sale, pay the parties, and the debtor gains title to the property again.

Refinancing When a borrower redoes or expands the loan on a property, usually to get a better interest rate or pay off other debts.

Rescind (Rescission) To take back or withdraw an offer or contract.

Reserve Requirements The percentage of customers' deposits that commercial banks are required to keep on deposit, either on hand at the bank or in a bank's own accounts. The money a bank cannot lend to other people.

Reserves Cash on deposit or other highly liquid assets a borrower must have in order to cover two months of PITI mortgage payments, after they make the cash down payment and pays all closing costs.

Residual Income The income a borrower has left after subtracting taxes, housing expense, and all recurring debts and obligations (used for VA loan qualifying). Also called the **cash flow** analysis method.

Right to Rescind The right of a consumer to rescind any credit transaction, except a mortgage, involving their principal residence as collateral, up to midnight of the third business day.

Savings and Loan Associations (S & Ls) Financial institutions that specialize in taking savings deposits and making mortgage loans. Traditionally, S & Ls were the major real estate lending institutions, investing roughly 75% of their assets in single-family mortgages. They were able to dominate local mortgage markets, even though commercial banks had more assets to invest, mainly because deposits placed with S & Ls were savings deposits less frequently subject to immediate withdrawal than demand deposits (checking) held by banks.

Secondary Financing The borrowing of money from another source in addition to the primary lender to pay for part of the purchase price or closing costs.

Secondary Mortgage Markets Private investors and government agencies that buy and sell real estate mortgages. The difference between primary and secondary markets is that secondary markets buy real estate loans from all over the country as investments, whereas primary markets are usually local in nature, with local lenders making local loans. Secondary mortgage markets were originally established by the federal government in an attempt to moderate local real estate cycles.

Secure and Fair Enforcement for Mortgage Licensing Act (SAFE Act) A key element of the Housing and Economic Recovery Act of 2008 (HERA) designed to enhance consumer protection and reduce fraud by requiring states to establish minimum standards for the licensing and registration of mortgage loan originators.

Securitization The act of pooling mortgages and then selling them as mortgage-backed securities.

Security Instruments Gives a creditor the right to have the collateral sold to satisfy the debt if the debtor fails to pay according to the terms of the agreement. Keep in mind, though, that a security instrument just describes collateral for a note. Even without a security instrument, the debtor is still obligated to pay the note.

Self-Employment Income Money someone earns working independently, either doing freelance work, as an independent contractor, or as the owner of a company. Self-employment income may only count as income if it's consistent. Tax returns are usually required proving consistency.

Self-Liquidating Description of a fully amortizing loan for which the total payments over the life of the loan pay off the entire balance by the end of the loan's term.

Seller Financing When a seller extends credit to a buyer to finance the purchase of the property, which can be instead of or in addition to the buyer obtaining a loan from a third party, such as an institutional lender.

Seller-paid Items Closing costs paid by the seller instead of the buyer. This usually refers to items normally paid by the buyer, but in some instances are paid by the seller to help close the sale. FHA and VA loans limit this.

Servicing The process of collecting payments, keeping records, and handling defaults for loans.

Sheriff's Deed A deed issued by the court to a purchaser of property from a foreclosure sale.

Sheriff's Sale A foreclosure sale held after a judicial foreclosure. Sometimes called an **execution** or an **execution sale**.

Steering Illegal activity of channeling prospective buyers or tenants to particular neighborhoods based on their race, religion, national origin, or ancestry.

Straw Buyer A person who receives payment from for the use of that person's name and credit history to apply for a loan, generally as part of a mortgage fraud scheme.

Subordination Clause Gives a mortgage recorded at a later date the right to take priority over an earlier recorded mortgage. Normally with mortgages, trust deeds, and other real estate contracts, the first instrument or document recorded gets lien priority. Lien priority is the order in which liens are paid off out of the proceeds of a foreclosure sale. This is important because the lien with the highest priority gets paid first out of the proceeds of a foreclosure sale.

Subprime Loans Loans that have more risks than allowed in the conforming market. Also called **B-C Loans** or **B-C Credit**.

Title The actual lawful ownership of real property. Title refers to holding the bundle of rights conveyed. Title is not a document, but rather a concept or theory of ownership.

Title, Equitable An interest created in property upon the execution of a valid sales contract, whereby actual title is transferred by deed at a closing. The buyer's interest in property under a land contract. Also called an **equitable interest**.

Title VIII Part of the Civil Rights Act of 1968; prohibits discrimination based on race, color, religion, sex, national origin, disability, or familial status. Also referred to as the **Federal Fair Housing Act.**

Title Insurance. Insurance that indemnifies against losses resulting from undiscovered title defects and encumbrances.

Title Report. A document stating the current title status of property. This report, also called a preliminary title report (prelim) or title guaranty, lists all encumbrances, covenants, and defects associated with the title and shown in the public record. A title report, however, does not detail the chain of title to property like an abstract of title does. Guarantees are limited to mistakes made in reading or interpreting items in the public record. Title reports must be current as of the day of settlement.

Total Debt to Income Ratio The relationship of a borrower's total monthly debt obligations, including housing and long-term debts with more than ten payments remaining, to income, expressed as a percentage. Also called **Debt Service Ratio.**

Trust Deeds Instruments held by a third party as security for the payment of a note. They are also called deeds of trust. Trust deeds are a three-party device. The borrower is called the **trustor**; the lender is the **beneficiary**; and there is an independent third party called the **trustee**. In states considered lien theory states, trust deeds create a lien against property in favor of the beneficiary. This lien gives the creditor the right to force the sale of the property if the debtor defaults on payments under the note or trust deed.

Truth In Lending Statement (TIL) Disclosure of the true costs associated with a residential loan, including the annual percentage rate, that is required to be given to prospective borrowers within three business days of applying for a loan.

Underwriting The process of evaluating and deciding whether to make a new loan.

Uniform Residential Appraisal Report (URAR) Also referred to as the Fannie Mae Form 1004 or Freddie Mac Form 70, it's the primary form used for single-family residential property appraisals. Its use must adhere to the standards set forth by the **Uniform**

Standards of Professional Appraisal Practice (USPAP), which is established and promoted by the Appraisal Foundation.

Unique Identifier A number or other identifier assigned by protocols established by the Nationwide Mortgage Licensing System and Registry that permanently identifies a mortgage loan originator.

Warehouse Lending When a mortgage broker uses his own funds to fund the mortgage loan and then sells the loan to the lender immediately after closing. The broker usually has a guarantee the lender will buy the loan and receives an additional fee for funding the mortgage loan.

Yield Spread Premium (YSP) A tool that mortgage loan originators can use to reduce the amount of money the borrower would pay toward their closing costs.

Appendix B:
Financial Calculations

Financial calculations are critical when originating and underwriting a loan. Mortgage professionals should be familiar with some of these basic calculations:

- Payments of principal and interest
- Interest per diem
- Loan-to-value and combined loan-to-value
- Qualifying ratios
- Discount points
- Closing costs and prepaid items
- ARMs (e.g., fully indexed rate)

Principal and Interest

Interest is the cost of borrowing money, while **principal** is the balance of the loan. To find the annual interest, simply multiply the principal by the interest rate.

Example

If the loan balance (principal) is $135,000 and the interest rate is 7.5%, the annual interest would be:

.075 x $135,000 = $10,125

That number, divided by 12, indicates the monthly interest on the loan balance. If the borrower makes a monthly mortgage payment of $985 (not counting insurance and taxes), it's possible to see how much of that payment is applied to the principal that month:

$10,125 ÷ 12 = $843.75 Monthly Interest

$985 - $843.75 = $141.25 Applied to Principal

Interest Per Diem

The interest on a mortgage loan is paid for the previous month. If interest on the outstanding balance of a seller's loan is collected at settlement, the seller is **debited** the daily interest amount based on the day of the month on which the loan closes. The first step is to determine the per diem amount:

Principal Amount (Loan Balance) x Interest Rate ÷ 365 = Per Diem Rate

And then determine the number of days in order to find the total debit:

Closing Day x Per Diem Rate = Amount Debited to Seller

Example 1:

The seller still owes $40,000 on his loan, which has an interest rate of 5%. The loan closes on June 10.

$40,000 x .05 = $2,000 Annual Interest

$2,000 ÷ 365 = $5.48 = Per Diem Interest

Closing Day = 10 Days Interest Due

10 Days x $5.48 = $54.80 Debited to Seller at Settlement

If the buyer had assumed the loan, the buyer would be credited with the same amount.

Sometimes, a buyer is required to prepay interest on a new mortgage loan as part of settlement. This accounts for the days from the close date to the last day of the month, since the first mortgage payment is usually not due in the first day of the *following month*. The borrower will be **debited** with the number of days from the close date to the last day of the month. The first step, again, is to determine the per diem amount:

Principal Amount x Interest Rate ÷ 365 = Per Diem Rate

And then determine the number of days in order to find the total debit:

Closing Day + # Days in Left in the Month x Per Diem Rate = Amount Debited

Example 2:

A borrower takes out a loan for $100,000 at 6% interest. The loan closes on June 10.

$100,000 x .06 = $6,000 Annual Interest

$6,000 ÷ 365 = $16.44 = Per Diem Interest

Closing Day + 20 Days Left in June = 21 days

21 Days x $16.44 = $345.24 Debited to Buyer at Settlement

Loan-To-Value

The **loan-to-value ratio** (LTV) refers to the amount of money borrowed for a first mortgage compared to the value of the property. Lenders use LTV to determine how much they are willing to loan on a given property based on its value. The lender will always use the lower of the appraised value or the sale price.

Example 1:

Sale Price:	$120,000
Appraised Value:	$125,000
Down Payment:	$24,000
Loan Amount:	$96,000

$96,000 ÷ $120,000 = .80 or 80% LTV

The loan-to-value may be used to find the required down payment as well.

Example 2:

Sale Price:	$148,000
Appraised Value:	$150,000
Required LTV:	85%

$148,000 x .85 = $125,800 Loan Amount

$148,000 - $125,800 = $22,200 Down Payment

Example 3:

Sale Price:	$220,000
Appraised Value:	$218,000
Required LTV:	80%

$218,000 x .80 = $174,400 Loan Amount

$220,000 - $174,400 = $45,600 Down Payment

Combined Loan-To-Value

The **combined loan-to-value** (CLTV) is the percentage of the property value borrowed through a combination of more than one loan, such as a first mortgage and a second mortgage home equity loan. The CLTV, sometimes called **total loan-to-value (TLTV)**, is calculated by adding all loan amounts and dividing by the home's appraised value or purchase price, whichever is lower.

Example:

Appraised Value:	$100,000
First Mortgage:	$80,000
Second Mortgage:	$10,000

$$\frac{\$80,000 + \$10,000}{\$100,000} = \textbf{90\% CLTV}$$

Both loan-to-value (LTV) and combined loan-to-value (CLTV) can be used to determine the amount of home equity a borrower has. So, that borrower with 90% CLTV has 10% equity in the property.

Qualifying Ratios

When considering a borrower's income, there are two important qualifying standards lenders look at: Housing expense ratio and total debt to income ratio (DTI). A borrower must qualify under **both** ratios. Different loan programs (e.g., conventional, FHA) accept different qualifying ratios.

Housing Expense Ratio

A borrower's housing expense ratio is the relationship of the borrower's total monthly housing expense (principal, interest, taxes, and insurances, or PITI) to gross monthly income, expressed as a percentage:

Total Housing Expense (PITI) ÷ Income = Ratio %

Debt to Income Ratio (DTI)

A borrower's total debt to income ratio (sometimes called debt service ratio) is the relationship of the borrower's total monthly debt obligations (including housing and long-term debts with more than ten payments left) to gross monthly income, expressed as a percentage:

Total Debt (PITI + all recurring monthly debts) ÷ Income = Ratio %

Example:

Gross Monthly Income:	$3,400.00	
Loan:	$120,000.00	at 5.5% (30-year fixed)
Principal & Interest:	$681.35	
1/12 Annual Taxes:	112.60	
1/12 Insurance:	+ 25.80	
PITI:	$819.75	
Monthly Debt:	$ 220.50	(Car Payment)
	35.00	(Revolving Credit)
	+ 145.00	(Child Support)
Total Monthly Debt:	$ 400.50	

$819.75 (PITI) ÷ $3,400 (Income) = 24.1% Housing Expense Ratio

$1,220.25 (PITI + Debt) ÷ $3,400 (Income) = 35.9% Debt to Income Ratio

Closing Costs and Prepaid Items

Proration is the division of expenses between buyer and seller in proportion to the actual usage of the item represented by a particular expense as of the **day the loan is funded.** In order to adjust a cost shared by both buyer and seller, it's necessary to determine whether the expense is accrued (paid in arrears) or prepaid (paid in advance).

- **Accrued expenses** are the items on a settlement statement for which the cost has been incurred, but the expense has not yet been paid; for example, mortgage interest. Accrued expenses are prorated on the settlement statement as a debit to the seller and a credit to the borrower.

- **Prepaid expenses** are the items on a settlement statement the seller has already paid; for example, homeowners insurance. Prepaid expenses are prorated on the settlement statement as a credit to the seller and a debit to the borrower.

Note that real estate taxes generally required to be prorated at closing. In some states, real estate taxes are paid in arrears (debit to seller), and in others, they are paid in advance (debit to borrower).

When performing proration calculations, expenses may be prorated using:

- A 360-day year, 12 months of 30 days each.
- A 365-day year, counting the exact number of days in each month (taking leap years into account).

Often, local custom dictates which factor is used. Either way, the steps to calculate the adjustment are similar:

1. Determine if the expense is accrued or prepaid.
2. Divide the expense by the appropriate period to find a monthly (daily) rate.
3. Determine how many months (days) are affected by the expense.
4. Multiply the monthly (daily) rate by the number of affected months (days).
5. Determine which party is credited and which is debited.

Example

Assume that property taxes of $1,234.42 are paid on June 30 for the first six months of the year (paid in arrears). The transaction closes on March 31.

1. The buyer pays on June 30, so the expense is accrued.
2. The $1,234.42 tax bill is for 181 days (Jan. 1 to June 30), for a daily rate of $6.82.
3. The seller lived in the house for 89 days (Jan. 1 to March 30).
4. The portion of the tax bill owed by the seller is $606.98 (89 days x $6.82).
5. Accrued expenses are a debit to the seller and a credit to the borrower.

Chapter Quiz and Exam Answers

Chapter 1 Federal Lending Legislation Review

1. C RESPA requires that the borrower have the right to inspect the HUD-1 one business day prior to closing, if requested.

2. C A borrower's legal source of income, including public assistance, cannot be an adverse consideration in loan underwriting, according to the Equal Credit Opportunity Act.

3. D An extended rescission period of three years is in place for borrowers to whom the APR has not been disclosed or for whom the true APR exceeds the APR on the TIL Statement by a certain amount.

4. A The Privacy Rule of the GLB Act requires that financial institutions provide the borrower with a Consumer Privacy policy before disclosing information to a non-affiliated third party. .

5. B Section 32 of Regulation Z prohibits excessive points and fees. Such high cost loans are defined in the Home Ownership and Equity Protection Act (HOEPA).

6. C The Home Mortgage Disclosure Act requires that this information be reported in order to determine whether discriminatory practices are being used.

7. D Title V, the Secure and Fair Enforcement for Mortgage Licensing Act, or SAFE Act, is a key component of the Housing and Economic Recovery Act of 2008.

8. A It is the Bank Secrecy Act/Anti-Money Laundering Act that includes this requirement.

9. B The National Do Not Call Registry includes provisions that could lead to a $16,000 fine for each instance of calling a number that is on the list.

10. D The Safeguards Rule (15 U.S.C. § 6801–6809) which is part of Title V protections included in the Gramm-Leach-Bliley Act requires all financial institutions and institutions that receive consumer's financial information to design, implement, and maintain safeguards to protect customer information while it is in the custody and control of the institution and its agents.

11. B Title X of the Dodd-Frank Act creates the Consumer Financial Protection Bureau (CFPB) as an independent entity with rule-making and enforcement authority over many consumer financial laws.

12. C The Mortgage Assistance Relief Services (MARS) Rule was established to protect distressed homeowners from mortgage relief scams that have sprung up during the mortgage crisis.

13. D Vacant land loans are not covered under the Home Mortgage Disclosure Act.

14. B The right to rescind this type of credit transaction extends until midnight of the third business day after a transaction closes. Business days do not include Sundays and federal holidays.

15. C The Equal Credit Opportunity Act requires that any decision be communicated to the applicant within 30 days.

16. C RESPA covers loans secured with a mortgage placed on a one- to four-family residential property.

17. D The Truth in Lending Statement (TIL) discloses the total cost of financing, including the annual percentage rate (APR).

18. A The information furnisher should complete their investigation within 30 days and either correct the credit report or explain why there is no error.

19. C FACTA requires that all consumer information be secured to avoid identity theft.

20. D MDIA requires that borrowers wait until the 7th business day after delivery of required disclosures before a loan can close, except possibly in the case of a bona fide financial emergency.

21. B Of these, only government recording charges may have a tolerance of 10%. Other charges that can show this tolerance include lender-required settlement services where the lender selects the provider or the borrower uses a provider identified by loan originator.

22. C RESPA requires most charges be available to the borrower for at least 10 business days.

23. B Only the fee for obtaining a credit report may be collected before the GFE, TIL, and other required disclosures are provided.

24. A The Real Estate Settlement Procedures Act prohibits kickbacks such as the one described.

25. B This would require an additional waiting period of three business days since the change exceeds the tolerance of .25% for a fixed rate loan.

26. A 2009 amendments to the Truth in Lending Act define a higher-priced loan as one with an APR that exceeds the applicable average prime offer rate by at least 1.5% on first lien loans or 3.5% for junior lien loans.

27. A Interest-only loans are prohibited by the qualified mortgage (QM) rule..

28. B Keeping records of cash purchases of negotiable instruments is a requirement of the BSA/AML..

29. C A loan originator's mistake such as this would not be considered a changed circumstance.

30. A. The new Federal Reserve Mortgage Loan Originator Compensation Rule prohibits a MLO from being paid based on any loan terms other than the loan amount. Any payment based on the fees or costs or other such loan terms is illegal.

Chapter 2 Nontraditional Loan Products Overview

1. C A fixed rate is one indicator of a traditional mortgage. A loan with any of these other characteristics would be considered nontraditional.

2. C The SAFE Act provides the definition of a nontraditional mortgage as anything other than 30-year fixed.

3. C A jumbo loan exceeds the limits of Fannie Mae and Freddie Mac and so is also known as a nonconforming loan.

4. A A blanket mortgage covers more than one parcel or lot and is often used for subdivision developments.

5. C A teaser rate is an introductory rate the lender approves on a mortgage loan. This is a short-term rate and can adjust according to the terms and conditions outlined in the note.

6. C Under the definition of qualifying mortgage provided by the CFPB in January 2013, interest only is considered to be a toxic feature that is prohibited in loans the CFPB would deem to be qualified loans.

7. A The Home Equity Line of Credit is just like a credit card; it can be used and paid off as needed. The main difference is the HELOC uses real estate as collateral and the credit card does not.

8. A If a borrower exercises his right to change from an ARM to a fixed rate mortgage, he has a convertible adjustable rate mortgage.

9. B A conforming loan follows the Fannie Mae and Freddie Mac criteria in order to be eligible for sale in the secondary mortgage market.

10. D The Guidance is concerned about borrowers suffering payment shock and being unable to repay a loan. A borrower with low debt income ratios would be a safer risk.

11. A If Stan has a low loan-to-value ratio, low debt to income ration, and a higher credit score, that will help him get approved for a simultaneous second loan. A high housing ratio is NOT a mitigating factor.

12. C The margin is added to the index to determine the adjustable rate.

13. D A reverse mortgage provides borrowers 62 years or older with a monthly check and the balance is owed at the end of the loan term or when the borrower dies.

14. C A loan that is fully amortizing means the total payments over the life of the loan will pay off the entire balance of principal and interest due at the end of the term.

15. B An index is a statistical report that is generally a reliable indicator of the approximate cost of money. Future interest rate adjustments for ARM loans are based on the up and down movements of the index.

16. B A reverse mortgage is a rising debt/falling equity loan.

17. B A homeowner who has a small balance on an existing mortgage may be able to get a reverse mortgage.

18. C If the borrower does not live in the home for 12 consecutive months, a reverse mortgage must be repaid.

19. B HECM loans are not available to those holding a proprietary lease on a cooperative.

20. B The borrower's credit history is not a factor.

Chapter 3 Ethics

1. B Refusing to make loans on property in certain neighborhoods for discriminatory reasons is called redlining.

2. D This could be an example of predatory lending.

3. A RESPA considers anyone who initiated, paid, or accepted a kickback to be in violation.

4. D An ad that claims "Only 10% down" is providing a triggering term—the amount of the down payment. Such a fact in an ad would trigger the required disclosures.

5. D When triggering terms are used in an ad, TILA requires the disclosure of the amount of down payment, terms of loan repayment, and annual percentage rate. The total closing costs are not required to be stated in the ad.

6. B While a lender should never make a loan to someone who is unqualified to repay it, someone should never be discouraged from making the application, according to the Equal Credit Opportunity Act (ECOA), on the basis of membership in a protected class.

7. D As of today, the federal Fair Housing Act prohibits discrimination in housing based on "race, color, religion, sex, national origin, disability, or familial status in the sale or lease of residential property."

8. A If the broker decided to ignore a critical fact, he could be accused of actual fraud.

9. C Steering relates to buyers or renters and is defined as channeling prospective buyers or renters to or away from specific neighborhoods.

10. D Requiring mortgage insurance does not indicate predatory lending.

11. D The Truth in Lending Act addresses advertising by creditors, including mortgage loan originators.

12. C Regulation Z implementing the Truth in Lending Act ensures that some borrowers have the right of rescission for three business days after a loan contract is signed.

13. D Appraisers are required to analyze the purchase contract, current listing, and recent prior sales for the past three years. As well, the URAR form asks for research of the subject's transfers from three years prior to the effective date of the appraisal.

14. B The Civil Rights Act of 1866 prohibits discrimination based on race. There are no exceptions to this law.

15. B In a loan flipping scam—a type of equity skimming—homeowners are encouraged to keep refinancing their property. Each time they refinance, they are charged points and closing costs, along with other fees. And each time, the equity gets smaller.

16. C The Fair Housing Act requires that the Equal Housing Opportunity logo be displayed in all printed material and the term "equal housing lender" must be used when broadcast over the airwaves.

17. A The Fair Housing Act was amended to include disability as a protected class. Persons with disabilities are not specifically named in the Equal Credit Opportunity Act.

18. D A straw buyer is someone whose name and personal information is used to obtain a loan, in this case, for property in which she will not live. This is also both identity theft and fraud.

19. A The Community Reinvestment Act was passed to encourage lenders to meet the needs of all of the communities in which they operate as a way address the illegal practice of redlining.

20. B Considering the borrower's receipt of public assistance if the applicant adequately met all other criteria would be a violation of the Equal Credit Opportunity Act (ECOA). All people must be considered for credit equally on the basis of income adequacy, sufficient net worth, job stability, and satisfactory credit rating.

Chapter 4 Mortgage Loan Origination Activities Review

1.   A   Savings, the previous sale of a home, or gifts are all acceptable sources of down payment, but the buyer is usually not allowed to use borrowed funds.

2.   C   The front ratio is calculated by dividing the total monthly housing (PITI, homeowners dues, PMI) by gross monthly income (before taxes).

3.   A   The cost approach is the most logical, since only a geodesic dome is comparable and the property is not being purchased as an investment property. There is no appraisal approach called the salability approach.

4.   B   To determine the loan-to-value ratio, you need to divide 118,000 by 131,000 (the lowest of the sales price or appraised value) to get an LTV of 90%.

5.   C   Market value is the theoretical price that a piece of real estate is most likely to bring in a typical transaction.

6.   A   Conventional ratios are 28/36, with 28% of the gross monthly income allowed for the total housing payment.

7.   D   The correct calculation is hourly rate x number of hours worked weekly x 52 (weeks in a year) ÷ 12 (number of months). Always calculate the income to the year and divide by 12. This will allow for the months that have more or less than exactly 4 weeks. Any other calculation will not give you the correct amount.

8.   B   A minimum of three comparables is required by most secondary market lenders to ensure an accurate appraisal from sufficient data.

9.   B   Consumer debts that have less than 10 months of payments remaining do not need to be included for the purpose of calculating debt ratios.

10.   C   FHA loans require income ratios of 31% for housing expense and 43% for debt to income.

11.   C   The USDA Section 502 loan program either guarantees loans made by approved private lenders or makes direct loans

12.   A   An FHA loan requires at least a down payment of 3.5% of the home's purchase price or appraised value, whichever is less.

13.   D   A Chapter 7 bankruptcy stays on a credit report for ten years.

14.   C   According to the new FHA rules, mortgage insurance must be paid for at least 11 years.

15.   C   The mechanics of closing are normally the responsibility of a closing or escrow agent or attorney, who simultaneously follows the instructions of both buyer and seller, as per the sales contract.

16.   A   An eligible veteran can use a VA loan to purchase a house with no down payment, which would be an LTV of 100%.

17.   C   A point is 1% of the loan amount, so $135,000 x .01 = $1,350 per point. Three points is $4,050.

18.   B   The Upfront Mortgage Insurance Premium is charged on all FHA loans and paid to HUD after the loan closing.

19.   D   When you purchase a house or car, you hypothecate it. You use it as collateral but keep possession of it.

20.   C   The borrower would need 15% of the $120,000 purchase price, or $18,000 plus the additional 2%, or $2,400 for closing costs that the seller is not providing.

Chapter 5 SAFE Act and UST Content Quiz

1. C The state regulatory authority may suspend or revoke a license for failure to provide proper disclosures to a borrower as part of a mortgage loan transaction.

2. D Of these, the only task that requires licensing is offering or negotiating loan terms.

3. B Of these choices, the underwriter may only consider the likelihood of continued income.

4. D Of these examples, only Trace is exempt from licensing requirements under the SAFE Act. An independent contractor who performs the activities of a mortgage loan originator is required to be licensed.

5. B Communicating prospective residential mortgage loan terms to a borrower whether directly or indirectly with a borrower is considered an example of the task of offering o negotiating the terms of a loan.

6. B Approving course offerings and course providers is the responsibility of the NMLS not the state regulatory authority.

7. C This responsibility of the states was included with the definitions in Section 1503 of the SAFE Act.

8. B An individual engaging solely in loan processor or underwriter activities, shall not represent to the public, through advertising or other means of communicating or providing information including the use of business cards, stationery, brochures, signs, rate lists, or other promotional items, that such individual can or will perform any of the activities of a mortgage loan originator.

9. A RESPA considers anyone who initiated, paid, or accepted a kickback to be in violation.

10. D These disclosures are not required if the borrower withdraws the application.

11. D Kirk is acting as a loan originator habitually or repeatedly. An individual who acts as a loan originator in providing financing for the sale of a property he owns is exempt from licensure unless that individual engages in such activity with habitualness as Kirk does.

12. D George was involved in a disqualifying association with a mortgage lender whose license was revoked. The state regulatory authority may refuse to issue finding that the applicant has been a director, partner, or substantial stockholder of an originating entity which has had a registration or license revoked by the state regulatory authority or of another state.

13. A The Real Estate Settlement Procedures Act or RESPA prohibits kickbacks such as the one described in this scenario.

14. A You would not be in violation of ECOA for asking a question about information that is offered on the loan application. The other questions, even if asked out of politeness or curiosity, would violate ECOA.

15. D Any mortgage loan that is NOT a 30-year fixed rate mortgage loan is considered a nontraditional mortgage product according to the SAFE Act definition.

16. D An individual act is for compensation or gain if the individual receives in connection with the individual's activities anything of value, including, but not limited to, payment of a salary, bonus, or commission. The concept anything of value is interpreted broadly and is not limited only to payments that are contingent upon the closing of a loan.

17. C The fingerprints/background check is a requirement under the SAFE Act. This requirement cannot be waived.

18. C The state regulatory authority will likely deny a mortgage loan originator license if, at any time preceding the date of application, an individual was convicted of a felony involved an act of fraud, dishonesty, a breach of trust, or money laundering no matter how long ago the offense occurred. Any felony conviction that occurred within the last 7 years would likely result in a denial but the state regulatory authority may, in his or her discretion, disregard a past felony conviction (10 years ago) that is unrelated to fraud or mishandling of money or for which the felon has been pardoned.

19. B An individual who fails to achieve a passing score of 75% on the MLO written test two consecutive times may retake the test after waiting 30 days. If an applicant fails the test three consecutive times, the individual must wait 6 months to retake the exam.

20. C To be in compliance, an organization should keep an internal Do Not Call list as well as an updated version of the national Do Not Call list.

Practice Exam #1: MLO National Test with UST

1. D If the referring party does not have an ownership or other beneficial interest, an Affiliated Business Arrangement (AfBA) disclosure is not required by RESPA.

2. B Assuming you provide the required disclosure, this is an example of an affiliated business arrangement, not a RESPA violation. The other three arrangements could be considered violations of RESPA. To violate RESPA, the thing of value does not have to be money.

3. C RESPA is also known as Regulation X.

4. B This provision in the MARS Rule is known as the Advance Fee Ban..

5. D The VA requires a non-refundable funding fee that varies based on the number of times the veteran has used a VA loan.

6. B An alienation clause requires the mortgagor to repay the entire balance of the loan if the property is sold, transferred, or otherwise abandoned.

7. D A zero tolerance applies to the sum of all state and local government transfer fees on mortgages and home sales.

8. A The Community Reinvestment Act is intended to ensure that all neighborhoods are served by financial institutions.

9. D The Safeguards Rule is a principal part of the Gramm-Leach-Bliley Title V privacy requirements..

10. A Traditionally, a loan is considered to be conforming when it meets Fannie Mae/Freddie Mac standards and can be sold on the secondary market.

11. C The Equal Credit Opportunity Act ensures all lenders must make credit available with fairness and without discrimination.

12. C A reverse mortgage allows qualified homeowners at least 62 years of age to convert equity in their home into a monthly income stream or line of credit.

13. D A buyer who has no intention of living in the property he or she fraudulently mortgages could be considered a straw buyer. While this situation may seem okay, since it's just one relative helping out another, it's still misrepresentation and, therefore, fraud.

14. D FHA loans are not just for low-income borrowers. They can be used to purchase a one- to four-family residence. FHA loans do require a down payment but allow borrowers to use a gift to cover that.

15. B Equity is the difference between market value of a property and the sum of the mortgages and liens against it.

16. A When refinancing, Regulation Z gives a borrower three business days to rescind after the contract is signed.

17. C The first mortgage is 80% of the sale price: $175,000 x 80% = $140,000.

18. A A convertible adjustable rate mortgage gives a borrower the right to change from an adjustable rate mortgage to a fixed rate mortgage one time during the loan term, provided certain conditions are met.

19. C Redlining is the refusal to make loans on property in certain neighborhoods for discriminatory reasons and is an illegal discriminatory act under federal, state, and local fair housing laws.

20. A His cable service payment is not considered part of his debt for qualifying purposes since cable service can be cancelled.

21. D HOEPA is an addendum to the Truth in Lending Act. HOEPA limits the amount of points that can be charged on loans without additional disclosures.

22. B The APR—annual percentage rate—takes into consideration the cost of borrowing and the total amount financed. It is represented as percentage and is the true cost of lending.

23. A A borrower's housing expense ratio is the relationship of the borrower's total monthly housing expense to income, expressed as a percentage.

24. D Any compensation that is based on loan terms or conditions such as interest rate, annual percentage rate (APR), loan-to-value (LTV), etc., is prohibited.

25. A The definition of appraisal is "an opinion of value."

26. B TILA law requires creditors to maintain records for two years after the disclosures were required to be made.

27. C Seven years is the maximum length of time such information can be reported on a credit report according to the Fair Credit Reporting Act,

except for criminal convictions, which can be reported indefinitely.

28. B Using the payment-to-income ratio of 31%, we get $1,240. But using the total debt to income ratio, we find: $4,000 (income) multiplied by 0.43, which equals $1,720. From that, you subtract monthly debts of $600, leaving $1,120.

29. C FACTA has provisions that allow consumers to freeze their credit under certain circumstances, such as when they have experienced identity theft.

30. B Two calculations need to be done: $5,200 x 28% = $1,456, then $5,200.00 x 36% = $1,872 - $950 = $922. Take the lower of the two. If you did not complete both calculations, you might have allowed Sue to have a payment of $1,456; by the time you added the debt and divided by the $5,200, your back ratio would be too high ($5,200 x 28% = $1,456 + $950 = $2,406 ÷ $5,200 = 46%).

31. D All consumers have the right to review their credit reports for accuracies, challenge inaccurate information, and receive a free copy of their credit report annually. They do NOT have the right to have bankruptcies removed after five years. That timeline is seven to ten years.

32. C Purchasing and remodeling a house and then selling it for a quick profit is the good side of flipping, which is perfectly legal. The illegal side of flipping is when colluding parties profit from the sale of property with an inflated appraisal that supports a loan. It may involve a series of sales and quick resales, with one property and a group of sellers and buyers changing ownership among them.

33. D A consumer who does not place his name on either the National Do Not Call Registry or a company's internal do not call list has no protection from phone calls. ABC can call the borrower indefinitely.

34. A The purpose of HMDA is to determine discrimination in lending for residential properties. This would not include commercial loans.

35. C Simply multiply the original loan amount by the interest rate for the annual interest, then divide by 2 to get six months' interest. In this case, $200,000 x 6.5% (0.065) = $13,000; $13,000 ÷ 2 = $6,500.

36. C Income from rental properties should be counted only at 75%; this allows for vacancy losses.

37. B The CFPB was given the task of finalizing the Qualified Mortgage (QM) definition which was provided as an update in January 2013,.

38. D Borrowers who meet the income limits in designated rural areas do not need a down payment to get a Rural Development loan.

39. A ECOA states that an MLO can ask if the borrower is married, unmarried, or separated. The MLO may not ask if the borrower is widowed or single.

40. B Regulation Z requires that once you state any type of credit terms in advertising such as 8% interest, you must disclose all finance charges and total annual percentage rate (APR).

41. A According to the Gramm-Leach-Bliley Act, this policy is required to be provided before disclosing information to non-affiliated third parties.

42. C With an LTV of 75%, the loan for this purchase is $150,000. On a $150,000 loan, a point costs $1,500 (150,000 x .01), so the borrower is paying $3,000.

43. A RESPA's Section 8 prohibits any kinds of kickback, unearned fee, or referral fee. Earned fees are certainly allowed.

44. A While other federal legislation prohibits discrimination due to age, the Fair Housing Act does not address age.

45. C The Home Mortgage Disclosure Act is a disclosure law that determines whether financial institutions are serving the housing needs of their communities.

46. A Blockbusting is soliciting others to sell their properties due to the changes in a neighborhood.

47. D Familial status refers to households that include individuals under the age of 18 who either live with parents or legal custodians. This protection also extends to pregnant women or any person in the process of obtaining legal custody of a child under the age of 18.

48. A First, determine the maximum loan amount the homeowner qualifies for: $125,000 x 85% = $106,250. Now, subtract the current debt and closing costs: $106,250 - $63,000 - $5,000 - $4,200 = $34,050 cash available.

49. D The Civil Rights Act of 1866 applies to anyone involved in any property transactions; there are no exceptions.

50. A Eligible veterans do not need a down payment to get a VA loan.

51. A The lender's right of acceleration can mean that a buyer who misses one or two payments may have to pay off the entire debt to save the home.

52. D RESPA and TILA require disclosure of loan terms. TILA requires the disclosure of the total finance charges and loan terms in the Truth in Lending Statement; RESPA requires lenders to provide a Good Faith Estimate of closing costs and a HUD-1 Settlement Statement.

53. D Tenure refers to the homeowners' stay in the house.

54. B Private mortgage insurance (PMI) is offered by private companies to insure a lender against loss by foreclosure on a loan by a borrower.

55. B A balloon payment is prohibited as it is considered a toxic loan feature under the qualified mortgage definition provided by the CFPB..

56. C The lender (mortgagee) provides this service to a mortgagor by adding one-twelfth of the insurance premiums and taxes to the monthly mortgage payment amount.

57. A The BSA/AML was originally passed by the Congress of the United States in 1970, and amended several times since then, including provisions in title III of the USA PATRIOT Act..

58. B The only correct way to ask about a client's marital status is, "Are you married, unmarried, or separated." Be sure to include all three of these words in the question.

59. C A margin, which is also sometimes referred to as a spread, is added to the selected index to determine the interest rate charged on an ARM.

60. B The interim final rule on Valuation Independence requires creditors and their agents to provide customary and reasonable compensation to fee appraisers. The other situations are prohibited.

61. B The borrower has a right to view a HUD-1 statement one business day before closing.

62. B The right of rescission is only in effect for refinances, not purchases. It applies to owner occupied refinances only, because a default on the loan results in the homeowner losing his or her house.

63. C Subprime loans fill a need for those with less than perfect credit who want to own a home. Some lenders and investors are willing to make these riskier loans because they can get much higher interest rates and fees than they can with other real estate loans.

64. C Under HMDA guidelines, Section X of the standard Residential Loan Application must be filled out even if the borrower does not wish to furnish the information. However, in the case of a face-to-face interview, the loan officer can still mark the "I do not wish to furnish this information" box, but must fill in the application according to a visual observation or the borrower's surname.

65. C The principal for the two loans is the same, $100,000, although Borrower B will potentially pay less interest, depending on how quickly he actually pays off the loan.

66. D FHA insures loans made and funded by approved lenders.

67. D Fixed rate loans have interest rates that remain constant for the duration of the loan.

68. D FCRA protects access to consumer credit files and allows a consumer reporting agency to provide information about a consumer only to people with a valid need. This man would have no permissible purpose to obtain his brother's credit information.

69. C Section 9 of RESPA Prohibits a seller from requiring the home buyer to use a particular title insurance company, either directly or indirectly, as a condition of sale.

70. C RESPA requires a Servicing Transfer Statement to be sent to the consumer if the loan servicer sells or assigns the servicing rights of the loan to another service provider.

71. B FCRA provisions entitle consumers to a free copy of their credit report if credit is denied based on what's in the report.

72. C This disclosure, as required by the Truth in Lending Act, must be provided to a borrower within three business days of a completed loan application.

73. B Occasional overtime would probably not be considered durable income.

74. A TILA does not apply to business, commercial, or agricultural loans, loans payable with four or less installments and without a finance charge, or to loans made to corporations, partnerships, associations, and agencies. The lender does have to follow the rules of TILA when the loan is for a residential property.

75. D To find monthly income, take weekly pay, multiply by 52 weeks, and then divide by 12 months ($750 x 52 = $39,000 / 12 = $3,250).

76. D The sales comparison approach is most common, since it compares the property to recent comparable property sales. There is no appraisal approach called the highest and best use approach.

77. A 2009 amendments to the Truth in Lending Act define a higher-priced loan as one with an APR that exceeds the applicable average prime offer rate by at least 1.5% on first lien loans or 3.5% for junior lien loans.

78. B The Financial Modernization Act of 1999 is usually referenced by the names of the legislators who sponsored it: Phil Gramm, Jim Leach, and Thomas Bliley.

79. A While you could make an argument that each of these questions might violate ECOA guidelines related to discrimination, the question about the applicant's age may be necessary to prove that the applicant is old enough to legally enter into a contract.

80. D Lenders offering residential financing, including ARMs, must comply with federal guidelines under Regulation Z of the Truth in Lending Act requiring certain disclosures be made to borrowers, including the annual percentage rate.

81. A The Equal Credit Opportunity Act requires the lender to provide the borrower an approval, notice of incomplete application, or a reason for rejection of credit in writing within 30 days of loan application.

82. A The CFPB does not enforce the Fair Housing Act.

83. D Negative amortization occurs when loan balances increase rather than decrease because the borrower is paying less than the minimum interest.

84. D FACTA addresses the problem of identity theft, and an office whose employee puts files in an unlocked drawer would not be in compliance. If someone does not personally secure his files, the confidential information could be accessed for identity theft after work hours by any unscrupulous office worker with keys or access codes to the building.

85. C These fees should be shown as a lump sum, not itemized.

86. D The settlement agent is responsible for tabulating all figures from the lender, broker, and government agencies, as well as any items being paid out to creditors.

87. C The SAFE Act requires at least 20 hours of prelicensing education for state-licensed MLOs. Individual states may impose additional educational requirements.

88. A The Equal Credit Opportunity Act requires that, if the borrower wishes to disclose this information on the loan application, it must be used in the underwriting decision.

89. B The Truth in Lending Act requires lenders to disclose consumer credit costs in a uniform manner to promote informed use of consumer credit, enabling them to compare credit costs and shop around for the best credit terms.

90. C She will pay $140,272 in interest for that 30-year loan (695.20 x 12 months x 30 years = $250,272 total payment – $110,000 principal = $140,272 interest).

91. A A blanket mortgage covers more than one parcel of land.

92. B The law that regulates credit bureau companies and users of credit reports is the Fair Credit Reporting Act.

93. D Information required to comply with the Home Mortgage Disclosure Act is gathered in part from Section X (Information for Government Monitoring Purposes) of the Uniform Residential Loan Application.

94. B The Secure and Fair Enforcement for Mortgage Licensing Act, or SAFE Act, is a key component of the Housing and Economic Recovery Act of 2008.

95. C The National Do Not Call Registry includes provisions that a telemarketer can be charged $16,000 for each instance of calling a number that is on the list.

96. A Section 10 of RESPA sets limits on the amounts that a lender may require a borrower to put into an escrow account while allowing a cushion of up to two months.

97. A Extending credit to people with little or no income and who have little chance of repaying the loan so the lender can foreclose on the property and keep the excess equity to cover costs is considered predatory lending, according to the

Interagency Statement on Subprime Mortgage Lending.

98. D The intent of the Mortgage Assistance Relief Services (MARS) Rule is to protect distressed homeowners from mortgage relief scams such as the ones that sprung up during the mortgage crisis.

99. A Someone who offers to negotiate the terms of a residential mortgage loan requires a license. These other tasks would be considered clerical or support duties that do not require licensure.

100. C The SAFE Act requires states to establish minimum standards for the licensing and registration of state-licensed mortgage loan originators.

101. D The state regulatory authority may conduct an examination of any licensed lender or broker as often as it deems necessary.

102. C A licensee that ceases to engage in business and desires to no longer be licensed must inform the state regulatory authority in writing and, at that time, surrender the license to the state regulatory authority. The licensee typically must file a plan for the withdrawal from regulated business, including a timetable for the disposition of the business and a closing audit/review performed by an independent accountant.

103. B If the MLO fails to file a required report with the state regulatory authority, the regulator has the authority to issue an order suspending the MLO's license if the mortgage loan originator fails to file any required report.

104. A The state regulatory authority does not have the authority to change the federally mandated NMLS testing requirements.

105. C The state regulatory authority does not typically provide loans.

106. C The unique identifier of any person originating a residential mortgage loan shall be clearly shown on all residential mortgage loan application forms, solicitations or advertisements, including business cards or websites, and any other documents.

107. A. An unlicensed mortgage loan administrator does not take loan applications or negotiate loan terms. The others could perform these activities as licensed professionals.

108. B A registered mortgage loan originator is an individual who is registered with and maintains a unique identifier through the Nationwide Mortgage Licensing System and Registry. A registered mortgage loan originator may not necessarily be licensed under the state regulatory authority. A registered mortgage loan originator could be exempt from licensure as an employee of a depository institution, a subsidiary that is owned and controlled by a depository institution and regulated by a federal banking agency; but still registered with the NMLS.

109. B Responsible for conducting the loan closing, the settlement agent or closing agent is considered a third party to the loan transaction.

110. C A dwelling is defined as a residential structure that contains one-to-four units, whether or not that structure is attached to real property. The term includes an individual condominium unit, cooperative unit, mobile home, and trailer, if it is used as a residence.

111. D An applicant for licensure may need to satisfy a net work, surety bond, or state fund contribution requirement.

112. C Of these scenarios, Ellen is the one who is communicating directly about loan terms with the borrower. That type of activity is considered part of taking a loan application, which requires Ellen to be licensed.

113. B The unique identifier is issued by the NMLS. The Nationwide Mortgage Licensing System and Registry (NMLS) was developed by the Conference of State Bank Supervisors and the American Association of Residential Mortgage Regulators, and was initiated as part of the SAFE. Act.

114. A The denial of an application must include a reason for the denial.

115. A A licensed mortgage loan originator may only receive credit for a continuing education course in the year in which the course is taken and may not take the same approved course in the same or successive years to meet the annual requirements for continuing education. This is referred to as the repeat rule. Courses taken may include any approved classroom, online, or correspondence studies.

116. B An applicant is not required to submit copies of other licenses. The other elements are required to be included. Applicants must also supply the current name and address and any other information requested by the state regulatory authority.

117. C Applicants must demonstrate they have financial responsibility, good character, and general fitness, including a satisfactory credit report.

118. D Real estate concepts is not a required pre-licensing topic. MLOs are required to complete 20 hours of pre-licensing education to obtain their license. At least 3 hours of this initial instruction must cover federal laws, 3 hours must focus on ethics, and 2 hours must cover on nontraditional mortgage products.

119. A Someone who offers to negotiate the terms of a residential mortgage loan requires a license. These other tasks would be considered clerical or support duties that do not require licensure.

120. C Advertisements soliciting mortgage business must include the name of the employing broker's principal place of business. A loan originator may not exclude this from an ad and use his or her own name instead.

121. A A mortgage loan originator who has become unaffiliated with an employing entity may not originate loans. After termination of employment with one broker, the licensee may request the transfer of his license to another mortgage broker or another entity by submitting a change of sponsorship application and paying any required fees as long as no violation is involved in the termination. If the MLO does not have an immediate job prospect, he may request to hold his license in inactive status. A licensee whose license is in inactive status must cease to engage in any activity as a mortgage loan originator. A licensee whose license is in inactive status will be required to apply for renewal annually and comply with the annual continuing education requirements. A mortgage loan originator will need to complete his annual continuing education requirements to reinstate his license when he resumes working as a loan originator.

122. B A business card is considered a type of advertisement under state law and the situation described would constitute a violation. An individual engaging solely in loan processor or underwriter activities is not permitted to represent to the public, through advertising or other means of communicating or providing information, including the use of business cards, stationery, brochures, signs, rate lists, or other promotional items, that he or she can or will perform any of the activities of a mortgage loan originator.

123. A Lenders not only should be checking one's ability to repay a loan, but are now required under law to do so. Several factors should be investigated to determine if a person has the ability to repay a loan.

124. A All of the choices are required by the GLB Act except for allowing consumers to add their number to a Do Not Call list, which refers to the Do Not Call Registry made permanent by the Do Not Call Improvement Act, which became law in 2008.

125. D When triggering terms are used in an ad, TILA requires the disclosure of the amount of down payment, terms of loan repayment, and annual percentage rate. The total closing costs are not required to be stated in the ad.

Practice Exam #2: MLO National Test with UST

1. C RESPA allows a mortgage broker to own a title company; however, the title company must be an actual company with a place of business, have employees, etc. If the title company is used in the same transaction, that relationship must be disclosed.

2. B The minimum down payment on an FHA loan is 3.5%, so $4,620 (if the FICO score is 580 or above).

3. D Of these, the Truth in Lending Act (TILA) contains very specific requirements for advertising the terms of a mortgage loan.

4. A Of these, only home equity loans are required to be reported under the Home Mortgage Disclosure Act.

5. D The lender must perform an escrow account analysis once during the year and notify borrowers of any shortage or excess overage and refund any amount held over 1/6th the annual amount held plus $50.

6. A There is an established business relationship (EBR) in this scenario. A company may call a consumer for up to three (3) months after the consumer makes an inquiry or submits an application to the company.

7. A A point is equal to 1% of the loan amount. So for this loan: $80,000 x 60% = $48,000 loan amount; so two points is $48,000 x 2% = $960.

8. D Regulation X (RESPA) requires the GFE and Regulation Z (TILA) requires the TIL.

9. C Nearly all mortgages are sold and the consumer is not affected by the selling of the mortgage. The consumer is only affected if the "servicing" of the mortgage is sold (who the customer makes the payments to).

10. B ECOA prohibits discrimination in granting credit to people based on sex, age (if at least 18), marital status, race, color, religion, national origin, receipt of public assistance, exercised rights under the Consumer Credit Protection Act.

11. B Title X of the Dodd-Frank Act established the Consumer Financial Protection Bureau (CFPB) as an independent entity within the Federal Reserve. .

12. C Of these, the MLO's mistake, even if done unintentionally, would not be considered a changed circumstance.

13. B The Safeguards Rule (15 U.S.C. § 6801–6809) requires all financial institutions and institutions that receive consumer's financial information to design, implement, and maintain safeguards to protect customer information while it is in the custody and control of the institution and its agents..

14. A Using the payment-to-income ratio of 31% for an FHA loan, we get $2,108. But using the total debt service ratio of 43% for this loan, we find: $6,800 (income) multiplied by 0.43, which equals $2,924. From that, you subtract monthly debts (485 + 200 + 1,500) which total $2,185, leaving $739.

15. D The Truth in Lending Act (TILA) allows for a three business-day right of rescission. Furthermore, the act specifies that the three business day time limit requires only notification and that the right-to-rescind document does not have to be delivered to the lender within that time as long as notification was provided by mail prior to midnight of the third business day.

16. B Escrow deposits are never part of calculating the APR.

17. C $100,000 divided by $125,000 (the lowest of the sales price or appraised value) equals 80%.

18. C Under the Fair Credit Reporting Act, consumer reporting agencies may not report negative information that is more than seven years old, in most cases.

19. A The Fair and Accurate Credit Transaction Act of 2003—also known as FACTA or the FACT Act—added new sections to the federal Fair Credit Reporting Act, intended primarily to help consumers fight the growing crime of identity theft.

20. D Under TILA, the earliest a loan may be consummated is the seventh business day after the applicant receives the required disclosures or the disclosures are mailed.

21. D Generic statements that do not state specific loan information are exempt from additional disclosing of referencing specific information concerning loan terms.

22. A The Bank Secrecy Act/Anti-Money Laundering Act requires financial institutions in the United States to assist U.S. government agencies to detect and prevent money laundering.

23. B The Equal Credit Opportunity Act requires lenders to accept any stable income that an applicant gets from public assistance.

24. C The Red Flags Rules are contained in the Fair and Accurate Credit Transaction Act, not the Gramm-Leach-Bliley Act.

25. B The rule mandates that creditors or settlement service providers who have information about appraiser misconduct file a report with the appropriate state licensing authorities.

26. B Although it might not be something a cautious lender would do, it is not illegal under fair housing and fair lending laws to disregard income that cannot be verified.

27. C The interest-only payment is calculated by multiplying the loan amount of $205,000 by the annual interest rate of 6% and dividing by the 12 monthly payments ($1,025 per month). Next, the taxes are quoted by the half-year so this amount is divided by 6 and not 12 ($300 per month). The hazard insurance is quoted annually so it must be divided by 12 ($35 per month). The mortgage insurance is quoted monthly ($65 per month). By adding these monthly amounts together, the total monthly payment is derived: $1,025 + $300 + $35 + $65 = $1,425 total monthly payment.

28. C RESPA allows the payment of fees to service providers for services rendered in connection with a mortgage loan.

29. A A subprime loan in and of itself is not evidence of predatory lending. The other situations should raise red flags, however.

30. C The purpose of the Truth in Lending Act is to let consumers know exactly what they're paying for credit, enabling them to compare credit costs and shop around for the best credit terms.

31. D The Truth in Lending Statement does not require that the interest rate appear since the TIL deals with the total cost of financing, which must be translated into an annual percentage rate.

32. C A mortgage is considered a voluntary specific lien, meaning that it is placed with the consent of the owner, and it applies to a specified property.

33. A An applicant is entitled to a free credit report if information in that report resulted in adverse action. Denying credit for another reason does not entitle the consumer to a free copy.

34. A Ann committed fraud by revising those income documents, but she did intend to buy and live in the house. The other situations all involved a borrower who did not intend to live in the house. In the case of Bob's brother, the straw buyer may not have even realized that he was part of a scheme.

35. C Redlining is a refusal to make loans or issue insurance policies on property located in a particular neighborhood for discriminatory reasons.

36. C The Home Ownership and Equity Protection Act (HOEPA) establishes disclosure requirements, prohibits deceptive and unfair practices in lending, and it requires verification of a borrower's ability to repay a high-cost loan.

37. A If Dave made the decision to ignore a critical fact, he could be accused of actual fraud.

38. B Only the fee to pull a credit report may be charged.

39. C The Home Mortgage Disclosure Act requires that the applicant be asked their race or national origin for monitoring purposes.

40. A A reverse mortgage is based on the equity in the home. It shrinks and the debt grows. .

41. A $95,000 X 95% = $90,250 - $70,000 - $3,000 = $17,250

42. A You would not be in violation of ECOA for asking a question that is on the loan application. The other questions, even if asked out of politeness or curiosity, would violate ECOA.

43. D HMDA data is found in section X of the 1003, titled Information for Government Monitoring Purposes. It gathers the information needed to make the lending practices public record.

44. B Section 114 of the FACT Act is known as the Red Flags Rules, which, among other things, requires financial institutions and creditors to implement a written identity theft prevention program.

45. D When a home is in such a designated flood zone, the lender will require some form of flood insurance for the life of the loan.

46. C A fully amortizing mortgage requires regular payment of principal and interest calculated to pay off the entire balance by the end of the loan term.

47. A The Fair Housing Act prohibits discrimination in housing based on "race, color, religion, sex,

national origin, disability, or familial status in the sale or lease of residential property."

48. B   The index added to the margin is the rate. The index is the variable portion of this formula that causes the rate to adjust.

49. B   A reverse mortgage borrower must be at least 62 years old and own a home with little or no outstanding mortgage.

50. D   Loans that have an adjustable interest rate or an interest only option can result in substantial increases in the monthly payment. A borrower with a reverse mortgage doesn't make a payment.

51. B   With a 2/6 rate cap, the rate can increase 2% each adjustment period to a maximum of 12% over the life of the loan (6% start plus 6% lifetime cap).

52. C   A nonconforming loan is one that does not follow Fannie Mae and Freddie Mac criteria, for example, for maximum loan amount. It is also known as a jumbo loan.

53. C   The most significant consumer protection under the FTC's MARS rule is the advance fee ban, which ensures that mortgage relief companies may not collect any fees until they have provided consumers with a written offer from their lender or servicer that the consumer decides is acceptable.

54. C   Some lenders and investors are willing to make these riskier loans because they can get much higher rates than they can with other real estate loans.

55. D   Points paid for loan origination fees, servicing charges, administration costs, documentation fees, and closing fees may be referred to as points but they are not discount points.

56. D   The requirements for financial institutions to assist in detecting and preventing money laundering are found in the Bank Secrecy Act/Ant-Money Laundering Act. All the others are parts of the Dodd-Frank legislation..

57. D   Religion is not a question that a loan originator may ask relevant to HMDA, since it is in no way included in government monitoring under the guidelines of the Home Mortgage Disclosure Act.

58. B   He would pay $1,900 because $95,000 x 0.02 = $1,900. Discount points are paid on the mortgage amount. The down payment is separate.

59. D   Once the difference is one-eighth percent (1/8%), a new TIL Statement must be issued.

60. B   RESPA applies to one- to four-family residential properties. Properties of five or more units are considered commercial. Unimproved land has no structure on it.

61. C   A package mortgage allows personal property to be packaged together and included in the mortgage loan.

62. B   The housing expense ratio for an FHA-insured loan is calculated by taking the borrower's stable monthly income and multiplying by 31% (0.31).

63. A   The APR or effective rate of interest is the total cost of the loan as an annual percentage of the loan amount and includes the loan fees, discount points, and other charges that must be paid by the borrower.

64. A   This would be considered a kickback, and it is prohibited under Section 8 of RESPA.

65. D   One of the objectives of the Dodd-Frank Wall Street Reform and Consumer Protection Act of 2010 was to address perceived unfair practices by mortgage loan originators related to steering practices related to compensation paid to loan originators by consumers.

66. A   Bankruptcy papers from 10 years ago would not be relevant today, because a bankruptcy does not show on a credit bureau report after 10 years. In rare cases, the papers may be needed for verification.

67. D   Total DTI ratio is calculated as: $2,500 (income) multiplied by (x) 0.36, which equals $900. From the $900, you must subtract his monthly debts ($250 + $100 + $50) which total $400. So, this leaves $500 to be used. If he could pay off some of his debts and reduce his total of other long-term monthly obligations, he would be able to qualify for a larger mortgage payment.

68. D   The SAFE Act mandates prelicensing and continuing education requirements for state licensed mortgage loan originators, as well as a national licensing exam. After the launch of the UST in April 2013, all applicants must take and pass the UST section of the national exam regardless of which state they are seeking licensure in.

69. B   Two full years of employment are required on the loan application, with an explanation of any gaps of 30 days or more.

70. D To find the monthly income for an hourly worker, multiply the hourly rate by 40 to find the weekly rate; multiply that by 52 weeks per year then divide by 12 months ($2,730). Then add the monthly amount of the overtime: $15.75 / 2 + $15.75 = $23.63 x 5 hours per week x 52 weeks / 12 months = $511.88; $2,730 + $511.88 = $3,241.88

71. D A borrower's total DTI ratio is the relationship of the borrower's total monthly debt obligations (including housing and long-term debts with more than ten payments left) to income, expressed as a percentage.

72. C The sales comparison approach looks at past sales that are similar to the subject property and that have recently sold in the area.

73. C Although prepayment penalties are generally prohibited by HOEPA, the prepayment penalty is not one of the triggers used to identify a high cost loan.

74. C A Home Equity Line of Credit (HELOC) is a mortgage loan (usually in second lien position) that allows a borrower to use and payoff, then use and payoff the loan up to a pre-determined amount. It is just like a credit card but secured by real estate.

75. B A Certificate of Eligibility (COE) is issued by the VA to those who qualify for VA loans and is required by a lender to establish the amount and status of the veteran's eligibility under the VA loan guarantee program. The DD-214 is the official military discharge paper.

76. C Salaried income can be considered and it is assumed that it will continue. Unemployment, disability, and alimony will need additional documentation to prove the likelihood that it will continue.

77. A The Civil Rights Act of 1866 prohibits racial discrimination in all property transactions in the United States.

78. C The income approach is a valuable appraisal method when determining the value of investment property.

79. B Mortgage insurance is required once the LTV reaches 80% for conventional loans.

80. C The lender's right of acceleration can mean that a borrower who misses one or two payments may have to pay off the entire debt to save the home.

81. B The HUD-1 must be made available one business day prior to closing. The other documents must be given to consumers within three business days of the completed loan application.

82. D The main advantage to a 15-year loan is that the total of the repayments or the total paid back to the lender is less because the borrower pays less interest over the life of the loan.

83. C The Equal Credit Opportunity Act requires the lender to provide the borrower a reason for rejection of credit in writing within 30 days of loan application.

84. A A deed proves ownership of a property and is transferred in the event of the sale of the property.

85. B The SAFE Act requires eight hours of continuing education for state-licensed mortgage loan originators.

86. A The Good Faith Estimate (GFE) is given to borrowers within three business days of applying for mortgage loan.

87. D FCRA provisions do not entitle consumers to a free copy of their credit scores.

88. A Red Flag Rules of the FACT Act require financial institutions and creditors to implement a written identity theft prevention program.

89. D Steering is when an MLO or real estate agent "advises" a borrower to move, or not move, to an area to "fit in."

90. C Form 4506-T gives the lender permission to request transcripts of federal tax returns from the IRS to document the borrower's income..

91. C HOEPA is also known as Section 32 of the Truth in Lending Act.

92. B $100,000 X 80% = $80,000 - $25,000 - $23,000 - $6,000 = $26,000

93. A Since the property is being used as collateral for the loan, certain determinations are made based on the accuracy of the appraisal. Property condition and loan-to-value are dependant on accuracy, and the Equal Credit Opportunity Act allows the borrower to challenge that information.

94. D Regulation Z does not apply to business, commercial, or agricultural loans, loans payable with four or less installments and without a finance charge, or to loans made to corporations, partnerships, associations and agencies.

95. C An appraisal is only an estimate or opinion. It is not a guarantee of value or the ultimate price that a buyer actually pays.

96. A A clear to close the loan is issued by the lender, giving permission to close the loan.

97. C The federal Gramm-Leach-Bliley Act, which was passed by Congress in 1999, regulates the handling and disclosure of consumers' private financial information.

98. D The Guidance indicates that institutions should avoid loan terms that rely on property sale or refinancing once amortization begins.

99. C Whenever a specific payment is quoted in an advertisement, the entire loan terms that determined that payment must be disclosed in the advertisement.

100. C The SAFE Act defines a nontraditional loan as anything other than a 30-year fixed rate loan.

101. C The state regulatory authority can impose fines and/or initiate suspension or revocation of a license.

102. C The unique identifier is issued by the Nationwide Mortgage Licensing System and Registry (NMLS).

103. D A state's system of supervision and enforcement should include the authority to examine, investigate and conduct enforcement actions as necessary to carry out the intended purposes of this Act, including the authority to subpoena witnesses and documents.

104. B The state regulatory authority may deny the renewal of a license if there is a finding that a licensee has demonstrated unfairness, unworthiness, incompetence, bad faith or dishonesty in the transaction of business.

105. B The person making an investigation or examination has the authority to administer oaths, examine persons under oath, and compel the production of papers and objects.

106. D Each state is authorized to write state-specific rules or regulations or adopt procedures related to licensing of persons covered under this Act.

107. B A registered mortgage loan originator is an individual who is registered with and maintains a unique identifier through the Nationwide Mortgage Licensing System and Registry. A registered mortgage loan originator may not necessarily be licensed under the state regulatory authority. A registered mortgage loan originator could be exempt from licensure as an employee of a depository institution, a subsidiary that is owned and controlled by a depository institution and regulated by a federal banking agency; but still registered with the NMLS.

108. B A loan modification refers to a modification or change made to an existing loan. The term does not include a refinancing transaction. Authorizing a mortgage lender to service a loan for more than four months is a service endorsement.

109. D FHA's Home Equity Conversion Mortgage (HECM) is the most common reverse mortgage program.

110. D The rate lock fee is paid to the lender and is not considered a third party fee.

111. A Mortgage brokers act as intermediaries.

112. A A licensed loan originator is a person—not an organization or entity—who takes a mortgage loan application or offers or negotiates terms of a mortgage loan for compensation or gain. Since Pam works for a federally chartered bank, she needs to be registered, not licensed. Since Tom originates only commercial mortgage loans, he also is exempt from needing a loan originator license.

113. C MLOs are required to complete 8 hours of approved continuing education to renew their license. At least 3 hours must be related to ethics, 3 hours on federal laws and regulations, and 2 hours on nontraditional mortgage products.

114. A Having a mortgage loan originator license revoked in another state due to a violation would definitely make Daryl ineligible to be granted a license by the state regulatory authority. Fern has attained the minimum written test score to be eligible for licensing. Although Joseph has omitted a material fact on his application, we can assume he made a bona fide error due to forgetfulness or haste and NOT an intentional misstatement or omission meant to deceive the state regulatory authority or conceal a disqualifying association. Zelda's criminal conviction occurred more than 7 years ago and did not involve fraud, theft, or mishandling of money and therefore would not necessarily prevent her from being licensed, especially if that past history was the only negative factor in her application.

115. D Working with an unlicensed and unregistered loan officer is a prohibited and punishable act under any circumstances.

116. B A past conviction for fraud would always be considered grounds for denial.

117. C The SAFE Act defines a nontraditional loan as anything other than a 30-year fixed rate loan.

118. D Of these, the only task that requires licensing is offering or negotiating loan terms.

119. D All advertisements must include the business location address of the licensee as it appears on the license. Using a post office box or newspaper box number constitutes placing a blind ad, which is a violation. Advertisements are also required to include the licensee's unique NMLS identifier.

120. C Assuming that Greg indeed left that key piece of information off the application by accident; his conduct could best be described as negligent. If it was intentional, however, he may have committed fraud.

121. A A mortgage broker is prohibited from directly collecting a rate lock-in fee, except where it is required by a governmental agency to be collected directly by the mortgage broker, issue a mortgage rate lock-in, or otherwise represent to a first mortgage loan applicant, or the applicant's representative, that the loan will be made at a specified rate if the loan is closed by the expiration of a specified period of time. A mortgage broker may provide a mortgage lender's mortgage rate lock-in to a mortgage loan applicant, or the applicant's representative, on behalf of such mortgage lender and collect a rate lock-in fee on the mortgage lender's behalf, payable to the mortgage lender.

122. A That is a provision included in the Dodd-Frank Act.

123. C A mortgage loan originator should never ask an appraiser to hit a mark by telling the appraiser the minimum amount the appraised value needs to be to get the loan approved. That is certainly unethical and if acted upon would be an example of collusion in appraisal fraud.

124. C The lender must respond with a decision within 30 days.

125. D An advertised interest rate must be made available to a reasonable number of qualified applicants.

UST Standalone Practice Exam #1

1. C The NMLS unique identifier is the number that should be used to identify a mortgage loan originator on any forms as well as business cards or other advertisements. The NMLS unique identifier is used to search for the MLO's name on the NMLS website.

2. C The state regulatory authority may suspend or revoke a license for failure to fully cooperate with any examination or investigation ordered by the regulatory authority.

3. D The state regulatory authority has the right to investigate a licensee's books at any time.

4. A The intent is that the state regulatory authority shall have a broad administrative authority to administer, interpret and enforce this Act.

5. D Each state must establish procedures for examining any books, papers, records, or other data of any loan originator operating in the state.

6. B The state regulatory authority does not have the authority to impose a prison sentence.

7. D A loan processor is a person who performs administrative or clerical tasks as an employee at the direction of and subject to the supervision and instruction of a person licensed, or exempt from licensing which includes the receipt, collection, distribution and analysis of information common for the processing or underwriting of a residential mortgage loan or the communication with a consumer to obtain the information necessary for the processing or underwriting of a loan if the communication does not include offering or negotiating loan rates or terms or counseling consumers about residential mortgage loan rates or terms. A mortgage lender is a person or company that directly or indirectly originates a mortgage loan. A creditor is a person who extends credit that is subject to a finance charge. A person who is obligated to repay a mortgage loan is called a borrower.

8. D As defined in the model state law language, the term person may refer to natural person,

corporation, company, limited liability company, partnership, or association.

9. C Of these scenarios, Rita is the only person who is NOT taking a loan application. All of the others in the situations described are considered to be taking loan applications and would require licensing to perform these particular tasks.

10. D Pleading guilty to a felony would not necessarily be the basis for denying a license, unless the felony involved fraud, dishonesty, breach of trust, or money laundering.

11. D If she is performing clerical duties, she is most likely to be a loan processor, and she is exempt from needing to be licensed.

12. C The state regulatory authority will likely deny a MLO license if, at any time preceding the date of application, an individual was convicted of a felony involving an act of fraud, dishonesty, or a breach of trust, or money laundering, no matter how long ago the offense occurred. The state regulatory authority may, in his or her discretion, disregard a conviction where the felon has been pardoned. Any felony conviction that occurred within the last 7 years is also grounds for denial.

13. D The license application fee to act as a mortgage loan originator in Connecticut is not refundable under any circumstance. This also applies to the associated fees for fingerprint processing and NMLS processing charged for the initial MLO application. These fees will not be abated by denial, surrender, suspension, or revocation of the license.

14. C A person who works part time as a mortgage loan originator has the same requirements as a person who works full-time as a mortgage loan originator. A part-time MLO requires licensing and must be registered with the NMLS.

15. B Licensees must meet the requirements for license renewal by December 31 each year. The license of a mortgage loan originator failing to satisfy the minimum standards for license renewal will expire at the close of business on December 31.

16. C A person may be approved for licensure in one state if he has a valid license in another state. However, if the applicant has had a license

denied, revoked, not renewed, or suspended in another state, the license likely will be denied in the current state of application.

17. A The SAFE Act does not require continuing education on conventional mortgage products.

18. C The SAFE Act requires states to establish minimum standards for the licensing and registration of state-licensed mortgage loan originators.

19. C Mortgage industry advertisements are considered deceptive or misleading if they include terms such as "immediate approval" or "immediate closing."

20. A Within 3 days of receiving a mortgage application from a borrower, the mortgage broker must clearly disclose to the borrower all material information that might affect the rights and interests of the borrower, including the total compensation that the broker would receive from any of the loan options that the lender or mortgage broker may present to the borrower.

21. C Disbursing the mortgage loan proceeds via direct deposit to customer's account is certainly allowable. The other choices describe conduct that is prohibited under state rules and regulations.

22. A If a licensee has a conflicting interest among providers in a mortgage transaction, the licensee must provide the following disclosures to the borrower in writing: The nature of the affiliated relationship, an estimated range of charges for using the affiliated provider's services, that use of the affiliated provider may result in a financial benefit to the licensee, and that alternative sources may be chosen by the borrower to provide the required products or services.

23. D An ad that contained the statement that the consumer should consult a tax advisor regarding deductibility of interest costs would not be considered misleading; the other statements are.

24. A An MLO cannot be held responsible if a client withholds material information.

25. D Overtime and bonuses would not be included.

UST Standalone Practice Exam #2

1. B Revocation is the permanent withdrawal of a license. When a state's regulatory authority revokes a license, the loan originator must be notified in writing that the license is revoked and that the individual may not engage in the business of loan originating in the state.

2. B While it is indeed a serious offense that may result in other lawful consequences, Marsha's citation for a traffic violation would not require filing a written report with the state regulatory authority. A written report describing the event and its expected impact on the activities of the licensee in this state must be after the filing for bankruptcy or reorganization by the licensee; the institution of revocation or suspension proceedings against the licensee by any state or governmental authority; the denial of the opportunity to engage in business by any state or governmental authority; any felony indictment of the licensee or any of its officers, directors, or principals; or any felony conviction of the licensee or any of its officers, directors, or principals.

3. B The mortgage broker or lender is liable for actual travel and reasonable living expenses incurred on account of its examination whether or not violations are discovered. These expenses should be paid within 30 days of the presentation of an itemized statement.

4. C In most states, Lisa would have the right to appeal a revocation of her license to the state Supreme Court.

5. C If an application has not been approved or denied within the allotted time frame, the MLO has the right to request a hearing with the state regulatory authority.

6. C Counseling is mandatory for consumers who are applying for Home Equity Conversion Mortgage.

7. D Taking a loan application or negotiating loan terms is part of the SAFE definition of a loan originator, which may also be a lender or broker. The SAFE definition of loan originator excludes those who act solely as a loan processor or underwriter or who extend credit for timeshare plans.

8. C A mortgage lock-in rate is defined as a written or electronically transmitted confirmation issued to a mortgage applicant by a mortgage lender prior to the issuance of a first mortgage loan commitment, stating that a particular rate, number of points or variable rate terms will be the rate, number of points, or variable rate terms at which the mortgage lender will make the loan, provided the first mortgage loan is closed by a specified date, and the applicant qualifies for the loan in accordance with the mortgage lender's standards of creditworthiness.

9. C If a licensee's son met the experience, responsible character and education requirements for the position, designating him as the principal loan originator would not be considered a conflicting interest for a licensee. The other choices involving relatives as stakeholders in companies providing products or services could all be considered having conflicting interests.

10. C A loan for a one to four family property which is to be lived is considered a residential mortgage loan.

11. B As defined in the model state law language, the term individual refers to a natural person.

12. B Administrative or clerical tasks refer to the receipt, collection, and distribution of information common for the processing or underwriting of a loan in the mortgage industry.

13. D A score of 70% is not a passing score for the written exam. Applicants must receive a score of at least 75% on each component of the written exam in order to pass and qualify for a license.

14. C A mortgage processor performs clerical or administrative duties including receipt, collection, distribution and analysis of information required for processing or underwriting or a residential mortgage loan. Individuals who perform this type of function are exempt from licensing.

15. C Applicants are required to a credit report primarily so that the state regulatory authority can evaluate their history of financial responsibility.

16. C The task of taking a mortgage loan application requires licensing. An individual is considered to take a residential mortgage loan application even if the individual receives the borrower request or information indirectly.

17. B No advertising copy shall be used after its use has been disapproved by the State Regulatory Authority and the licensee is notified in writing of the disapproval. To be in compliance, the company should stop running the disapproved advertisement altogether. Any changes to remedy

an objectionable ad should be approved by the State Regulatory Authority before continuing to use the advertisement.

18. D General statements, such as "terms to fit your budget," "take years to pay," or "low down payments accepted" do not trigger further disclosure in advertisements of closed-end credit because they do not state or suggest the period of repayment or amount of required down payment. All the other choices contain triggering terms.

19. C Rules and regulations for high cost loans never apply to reverse mortgage loans.

20. A According to the Gramm-Leach-Bliley Act, this policy is required to be provided before disclosing information to non-affiliated third parties.

21. D Under TILA, the earliest a loan may be consummated is the seventh business day after the applicant receives the required disclosures or the disclosures are mailed.

22. B Creditors are not permitted to ask a potential borrower whether he or she receives child support.

23. B The only correct way to ask about a client's marital status is, Are you married, unmarried, or separated. Be sure to include all three of these words in the question.

24. A The new Federal Reserve Mortgage Loan Originator Compensation Rule prohibits a MLO from being paid based on any loan terms other than the loan amount. Any payment based on the fees or costs or other such loan terms is illegal.

25. A Offering a subprime loan to a borrower who is coming out of bankruptcy is an acceptable practice because of the risk associated with this borrower. The other scenarios include elements that would be considered predatory lending tactics.